SISTER LIGUORI

The Nun Who Divided a Nation

JEFF KILDEA

connorcourt
PUBLISHING

Published in 2024 by Connor Court Publishing Pty Ltd.

Copyright © Jeff Kildea

ALL RIGHTS RESERVED. This book contains material protected under International and Federal Copyright Laws and Treaties. Any unauthorised reprint or use of this material is prohibited. No part of this book may be reproduced or transmitted in any form or by any means, electronic or mechanical, including photocopying, recording, or by any information storage and retrieval system without express written permission from the publisher.

Connor Court Publishing Pty Ltd.
PO Box 7257
Redland Bay QLD 4165
sales@connorcourt.com
www.connorcourt.com

ISBN: 9781923224063

Cover Design: Ian James

Printed in Australia.

Contents

Preface	vi
Introduction	1
1 Flight	17
Winter of discontent	17
First flight	19
Second flight	24
Raising the alarm	26
2 Evasion	29
Sunday, 25 July	29
Monday, 26 July	38
Tuesday, 27 July	38
Wednesday, 28 July	43
Thursday, 29 July	44
Friday, 30 July	47
Saturday, 31 July	48
3 Arrest	53
Sunday, 1 August	53
Monday, 2 August	54
Tuesday, 3 August	55
Wednesday, 4 August	57
Thursday, 5 August	61
Friday, 6 August	63
Saturday, 7 August	63
Sunday, 8 August	65

4 Release — 71

Monday, 9 August — 71
Tuesday, 10 August — 74
Wednesday, 11 August — 75
Thursday, 12 August — 79
Friday, 13 August — 81

5 Crusade — 91

'This business is not finished with' — 91
The gunmen of Berry and the wreckers of Mount Erin convent — 95
Enter Charles Heydon — 100
A 'fistic encounter' in Parliament — 102

6 Reunion — 109

Arrival of Joseph Partridge — 109
Armageddon — 118
'A veritable hurricane of sectarian strife' — 122

7 Trial – Part One — 125

Writ of Summons — 125
The build-up to the trial — 126
Dramatis personae — 129
Day 1: Thursday, 30 June — 131
Day 2: Friday, 1 July — 139
Day 3: Monday, 4 July — 141
Day 4: Tuesday, 5 July — 143
Day 5: Wednesday, 6 July — 146

8 Trial – Part Two — 149

Day 6: Thursday, 7 July — 149
Day 7: Friday, 8 July — 155

Day 8: Monday, 11 July	158
Day 9: Tuesday, 12 July	163
Day 10: Wednesday, 13 July	165
9 Aftermath	**177**
The Jury's Verdict	177
Sectarian violence in the Riverina	180
Joseph Partridge's continued pursuit of his sister	185
The Abduction of Bridget Partridge	191
A censure motion in Parliament	200
The End of the Affair	202
10 Conclusion	**207**
Epilogue	**213**
Appendix: Magdalen laundries, orphanages, and industrial schools	**219**
Note on Sources	**225**
Index	**229**

Preface

I first came across the Sister Liguori story in the late 1990s when researching religious sectarianism in Australia. At the time I was told by a local historian in Wagga Wagga that the town was still divided over the affair, a claim I found incredible. How could an event that occurred nearly eighty years before still generate controversy? Yet, twenty-five years after that conversation, the Sister Liguori affair continues to do just that, as evidenced recently by a sensational news story about the affair appearing in the *Sydney Morning Herald*.[1]

The story of Sister Liguori, whose baptismal name was Bridget Mary Partridge, is a remarkable tale which, if written as a novel, would be considered too far-fetched to be acceptable as a serious work of fiction. Yet it is a true story, full of tragedy and farce with a mix of politics and religion, though not sex, as the *Herald*'s article would have us believe.

On many occasions during the past twenty-five years, I have sat down to write a book on the Sister Liguori story, only to be diverted by other projects. The recent report in the *Herald* firmed up my resolve to complete it. The article contained the novel but unsubstantiated claim that Sister Liguori had fled her convent because she had been made pregnant by a priest and had refused to give up her child for adoption. I decided it was time for me to publish a complete and accurate account of the story – 'the true history of the Sister Liguori affair'. I was also persuaded of the continuing relevance of the story on learning that in 2021 an artist, Amanda Bromfield, had marked the 100th anniversary of the affair with an exhibition at the Wagga Wagga Art Gallery incorporating ceramics, found objects, and a video performance.

Many of my contempories tell me they grew up with stories of the Sister Liguori affair. Over the years it has been the subject of popu-

---
[1] 'Pregnant to a priest, nun on run defied church over child', *Sydney Morning Herald* 3 April 2023, pp. 14-15.

lar articles in newspapers and magazines as well as scholarly articles in academic journals. In 2017 Maureen McKeown, a great-niece of the nun, wrote *The Extraordinary Case of Sister Liguori*. Published in Ireland as 'narrative non-fiction', the book does not pretend to be a true history of the affair, being more imaginative than real. Even so, it demonstrates that after a century the story continues to resonate. As with the *Herald* article, the shortcomings in Ms McKeown's book reinforces the need for a full and factual account.

The Sister Liguori affair provides a lurid illustration of Australia's sectarian past. But it is more than just an episode in Australia's political and religious history. It is also a very personal story of a young woman who, in attempting to leave a system she finds oppressive, ends up in no-man's land, caught between two powerful forces keen to use her to advance their ends. The story has recently found a contemporary idiom, with Amanda Bromfield telling the Australian Broadcasting Corporation during an interview about her exhibition that Bridget's story is profoundly engaging as a feminist parable: 'A young woman, a nun, taking on the Bishop and the Catholic Church, she was a very brave young woman to do this. I see Brigid as a real heroine. Her story is fantastical—I think she's a very strong woman who needs to be put up on a pedestal. Her story must be known to the world.'[2] It is no wonder the Sister Liguori story continues to captivate the imagination.

Many people have assisted me in researching and writing this book. In particular, I am indebted to the late Bishop William Brennan, Bishop of Wagga Wagga from 1984 to 2002, who gave me full access to the diocesan archives relating to the Sister Liguori affair. I also express my appreciation to Ian Kells, Grand Secretary of the Loyal Orange Institution of New South Wales, who gave me access to the institution's archives. Others who provided assistance include Sister Margaret Barclay and Sister Rosaria Connell of the Presentation Sisters Wagga Wagga, Eithne Flanagan (daughter of Joseph Par-

---

[2] https://www.abc.net.au/news/2021-07-22/nun-in-the-nightgown-scandal-that-put-wagga-on-the-map/100311566.

tridge), Maureen McKeown (great niece of Sister Liguori), and Dr Perry McIntyre AM. Also, thanks to Michael Kildea, Robyn Kildea, and Professor James Franklin, who read and commented on drafts of the book.

Introduction

The Sister Liguori story, strange but true, concerns a Catholic nun, a Catholic bishop, and a Protestant parson. Arrayed behind them are the parson's wife, the grand master of the Loyal Orange Institution, and numerous priests, politicians, and policemen, not to mention the press and the public. For more than fifteen months in 1920-21 they worked themselves into such a lather over the fate of the nun that many feared the consequences not only for her but for the social harmony of the country as well.

If that sounds far-fetched, it must be remembered that Australia in the early twentieth century was a very different place to what it is now, no more so than in matters pertaining to religion. Unlike today, most people then regarded religious affiliation as a significant marker of their identity. And for many Australians the Sister Liguori affair was a Manichean morality play, a struggle between good and evil, in which the players on both sides sought to pluck the mote from the eyes of the other without beholding the beams in their own.

At one level, the Sister Liguori affair is the story of the personal crisis of a young Irish woman, Bridget Mary Partridge, who wished to quit the religious life she had embraced as Sister Liguori a decade before, but who felt trapped by the system she wanted to abandon. At another level, the affair is arguably one of the most significant events in the history of religious sectarianism in Australia. And, at yet another level, it is an episode in the ongoing struggle for political power. It is the intertwining of these three strands that makes the Sister Liguori story so compelling.

Not since the infamous Coningham affair of 1900, when Cardinal Patrick Moran's secretary, Monsignor Denis O'Haran, was named as co-respondent in a divorce case, had public interest in the religious life been so aroused. Arthur Coningham was an Australian test cricketer who commenced proceedings to obtain a divorce from his wife Alice on the grounds of her alleged adultery with Monsignor O'Haran. When the matter came to court, the jury were unable to reach a verdict. However, following a second trial the jury rejected Coningham's allegations against the priest. O'Haran emerged with his reputation intact and a hero to his fellow-Catholics, whose monetary contributions covered all his court costs.[1] Just as the forces of Protestantism and Catholicism had lined up against each other in that affair, so too would they do so 20 years later in the case of Sister Liguori.

Our story begins on a wet Saturday afternoon in July 1920 in Wagga Wagga, a town on the banks of the Murrumbidgee River in the Riverina district of New South Wales. The town's name means 'where crows gather' in the language of the local Aborigines, the Wiradjuri. Soon it would appear in newspaper headlines across Australia and around the world. Not since the Tichborne affair 50 years before, when Thomas Castro, the town's butcher, claimed to be the missing heir to the Tichborne fortune, had Wagga Wagga excited such national and international interest. After commencing a civil action in the English courts to claim his inheritance, Castro was exposed as a fraud. Identified as London-born Arthur Orton, he lost his case and he was tried and convicted of perjury. In the aftermath of the affair, Wagga Wagga attracted a number of overseas visitors, including the American writer Mark Twain.

At the northern end of the town is a rise known as Mount Erin on which the Sisters of the Presentation of the Blessed Virgin Mary had erected a convent and school in 1876. By 1920 the convent housed almost 80 nuns and 90 resident boarders. In addition, between 300 and 400 pupils attended day school. The Presentation order had been founded in Ireland in the eighteenth century and its mother house, named for one of Ireland's patron saints, Bridget,

---

[1] Anne E. Cunningham, *The Price of a Wife?: The Priest and the Divorce Trial*, Anchor Books Australia, Spit Junction, NSW, 2013. Cyril Pearl includes a chapter on the Coningham affair in *Wild Men of Sydney*, W.H. Allen, London, 1958. A contemporary account from the Catholic point of view is Zero, *The Secret History of the Coningham Case*, Finn Brothers, Sydney, 1901.

was in the town of Kildare. It was there in 1908 that Bridget Mary Partridge, first entered religious life.

Born at Newbridge, County Kildare on 21 October 1890, Bridget was the second of five children of an English father, Edward Partridge, a soldier in the Royal Engineers, and an Irish mother Anne (née Cardiff).[2] She would later explain, 'My mother was a devoted Catholic. My father was also, but he was brought up a Protestant and changed his religious faith on marrying my mother'.[3] Bridget's older sibling, Susan, was born at the Curragh camp, County Kildare, just 13 months before her. When Bridget was seven months old her father resigned from the army and the family moved to Warrington in Lancashire, England, where he worked as a wheelwright and coach builder. It was there that the three youngest children were born: Catherine (known as Kathleen) in 1893, Elizabeth (known as Lizzie) in 1894, and Joseph in 1897. Joseph will figure prominently in the story to come. In 1901 Edward re-enlisted in the Royal Engineers and was posted to the Curragh. The family moved back to Ireland residing first at Kilcullen and then at Brownstown.

Bridget left school at age 14 and helped her mother in the family home until she was 17 when she entered St Bridget's convent. Three months later she was on her way to Australia on board the steamer *Oroya*, landing at Melbourne in February 1909. A fortnight later she arrived in Wagga Wagga and entered the Mount Erin convent as a postulant. In September 1909 she received the habit of the order as a novice and after a further two years she took her final vows on 25 September 1911.[4] She also took the name Sister Liguori, in honour of St Alphonsus Liguori, an Italian Catholic bishop and

---

[2] On her birth certificate her name is spelt 'Bridget', the anglicisation of the original Irish 'Bríd' (pronounced 'Breed') whose spelling in modern Irish 'Brigid' or 'Brighid' led to the silent g/gh being sounded. In some documents, including her baptismal and death certificates, Sister Liguori's name is spelt 'Brigid'. Along with most writers on the subject, I have adopted 'Bridget' throughout except when quoting a document in which 'Brigid' is used.

[3] *Evening News*, 9 August 1920, p. 1.

[4] *Wagga Wagga Express*, 26 September 1911, p. 4.

spiritual writer who lived from 1696 to 1787. He was canonised a saint in 1839. In 1911 Sister Liguori spent six months teaching primary school children at Lockhart, a town 65 kilometres west of Wagga Wagga, before being sent to the convent school at Ganmain, 55 kilometres to its north. There she remained for five and a half years. These were relatively happy years for the young nun. However, the diocesan inspector, Father Patrick Hartigan, better known by the pen name 'John O'Brien' which he used when writing poetry, found her teaching to be below standard. When she asked him how the inspection went, he simply said, 'You'll be right, Sister'. It seems she took Hartigan's non-committal answer to be 'some kind of testimony of her suitability', for she would later claim, 'At Ganmain the father was quite pleased with my teaching'. This was not the case. In his report to the mother superior, Hartigan recommended that Sister Liguori be removed from teaching duties, with the result she was recalled to Mount Erin and assigned to domestic duties in the convent.[5] The misunderstanding likely added to Sister Liguori's disenchantment with religious life.

Compared to many other places around the world, Wagga Wagga in July 1920 was a haven of peace and harmony. The international news pages of the town's two newspapers, the *Daily Advertiser* and the *Daily Express* carried reports of anarchy and civil unrest in many countries, such as China, Turkey, Germany, Russia, and Ireland. Yet, beneath the calm surface lay divisions that reflected troubles elsewhere, especially in Ireland, which was then in the grip of a war in which Irish republicans were fighting for their nation's independence from the British Crown. Wagga Wagga's Irish Catholic community strongly supported Ireland's struggle while the town's Protestant majority, whose loyalty to the Crown was unswerving, regarded their neighbours' support of the rebels as treasonous.

This division of opinion was not new. For decades events in Ireland had had a significant impact on relations between Australia's

---

[5] *Daily Telegraph*, 7 July 1921, p. 5; Frank Mecham, *"John O'Brien" and the Boree Log*, Angus & Robertson, Sydney, 1981, pp. 125-127.

Catholics, mostly of Irish descent, and its Protestants, mostly of British descent. Ethno-religious rivalry had been a feature of Australian history since the founding of the colony at Sydney in 1788. For the most part it simmered below the surface. But every now and then it would bubble up and boil over, sometimes around the Twelfth of July, the anniversary of the Battle of the Boyne, as in Melbourne in 1846 when shots were fired, or on St Patrick's Day, as in Sydney in 1878 when rioting broke out in Hyde Park. But the conflict was mostly rhetorical, erupting particularly when the Irish in Ireland stepped up their campaign for self-government, such as during the debates over home rule and land reform in the 1880s, or following the Easter rising in Dublin in 1916, or during the Irish War of Independence, which began in January 1919.

Divisions over Ireland often became entangled with local issues such as the campaign for state aid for Catholic schools. State financing of denominational schools had ended in 1880. Since then, the Catholic Church had run its own school system funded by the generosity of the Catholic people and the self-sacrifice of the teaching orders of brothers and nuns who taught the children unpaid. Every now and then, particularly during election campaigns, the church would demand a return to state funding of denominational schools. Protestants strongly resisted these demands arguing that the Catholic church 'seeks to segregate its young people, and to bring them up under influences which imbue their minds with the narrowest and most bigoted notions, separating them in the most sacred relations of life from the rest of the citizenship of the State'.[6]

Another issue that had divided Australian Catholics of Irish descent from Protestants of British descent was the Australian government's plans to introduce conscription for overseas service during the First World War. Many Irish Australians fervently opposed the measure. At referendums in October 1916 and December 1917 the Australian people voted against conscription. Militant Protes-

---
[6] *Methodist*, 21 January 1911, p. 1.

tants blamed their Irish Catholic compatriots for the defeat of the referendums, declaring them to be disloyal to the British Empire. The people of Wagga Wagga were divided over the issue. In 1916 53.58 per cent of the town's voters supported conscription, but in 1917 57.74 per cent voted against it.

Politically Wagga Wagga in 1920 was also evenly divided in terms of party and denominational representation. At the federal level the Labor Party's Parker Moloney, a Catholic of Irish descent, had won the seat of Hume at the December 1919 elections with 52.53 per cent of the vote, whereas at the previous election in 1917 the Nationalist candidate Franc Falkiner, an Anglican of Irish descent, had won the seat with 51.86 per cent. At the state level the March 1920 elections were conducted using proportional representation with three members to be elected to the Legislative Assembly for the seat of Murray. The Labor Party's William O'Brien, a Catholic of Irish descent, won one of the seats with 45.58 per cent of the vote and two non-Labor candidates, George Beeby, an Anglican of English descent, and Richard Ball, a Baptist also of English descent, won the other two seats with 31.17 per cent and 22.95 per cent, respectively. In the town itself the Labor Party did slightly better with 48.49 per cent.

The divisiveness of the war years continued in Australia long after the armistice of 11 November 1918. Wagga Wagga exemplified this continuing disharmony when two committees vied for approval to erect the town's war memorial. One comprised Protestants, the other Catholics. The dispute was brought before the Supreme Court but the judge declined to give preference to one side over the other. In the end, one committee erected a pillar and the other an arch.[7] Visitors to Wagga Wagga today are likely to be impressed by the patriotism of a town that has two war memorials, not appreciating that they stand as memorials not only to the 200 townsmen who did not return from the war and the 800 who did, but also

---

[7] K. S. Inglis, *Sacred Places: War Memorials in the Australian Landscape*, Melbourne University Press, Carlton, 2001, p. 128.

to the sectarian schism that had infected the act of remembrance itself. Wagga Wagga's two newspapers also reflected the town's divisions, with the *Daily Express* regarded by Catholics as hostile. In the wake of the Sister Liguori affair, the Mount Erin convent would boycott the *Express*, which in turn would boycott covering Catholic news such as school graduations and prize givings.[8]

In the months before our story begins, the situation in Ireland deteriorated. To counter the Irish Republican Army's guerrilla tactics, the British government in March 1920 introduced the Black and Tans, an ill-disciplined force of ex-servicemen recruited to reinforce the Royal Irish Constabulary. Their deployment added a new dimension of horror to the bitter struggle that was taking place in Ireland. It also fanned the flames of the sectarian conflict in Australia which was being fuelled by the war in Ireland. Just a week before our story begins, Wagga Wagga's newspapers carried daily reports of atrocities in Ireland. One report told of the IRA's assassination of Colonel Smythe VC, the Commissioner of Police in Cork, while another described how police ran amok in Tuam, County Galway after attending a wake for two of their colleagues killed by the IRA: 'The police got completely out of control and spent the day in an orgy of shooting, bombing and burning,' reported the *Daily Advertiser* quoting from Reuters.

It was not only foreign news that aroused fears in the community of growing social disorder. That week the *Advertiser* reported that trade unionists were threatening to black ban a ship that was being used to deport Father Charles Jerger, a Catholic priest of German birth who had been interned during the war for allegedly making disloyal statements from the pulpit. Loyalist Protestants had demanded the government act against Jerger, which it did, first by interning him in 1918 and then by deporting him in 1920 even though the war was over. In May 1920 an estimated 150,000 Catholics of Irish descent had rallied in Sydney's Moore Park to protest the priest's deportation. Scuffles had broken out when men of the

---

[8] *Daily Express*, 14 December 1920, p. 1.

King and Empire Alliance stormed the speakers' platform in an attempt to break up the meeting.⁹

The most prominent of Jerger's antagonists was Alderman John Thomas Ness, a real estate agent. Born at Young, New South Wales, in 1871, Ness was a Presbyterian who in 1920 became president of the Protestant Federation. His business partner from 1913 to 1919 was Robert Elvin Barton, who would play a leading role in the Sister Liguori affair. Born in Christchurch, New Zealand in 1865, Barton moved to Victoria in 1882 and to Sydney in 1892. He was initiated a member of the Loyal Orange Institution of New South Wales in 1905 and became a member of the Grand Lodge in 1907. He held many leadership roles in the Orange order before being appointed grand master at the beginning of 1920.

Another Catholic priest to figure in newspaper reports at this time was the Irish-born Archbishop of Melbourne, Daniel Mannix. During the war he had been a strong opponent of conscription, often clashing publicly with Prime Minister Billy Hughes. He was also an outspoken supporter of Irish independence. At the 1918 St Patrick's Day parade in Melbourne, he had earned the ire of loyal Protestants when he saluted the Sinn Féin flag but failed to remove his hat during the playing of *God Save the King*. As our story unfolds Mannix was a passenger on the S.S. *Baltic* sailing from New York to Ireland. The *Advertiser* told its readers that the British cabinet had resolved not to allow Mannix to land in the country of his birth, a decision with which Prime Minister Hughes was in complete agreement, judging by a report in the *Express*. The report carried Hughes' scathing attack on the Catholic prelate, whom he described as worse than the Kaiser and willing to plunge a dagger into the heart of the Empire. The Royal Navy's arrest of Mannix on the high seas on 8 August would have repercussions around the world and would inflame passions aroused in Australia by the Sister Liguori affair.¹⁰

---

⁹ Jeff Kildea, *Tearing the Fabric: Sectarianism in Australia 1910-1925*, Citadel Books, Sydney, 2002, pp. 213-217.
¹⁰ Kildea, *Tearing the Fabric*, pp. 217-218.

In November sectarian bitterness would again rise to the surface with the expulsion from the federal parliament of Hugh Mahon, the Irish-born Labor member for Kalgoorlie. At a public meeting in Melbourne, Mahon had criticised British rule in Ireland, referring to the British Empire as 'this bloody and accursed empire'. Protestant, loyalist, and ex-service organisations inundated the government with letters, telegrams, and public protests demanding the government act against Mahon. Hughes willingly obliged, moving Mahon's expulsion and picking up his seat at the ensuing byelection fought on Empire-loyalty lines, thus securing for his government a majority in the House of Representatives.[11] Mahon's expulsion finished off a year that was arguably the worst in Australia's long history of sectarianism. New South Wales Attorney General Edward McTiernan described the year's accumulated events as 'a hurricane of sectarian strife'.[12]

Party politics also played a part in polarising New South Wales society along sectarian lines. At the elections in March 1920, neither major party won a majority of seats but Labor was able to form a minority government with the support of independents. Of the 43 members in the Labor caucus, 25 were Catholics, while five of the 13 ministers in the cabinet were Catholics, including the treasurer, the attorney general, and the chief secretary, who was in charge of the police.[13] Although Catholics were less than 25 per cent of the population of New South Wales, they constituted 56 per cent of the Labor Caucus and held 38 per cent of the cabinet positions in the state government. To many Protestants, this was a potentially menacing situation. In the past, Protestant spokesmen who raised the spectre of 'Rome rule' in Australia could be dismissed as alarmist and irrational—after all, Catholics were a minority. The year 1920 demonstrated the dangers of such complacency. To these troubled Protestants, militant Catholicism was on the march.

---

[11] Ibid., pp. 226-227.
[12] *Catholic Press*, 16 December 1920, p. 17.
[13] *Catholic Press*, 8 April 1920, page 27; *Freeman's Journal* 15 April 1920, p. 18.

Even before the Sister Liguori affair hit the headlines in August 1920, both sides of the ethno-religious divide were organised and lining up for a showdown. Some people were predicting a violent conflict. A correspondent to the *Australian Christian World* wrote: 'Australia will be embroiled in a war such as that now being waged in Russia; in other words, Australia will have a bloody time with Bolshevism and Sinn Féinism arrayed on one side and constitutionalism and Protestantism on the other'.[14]

On the Catholic side was the Catholic Federation. Formed in 1912 to advance Catholic interests, particularly state aid for Catholic schools, it represented to Protestants the spectre of Roman domination. This view was confirmed in March 1920 when the federation ran candidates under the banner of the Democratic Party at the New South Wales state elections. To defend themselves from organised Catholic militancy, Protestants had formed the Protestant Federation in 1917. Its purpose was to 'conserve and preserve the rights and liberties possessed by us under the British flag', and its principal objective was 'To maintain loyalty to the Throne, the unity of the Empire, and to promote the national development of Australia'.[15]

Another Protestant organisation that took up the cudgels against the Catholic Federation and the perceived malign influence of the Catholic church was the Loyal Orange Institution (LOI).[16] It had been established in Ireland in 1795 following the 'Battle of the Diamond', a sectarian affray near Loughgall, Co. Armagh, in which the Protestant Peep o' Day Boys beat off a large force of Catholic Defenders, killing thirty or more. Its name derives from William of Orange, whose victory over the Catholic King James II at the Battle

---

[14] *Australian Christian World*, 12 November 1920, p. 10.
[15] Kildea, *Tearing the Fabric*, p. 162.
[16] To resist what they saw as the growing threat of 'Romanism', the two organisations, together with the Australian Protestant Defence Association and the Evangelical Council, joined forces in 1921 to form the United Protestant Council (Minutes of the Executive Committee of the Loyal Orange Institution of NSW, 5 April 1921).

of the Boyne in 1690 ensured Protestant ascendancy in Ireland. It grew to become 'an important and elaborately structured religious and political institution, represented in all English-speaking countries'.[17] The LOI, sometimes known as the Orange order, found its way to Australia in the form of Orangemen serving in British regiments posted to New South Wales. In 1845 Sydney's No. 1 Lodge, later known as the District Grand Lodge, was formed. Thereafter, the order established a presence in all the colonies.[18]

As an ultra-Protestant organisation, the LOI proclaims 'its devotion to the ideals of civil and religious liberty, which it associated with the Glorious Revolution and the preservation of Protestant Ascendancy in Church and State'.[19] While espousing love for individual erring Roman Catholics, it requires of each Orangeman that 'he should strenuously oppose the fatal errors and doctrines of the Church of Rome, and scrupulously avoid countenancing (by his presence or otherwise) any act or ceremony of the Roman Catholic worship. He should, by all lawful means, resist the ascendancy of that Church, its encroachments, and the extension of its power'.[20] Membership is thus confined to Protestants, which is not the case with freemasonry, which is sometimes wrongly associated with Orangeism. Although individual masons might also be members of the Orange order, freemasonry does not espouse Protestantism or condemn Catholicism, nor does it exclude Catholics from its ranks. Rather it was the Catholic church which condemned freemasonry as incompatible with Catholic teaching and banned its adherents

---

[17] David A. Roberts, 'The Orange Order in Ireland: A Religious Institution?', *The British Journal of Sociology*, Vol. 22 No. 3, 1971, pp. 269-282, p. 269.
[18] Loyal Orange Institution of N.S.W., *Early History of the Loyal Orange Institution N.S.W.*, Grand Lodge of New South Wales, Sydney, 1926; Tas Vertigan, *The Orange Order in Victoria: Origins, Events, Achievements, Aspirations, and Personalities*, Loyal Orange Institution of Victoria, Melbourne, 1979; David Fitzpatrick, 'Exporting Brotherhood: Orangeism in South Australia', *Immigrants & Minorities*, Vol. 23, No. 2-3, 2005, p. 277-310; Richard P. Davis, *Orangeism in Tasmania, 1832-1967*, University of Ulster, Newtownabbey, Co. Antrim, 2010.
[19] Fitzpatrick, 'Exporting Brotherhood', p. 278.
[20] *Early History of the Loyal Orange Institution*, p. 5.

from joining masonic lodges.[21] Consequently, few Catholics are masons so that masonry and Catholicism are often seen as being in conflict.[22] But their rivalry pales in comparison to the antagonism that occurred between Irish Catholics and Orangemen in Australia during the nineteenth and early twentieth centuries, including bitter confrontations both rhetorical and violent.[23]

It was in this poisoned atmosphere of ethno-religious sectarianism that our story begins with Sister Liguori fleeing her convent and going into hiding under the protection of Robert Barton and the LOI. This prompted her bishop, Dr Joseph Wilfrid Dwyer, to have her arrested under the Lunacy Act. Born in 1869 at East Maitland of Irish parents, Dwyer was appointed the first bishop of Wagga Wagga in 1918. When the Lunacy Court declared Bridget sane, she was released and went to live in the Protestant home of Rev. William Touchell and his wife Laura. The affair rose to prominence in the press, parliament, and at protest meetings nationwide. Bridget later sued Dwyer in the Supreme Court, claiming damages for falsely and maliciously procuring her arrest and imprisonment. This would be no ordinary court case between two individuals. As Sydney's *Sun* newspaper told its readers during the trial:

> Behind the simple figures of ex-Sister Liguori and of Bishop Dwyer stand two great antagonistic forces, unseen, undemonstrative, and impersonal, which sway and seem to compel the action that goes on on the little stage.[24]

The Sister Liguori affair was not unique. The 'escaped' nun was

---

[21] José A. Ferrer Benimeli, 'La Iglesia Católica y la Masonería: Visión Histórica', in . José A. Ferrer Benimeli (ed.), *Masonería y Religión: Convergencias, Oposición, ¿Incompatibilidad?*, Madrid, 1996, pp. 187–201 (English translation in *Ars Quartor Coronatur*, Vol. 119, 2006, pp. 234–55.

[22] James Franklin, 'Catholics versus Masons', *Journal of the Australian Catholic Historical Society*, Vol. 20, 1999, pp. 1-15.

[23] Henry William Cleary, *The Orange Society*, Bernard King & Sons, Melbourne, 1897; Rev. A. Madsen, *The Loyal Orange Institution: Facts v Fables A Rejoinder to the Rev Father Cleary's Book the Orange Society*, C.W. Burford, Melbourne, 1898.

[24] *Sun*, 1 July 1921, p. 7.

a trope that had excited sectarian divisions over the years in many countries. As noted by historians Nancy Blacklow and Elizabeth West:

> Whether through the penny press of the early nineteenth-century scandal sheets or the enormously popular 'Awful Disclosures', alleged and real ex-nuns of the likes of Maria Monk (1836), Rebecca Reed (1835), Edith O'Gorman (1886), and Josephine Bunkley (1855), and the 'plight' of women incarcerated in convents, were appropriated by the Protestant crusade.[25]

Writing about the Sister Liguori affair in 1980, journalist Alan Gill observed that in the 1920s:

> Nuns were, to the general public, objects of fascination and myth. They were confined, in popular view, to the cloister. Those who found the life unsuited did not 'leave' their convents – they 'ran away', 'escaped', or 'jumped over the wall'. The mystery surrounding nuns was exploited for sectarian interests.[26]

Embittered ex-nuns willing to tell their stories were grist to the mill of the anti-Catholic press. One of the many such stories was the 'Great Convent Case' of 1869 in England. It has some features in common with the Sister Liguori story. In that case, Sister Mary Scholastica, whose baptismal name was Susanna Mary Saurin, claimed she had been subjected to numerous petty but vindictive actions by her mother superior and that she had been given humiliating physical work not allocated to others in the convent. When the bishop learned of the contretemps he instituted an inquiry that sided with the convent and ordered that Saurin be discharged from her vows. When the nun refused to leave the convent, she was subjected to a campaign of petty cruelty. After several months of mistreatment, she fell ill and her family brought her home. Maligned as an ex-nun thrown out of her order, she sued to clear her name. The

---

[25] Nancy Blacklow and Elizabeth West, 'Sectarianism and Sisterhood: Research in progress', *Rural Society*, Vol. 10, No. 2, 2000, pp. 243–248, p. 243.
[26] *Sydney Morning Herald*, 19 July 1980, Good Weekend section, p. 14.

jury found in her favour on the counts of libel and conspiracy and awarded her £500 in damages. The trial judge severely criticised the bishop for not carrying out suitably and fairly his duty to investigate properly the 'miserable squabbles of a convent'.

Another 'escaped' nun, Irish American Edith O'Gorman toured Australia in 1886 giving lectures on 'How I escaped the convent'. The LOI in Sydney sponsored her visit as part of its campaign against Catholic convents. The campaign featured reports of the iniquities of religious life for women and demands for government inspection of religious institutions. O'Gorman's lectures attracted strong opposition from Catholics and sometimes resulted in violence. Historian Dianne Hall provides a vivid description of one such event in Lismore in northern New South Wales:

> Before [O'Gorman] had even appeared on stage, groups of men, with hats ostentatiously on their heads, began throwing eggs and shouting. Sitting on the left-hand side of the stage were Orangemen Christopher Hetherington and his relative John Johnstone, while Charles Staff the Master of the Lodge no. 99 was taking tickets at the door. Once O'Gorman appeared on stage, the hall erupted into a full-scale riot. The Catholics, armed with sticks, whips, bottles, chair legs, and horseshoes, gained possession of the hall and the Orangemen beat a hasty and unarmed retreat, escorting O'Gorman and other women out of the stage door. Hetherington was covered in blood from a head wound, Johnstone was also wounded. Edith O'Gorman's husband Professor Auffray described it as the worst riot they had ever seen.[27]

A more recent example of a nun who claimed to be mistreated by her mother superior and her bishop is the story of Sister Mary Basil of the Sisters of Charity in Quebec. In 1917 she was awarded $20,000 in damages against her bishop and her mother superior after she sued them for abducting her from her convent to place her

---

[27] 'Dianne Hall, Defending the Faith: Orangeism and Ulster Protestant Identities in Colonial New South Wales', *Journal of Religious History*, Vol. 38, No. 2, 2014, pp. 207-223, p. 220.

in an asylum. The Grand Orange Lodge of British America published a pamphlet entitled *Attempted Abduction of Sister Mary Basil*, which contained a transcript of the evidence given in court. The story of Sister Basil was well publicised in Protestant newspapers in Australia. The *Watchman*, the official organ of the Australian Protestant Defence Association and the LOI, observed, 'The whole affair is a terrible revelation of the possibilities of wrongdoing and cruelty within convent walls and is yet another clear call for Government inspection of these institutions'.[28]

'Escaped' nun stories were also good box office. By coincidence or, more likely, by clever marketing, Leila Zillwood's play *The Broken Rosary* was performed at Sydney's Grand Opera House during the trial of Sister Liguori's action for damages against Bishop Dwyer. Advertisements in the newspapers described it as:

> The extraordinary story of a girl who ran away from a Convent, told in ten scenes, including the Convent Grounds, the Call of the World, the Runaway, the Futile Search, the Broken Rosary, the Forced Marriage, the Lovers' Quarrel, the Twins, the Wanderer's Return.

With the flight of Sister Liguori from her Wagga Wagga convent and her taking refuge in the house of Robert and Mary Thompson, a Protestant family associated with the LOI, Australia now had its own homegrown 'escaped' nun story. For militant Protestants, it was an opportunity, too good to pass up, to renew their attack on the Catholic convent system. In the press and in parliament they called for a royal commission into convents. Predictably, Catholics fought back and the passions aroused by the O'Gorman visit were re-ignited. Like Helen of Troy, Bridget Partridge would become the occasion of a conflict between two powerful forces, her personal crisis subordinated to the broader contest. Instead of helping the young nun sort out her troubles in dialogue with the convent, the Thompsons lied to her bishop and the police as to her whereabouts,

---

[28] *Australian Christian World*, 30 August 1918, pp. 7-8; 6 September 1918, pp. 7-8; *Watchman*, 26 September 1918, p. 6; 3 July 1919, p. 1.

spirited her out of Wagga Wagga, and despatched a messenger to Sydney requesting the assistance of the LOI, which resulted in the intervention of Grand Master Barton, who sent her into hiding in Sydney. Thus, the die was cast and the apocalyptic battle begun. Protest, disorder, and the threat of violence soon emerged to shatter the peace and harmony of the local community and send shockwaves through the country.

Yet, in Wagga Wagga that July weekend in 1920, one might be forgiven for failing to foresee the dark clouds of discord that soon would gather. The back pages of that weekend's *Advertiser* and *Express* informed their readers that show season was about to begin in the Riverina. Advertisements reminded them that entries for the fine arts, needlework and cookery competitions at the Wagga Wagga show would close on Monday, 26 July. Readers also learned that the School of Arts and the Wagga Literary Institute had just elected new committees. For those who liked to spend their Saturday afternoons playing or watching football, the town's newspapers reported that the local Australian Rules football teams, the Federals and the Lillies, would be battling it out at the Wagga Cricket Ground. And, for those who preferred their entertainment indoors, the Strand cinema would keep the citizens of Wagga Wagga entertained during the week with the latest movies from overseas. With a lovely touch of irony, the Strand's movie due for screening on Monday night, when many of the town's citizens would be out searching for the 'escaped' nun, was *Manhattan Knight*, an adaptation of Gelette Burgess's popular novel *Find the Woman*.

1
FLIGHT

Winter of discontent

It was one of those dreary, damp, winter days when the hearts of men and women are as heavy as the leaden skies above. It is not easy to be joyful when day after day the weather is poor, particularly if your life is a misery and you have been feeling unwell for longer than you can remember. At such times, the smallest of incidents, which on happier days you might shrug off with a laugh, can be overwhelming.[1]

Why, for instance, would anyone get upset over a broom that had gone missing, particularly when any rational person would work out that it cannot have gone far? Surely, it is just a matter of looking and it would eventually turn up—in a cupboard, behind a door or leaning against a wall somewhere. But, judging by the noise that echoed that morning through the convent at Mount Erin, one could be forgiven for believing that Sister Joan and Sister Liguori were arguing about life itself, rather than who was responsible for the missing broom. But trivial though it might seem to the objective observer, this altercation over the broom, in which Sister Joan accused Sister Liguori of lying, was the last straw for the depressed and ailing nun, who only that morning had complained to the mother superior of a headache.

Sister Liguori's reaction to the incident of the broom would be followed over the next few weeks by a cascading series of actions, each minor in itself, that would together result in one of Australia's most bitter sectarian conflicts. Readers of Erik Durschmied's *The*

---

[1] Unless otherwise indicated, the narrative in this and following chapters is taken from the detailed newspaper accounts of the trial of Bridget Partridge's action for damages against Bishop Joseph Dwyer. See the note on sources at the end of the book.

Hinge Factor: How Chance and Stupidity Have Changed History (Hodder & Stoughton, 2013) will recognise the phenomenon. It is akin to 'the butterfly effect' in Chaos Theory, sometimes expressed in terms of the proverb 'For Want of a Nail':

> For want of a nail the shoe was lost.
>
> For want of a shoe the horse was lost.
>
> For want of a horse the rider was lost.
>
> For want of a rider the message was lost.
>
> For want of a message the battle was lost.
>
> For want of a battle the kingdom was lost.
>
> And all for the want of a horseshoe nail.

Following her altercation with Sister Joan, Sister Liguori left the refectory and walked through the paddock surrounding the imposing buildings of the Mount Erin convent. It was a wonder she was not observed. But, then again, any sensible person would have been indoors on such a miserable day, perhaps cooking a batch of scones or sitting in front of the fire reading a book. Not so the troubled nun who was pre-occupied with thoughts as to what she could do to end her misery. She had heard stories of another nun who had felt so miserable she had thrown herself into the waterhole on the property. But Sister Liguori was not suicidal – she wanted to live, to be free.

Eventually she determined on a plan. She would tell her bishop of her problems. She had no reason to believe he was other than a kindly man, surely he would listen sympathetically to her story. She would tell him that the diocesan inspector had been pleased with her teaching and she did not understand why she had been removed from teaching at Ganmain and put in charge of the refectory at Mount Erin. She would say that her new duties included scrubbing, sweeping, washing up dishes, waiting on tables, and taking trays to any of the sisters who might be ill - the work of a lay-nun not that of a choir-nun, the status which she had achieved.

She would let him know that she loved teaching and her pupils had loved her and that now her only contact with the children was during playground duty. She knew she had missed an opportunity to tell him all this when he had come in May on his annual visitation to interview each nun privately. But the way he put the three standard questions seemed so formal:

'Are you in good health?';

'Have you any complaints of any sort to make to me as bishop?'; and

'Are you perfectly happy and contented?'

She realised now she should have told him she was not well, that she was not happy and that, yes, she did have complaints. But when he asked her the three questions that day she had meekly answered in turn, 'Yes, my Lord', 'No, my Lord' and 'Yes, my Lord.' Since then, she had become more miserable, her health had deteriorated, and she had become run down. Dr William Leahy, who had practised medicine in Wagga Wagga for about 25 years and was the district's government medical officer and the convent's visiting medical practitioner, had come to the view that Sister Liguori's general physical condition was not very strong and he had diagnosed her as being neurasthenic with a neurotic temperament.

First flight

Sister Liguori now made up her mind. She would set the record straight. She would go to a nearby house and telephone the bishop. For the young nun this was a big step. She was a member of an enclosed order, whose rules forbade her leaving the convent without permission and, even then, only in exceptional circumstances. As for telephoning the bishop, it was unheard of. But, after the incident with the broom, she felt desperate and determined. Turning her back on the brick and stone edifice on the hill, she walked with purpose across the paddock toward Coleman Street. At a time when Wagga Wagga had no electric light or power, it was easy to see which houses had telephones by the overhead telephone wires. She made her way to the house of the Burgess family and pushed on the side gate. One of the children playing in the yard ran inside the house and fetched her mother.

Forty-year-old Jessie Ada Burgess (née Taylor) was originally from Victoria. She and her husband, Clarkson James Burgess, had moved to Wagga Wagga a few years before with their three children: Roderick now aged 15, Walter 13, and Jessie Marjorie 9. Forty-two-year-old Clarkson was the manager of T. Edmondson & Co., Wagga Wagga's earliest and largest department store. The Burgess family were active members of St John's Church of England parish and Jessie and Clarkson were on the management committee of St Margaret's Hostel for girls, which the church had established at the start of the year not far from their house.

Sister Liguori asked Mrs Burgess whether she could use the telephone. Mrs Burgess observed the nun's distress but she did not question her for she seemed determined to make her phone call. After calling the exchange, Mrs Burgess left the young woman alone. Sister Liguori asked to speak to Bishop Dwyer but when informed he was in Albury she agreed to speak instead to Father Thomas Barry, one of the assistant priests at St Michael's cathedral. She told him who she was and that she was not in the convent, though not far from it.

How disappointed and bereft she must have felt, after having determined on this extraordinary method of contacting the bishop to retrieve the opportunity she had passed up three months before, to speak to him in confidence and tell him of her worries and concerns. She must have realised then that her superior, Mother Stanislaus, would soon hear of what she had done and no doubt she feared she would end up in more trouble. Mother Mary Stanislaus, a native of County Kildare, was one of the original five pioneering nuns who had arrived in Australia from Ireland in 1874 to establish a convent and schools in the Wagga Wagga district. She had recently advised Sister Liguori she might be better off returning to her family in Ireland, but the young nun had baulked at the suggestion, saying she wanted to remain at Mount Erin. The council of the senior sisters who shared the decision-making role at the convent recommended that Sister Liguori be permitted to stay and Mother Stanislaus had relented.[2]

When Sister Liguori hung up the phone she asked Mrs Burgess whether she could stay at the house a while as there had been a little trouble at the convent, and she would like to be away until it blew over. The nun remained at the house for about three hours, passing the time looking at photographs with Jessie Marjorie, the youngest of the Burgess children. Meanwhile, Father Barry telephoned the convent and told Mother Stanislaus of his telephone conversation with Sister Liguori and of his belief that she was at a house near the convent. Mother Stanislaus ordered a search be made of the convent and when it confirmed that Sister Liguori was not there the search was widened. During the course of the afternoon the groom from the convent called at the Burgess house. Sister Liguori pleaded with Mrs Burgess not to let him in and, in a pathetic gesture, locked herself in the dining room.

Soon after, Mother Stanislaus telephoned Mrs Burgess who confirmed that Sister Liguori was at her house. A little later, Mother Clare and Sister Brendan arrived there in the convent's bus. After Mrs Burgess let them in, Sister Liguori opened the door of the dining room and Mother Clare went in, while Mrs Burgess and Sister Brendan remained outside the room. Mother Clare was the bursar at Mount Erin. She had been the mother of novices when Sister Liguori was in the novitiate. She had been very strict.

'Sister, you do not look well,' Mother Clare said. 'I think you are ill.'

Sister Liguori replied, 'I wanted a rest. I was tired.'

---

[2] B. T. Dowd and Sheila E. Tearle, *Centenary, Sisters of the Presentation of the Blessed Virgin Mary, Wagga Wagga, New South Wales, 1874-1974*, The Sisters of the Presentation of the Blessed Virgin Mary, Wagga Wagga, N.S.W., 1973, p. 65.

Mother Clare said, 'If you come back the doctor will give you something to relieve you.'

'I do not want to see the doctor,' replied the young nun.

Mother Clare said, 'Reverend Mother is very anxious to see you.'

Sister Liguori had not yet made up her mind to quit convent life. Overwhelmed by her failure to communicate with the bishop, she felt powerless. She replied, 'I will go back.'

When Mother Clare and Sister Liguori emerged from the dining room the four women stood talking for a while before moving towards the gate. As she left, Sister Liguori squeezed Mrs Burgess's hand and said goodbye. Sister Brendan, who had known Sister Liguori since they were novices together, thought that her companion looked ghastly and seemed in a very agitated state of mind. However, as they proceeded toward the convent, she observed that Sister Liguori became more composed.

On reaching the convent, Sister Liguori was ushered into the mother superior's office. It was just before 5 pm. Recently, Mother Stanislaus had been away from the convent for three weeks. On her return the previous Wednesday, she had noticed that Sister Liguori was in a very excited state, was flushed, and altogether out of sorts. The troubled young nun had asked her several times whether non-Catholics could be baptised in the boarding school. When she explained that it could not be done without the consent of the parents, Sister Liguori had waxed warm, saying she knew it could. Sister Liguori had previously told Mother Stanislaus that she had heard there was a girl at the convent school whose father intended to remarry and that the girl had said she wanted to be baptised into the Catholic Church. Eventually, Mother Stanislaus had tired of Sister Liguori's obsessive questioning and told her to leave such things to her as it was her business.

Upon entering the mother superior's office, Sister Liguori came across to Mother Stanislaus and said, 'Mother, I am sorry.' Mother

Stanislaus did not scold her. Rather, observing that her habit was wet, she looked at her sadly and said, 'Now go and change your clothing.' When Sister Liguori left the room, Mother Stanislaus telephoned Dr William Leahy and asked him to come to the convent.

Sister Brendan made Sister Liguori a cup of tea, some toast, and an egg, which she ate with Mother Clare. Sister Liguori asked the older nun whether she had heard the disturbance that morning over the broom but Mother Clare said she had not. Sister Brendan then took Sister Liguori upstairs and helped her to change out of her wet and muddy clothes and obtained some warm water for her to wash in. As Sister Liguori was about to get into bed, she was summoned back to the mother superior's office where the doctor was waiting for her.

She related to Leahy what had happened that day when she had left Mount Erin. When asked by Mother Stanislaus whether anyone in the convent had done anything to make her go away, she at first replied that they had all been very kind to her but then told her about the argument over the broom. Mother Stanislaus said it did not matter but Sister Liguori insisted it had worried her. Sister Liguori also told them that another sister had upset her by asking at what time dinner would be. Mother Stanislaus told her that there was no harm in that but again Sister Liguori replied that it had worried her.

Throughout this exchange Dr Leahy observed that Sister Liguori was ghastly pale, nervous, and excited. He had known the young nun for years and had treated her for insomnia, nervousness, and headaches. After examining her, he said she was run down and asked whether she had been taking the medicine he had previously prescribed. She told him she had not because she had asked for a tonic and he had only given her medicine to be taken at night. She thought it was a sleeping draught. From his observations that evening and his previous knowledge of Sister Liguori, Dr Leahy formed the view that she was of unsound mind and suffering from delusions and that she was 'mentally unhinged'. Mother Stanislaus told Sister Liguori to return to her room.

Second flight

When Sister Liguori returned to her room, she found that Sister Brendan had prepared her bed, which was on an enclosed balcony upstairs. This was another source of grievance for Sister Liguori, who resented the fact she did not have a room of her own even though sisters less senior than her had separate rooms. Sister Brendan said she would fetch her a dose of castor oil. Castor oil was a multi-purpose medicine that used to be given for a host of ailments. It tasted vile and, in the case of children, the threat of its administration was usually enough to ensure they were not faking an illness to get time off school. At Mount Erin the practice was to administer castor oil in black coffee in order to mask its unpleasant taste. When Sister Brendan returned with the mixture and a biscuit, she helped her sad friend to sit up and placed her arms around her while she drank the mixture. According to Sister Brendan's account of the evening's events, Sister Liguori did not complain about the dose or tell her that there was anything unusual in its flavour. But later Sister Liguori would claim that she suspected the darkish liquid mixed with the castor oil was something other than coffee. To her, it tasted like ink and made her feel weak. For nearly a week afterwards she felt ill because of it.

Thinking that Sister Liguori should get some sleep, Sister Brendan made her comfortable and, as was customary when a sister was indisposed, sprinkled holy water around the bed. Sister Liguori would later allege that Sister Brendan's actions were sinister, claiming she removed her pillows, placed her arms by her side and said, 'You won't get out of bed for the next six months.' Sister Brendan sat with her charge for about twenty minutes and then retired to another part of the room. While there she heard a noise. She went to investigate and saw Sister Liguori getting out of bed. Sister Liguori said she wanted a cup of cocoa. Sister Brendan put her back to bed, saying it was too soon after the medicine, but she would bring her some later. Not long after, she noticed that Sister Liguori was tossing about a good deal and told her that if she would lie still the oil would not repeat on her.

At about 7.30 that night, Mother Stanislaus sent for Sister Brendan. When she had gone, Sister Liguori leapt out of bed. Seized with the fear that her mother superior, Sister Brendan, and Dr Leahy had conspired to poison her, she ran to the bathroom, where she proceeded to drink three cups of soapy water in order to induce herself to vomit the oily mixture. Meanwhile, Sister Brendan, whose normal duties required her to supervise the boarders, had persuaded Mother Stanislaus to allow her to remain with her companion through the night. When she returned upstairs she found Sister Liguori in the bathroom and scolded her for risking a chill. As they made their way back to the veranda, Sister Liguori asked Sister Brendan to fetch a hot water bottle as her feet were cold. She promised she would be in bed by the time her friend returned. When Sister Brendan left to obtain the hot water bottle Sister Liguori ran down the stairs and out the door of the convent. Clad only in her nightdress and in her bare feet she plunged into the fog-shrouded darkness of the cold winter's night.

It was only a slight knocking but Mrs Burgess heard it coming from the back door. On investigating, she found Sister Liguori standing in her yard. 'Here I am frightening you again,' the young woman said. Mrs Burgess could see she had been crying. She brought her inside and gave her shoes and warm clothes to wear. 'You must stay the night,' Mrs Burgess said but Sister Liguori shook her head, saying she was afraid the sisters would know where to look for her. She begged Mrs Burgess to take her somewhere else. The two women left the house, Bridget now clothed in a coat and buggy rug for warmth. At first they went, running and walking, to the Church of England hostel, but it was locked up. They returned to Coleman Street but instead of returning to her house, Mrs Burgess took Sister Liguori to the house of a neighbour, Mrs Thompson.

Born in 1881 at Cootamundra, Mary Eliza Thompson (née Heathwood) was the second wife of Robert Thompson, a Yorkshireman born in about 1844, who had come to Australia as a young man. He travelled the country hoping to make his fortune from mining and prospecting before settling in Wagga Wagga as a local agent for a grocery wholesaling business. His first wife, Cecilia Grace Graham, whom he married in 1886, had died in 1906. Robert inherited her house in Coleman Street, known as 'Bredagh', which sat on three acres of land. Robert and Mary married the following year in Victoria. They had five children, who were aged from 13 down to 5 when Mrs Burgess and Sister Liguori came knocking at Bredagh's door. Like the Burgess family, the Thompsons were Protestants. In fact, Robert was a member of the Star of Wagga Lodge No. 103 of the Protestant Alliance Friendly Society, an offshoot of the Loyal Orange Institution.

When Mrs Thompson opened the door, the two women stepped inside. Bridget said, 'Don't let them take me back again'.[3]

Raising the alarm

When Sister Liguori's absence was discovered, the sisters in the Mount Erin convent became apprehensive. A search was mounted of the convent but the missing nun could not be found. Becoming increasingly alarmed, Mother Stanislaus telephoned the police, Father Barry, and several Catholic homes asking for assistance in finding the missing nun. She also rang Dr Leahy. He too joined the searchers. They would be out all night, scouring the paddocks, searching the dams and railway cuttings, and other dangerous places.

On being told that a nun had gone missing from the convent, Sergeant Sam Gallaher, the officer on duty at the police station, despatched Sergeant Patrick O'Rourke and Constable James Brownlee to the convent and they joined the search party. Gallaher and O'Rourke were both from Ireland. Gallaher had started his police career in the Royal Irish Constabulary and joined the local force in

---

[3] *Daily Express*, 14 August 1920, p. 1.

1893. A Protestant and a freemason, he had been posted to Wagga Wagga from Sydney in 1916. O'Rourke, like Sister Liguori a native of County Kildare, was a Catholic. He had been in Wagga Wagga since 1915, having joined the police in 1889. Brownlee was a New South Welshman and a Catholic who joined the police force in 1904.

During the search, Father Barry and Dr Leahy apprehensively made their way towards the waterhole on the Mount Erin property, looking for footprints near the bank. Having found none, the two men separated. Dr Leahy went with another searcher, John O'Regan, across a paddock that separated the convent from Mrs Burgess's house. On the way they found a head dress, which the sisters later identified as belonging to the missing nun. By then several others had joined in the search, including Michael Ferry, the 48-year-old secretary of the Wagga Racing Club. Ferry was from a leading Catholic family in Wagga Wagga. He and his father Bryan were founding members of the Wagga Wagga branch of the Catholic Federation.

From the Thompson house, Sister Liguori could see the torchlights of the searchers coming closer. When some of them spoke to Mrs Burgess, she assured them Sister Liguori was in good hands, though she did not reveal her whereabouts. But some of the searchers had worked that out for themselves and had surrounded the Thompson house. When the police came knocking on the front door, Sister Liguori begged the Thompsons not to disclose her presence. She was relieved to hear them telling the police she was not in the house. Then she heard Mr Thompson's agitated voice, demanding the searchers leave his property or he would set his dogs on them. The decision of the Thompsons to lie to the police about Sister Liguori's presence in the house was the first of a series of fateful decisions that would transform the personal travails of a troubled young woman into Australia's most bitter sectarian conflict of the twentieth century.

2
Evasion

Sunday, 25 July

Throughout Saturday night and into Sunday the searchers maintained a vigil around the Thompson house in Coleman Street. Mrs Thompson later recounted:

> No one slept in my house that night. We were all too excited, and the mysterious noises of the search parties kept us on the alert. A fog enveloped everything. In the morning, when the fog had lifted, we found a search party in the back yard.
> 'Good morning,' said the leader of them.
> 'What do you want here?' was the question I put to them.
> 'It's this way, Mrs Thompson,' was the reply. 'We've lost some turkeys and we thought they might be here.'
> 'Well, they're not. But it strikes me you are looking for another bird – a partridge, perhaps. So, get out.'[1]

Michael Ferry had been keeping a close watch on the entrance to the property. As dawn broke, Mrs Thompson sent her sister, Ethel Heathwood, to the hostel to ring Dr Eric Tivey, a 33-year-old general practitioner who had practised at Wagga Wagga for six of his eight years as a doctor. As Miss Heathwood was leaving the property, Ferry approached her and asked whether Sister Liguori was in the house. She said she was not.

At about this time, Inspector Duprez came on duty at the police station, where Sergeant O'Rourke briefed him on the night's events. Aged 58, William Alexander Duprez was an experienced police officer who, after more than 30 years in the police force, four of them

---
[1] *Sun*, 13 August 1920, p. 5.

in Wagga Wagga, was close to retirement. He was also a prominent freemason.

Using the hostel phone, Miss Heathwood asked Dr Tivey to come to the Thompson house but she said he should first call at the police station to pick up Inspector Duprez. When Tivey inquired what was wrong she said, 'I cannot tell you over the telephone, but there is nothing wrong with any member of the family'. When Tivey arrived at the police station Inspector Duprez told him, 'A nun has escaped, and search parties have been out all night. The police were informed and two constables were detailed to join the search.' Dr Tivey would later give evidence at the trial that Duprez's use of the word 'escaped' had led him to assume that she was an escapee from forcible detention, which to him was a significant fact bearing on her mental condition in that it provided a rational explanation for the unusual manner in which she had left the convent.

Duprez and Tivey accompanied by Constable Cooper proceeded to the Thompson property. As they were walking towards the house, Ferry, who had been standing with two constables, approached Tivey. He told the doctor that he and others had been searching all night for the missing nun adding, 'She has been wandering about these paddocks in her nightgown. She must be mad.' Ferry asked whether he had come to the house to visit her. Tivey denied he was there to see the nun. Later, after Duprez had spoken with Mrs Thompson, the inspector informed the searchers that Sister Liguori was safe, whereupon most of them withdrew.

When Tivey and Duprez arrived at the house, Miss Heathwood opened the front door and said, 'Oh, come in doctor. We've got an escaped nun here. They say she is mad.' Once inside, Tivey spoke with Mrs Thompson, who said, 'People have been round the house all night trying to get in and saying that the girl who is in here is mad. We would like to have her examined to see if you can find any evidence of madness.' When Tivey was introduced to Sister Liguori, she asked him whether he had come to take her back to the convent.

Tivey reassured her, saying that Mrs Thompson had only called him to examine her. The doctor then had a conversation with Bridget in the presence of Mrs Thompson and her sister, following which he and Sister Liguori went into another room. Tivey asked her why she had left the convent. She answered, 'I have been rather run down in health lately and the work I have been called on to do has been heavier than my health would stand.' She did not tell him that an attempt had been made to murder her. Dr Tivey then briefly examined her and formed the opinion that she was showing no signs of illness – physical or mental. After the examination, Tivey and Sister Liguori returned to the room where Inspector Duprez and Mrs Thompson were waiting. The inspector was introduced to her. Duprez asked,

> 'Are you the nun who left the convent yesterday?'
>
> She replied, 'Yes.'
>
> Duprez inquired, 'How long had you been in there?'
>
> Sister Liguori said, 'About ten years.'
>
> 'By Jove,' said the inspector. 'You look very young. How old are you?'
>
> She replied 'I am 28. I was 18 when I went into the convent.'
> (She was actually 29 by the date on her birth certificate.)

She informed the inspector she had no relatives in Australia, but she had a brother in China. She told the inspector she did not like the convent.

> Duprez asked, 'Do you not want to go back?'
>
> She answered, 'No, not if I can help it.'
>
> Duprez said, 'I do not know any law to compel you to go back, if you don't want to.'
>
> Sister Liguori said, 'Mrs Thompson is going to look after me for the present.'
>
> The inspector turned to Mrs Thompson and asked, 'Is that right?'
>
> Mrs Thompson replied, 'Yes.'

Upon leaving the house, Dr Tivey was again approached by Ferry who asked whether Sister Liguori was inside. This time Dr Tivey said she was. Ferry then suggested that the mother superior of the convent should be informed of the nun's whereabouts. Accompanied by Ferry, Inspector Duprez, Dr Tivey, and Constable Cooper went up to the convent where they met with Mother Stanislaus and Mother Clare. Mother Stanislaus was in an agitated state.

> 'Where is she?' she asked Tivey. 'Have you seen her? Is she all right?'
>
> Tivey replied, 'She is at Mrs Thompson's house, and is being well cared for there.'
>
> Tivey then asked, 'How did the sister leave the convent?'
>
> Mother Stanislaus said, 'Yesterday morning we received a telephone message from the presbytery saying she was at Mrs Burgess's house, and I sent two sisters over, and they brought her back. I summoned Dr Leahy and he saw her, and she was ordered to bed. A sister was left in charge. Sister Liguori asked her to get a hot water bag, and while she was gone she left the convent again in her nightgown.'

Tivey inquired as to Sister Liguori's duties and was told that she was a lay sister who did sweeping, scrubbing, washing up, and also took trays to the sick sisters.

> Mother Stanislaus said, 'She was tried as a teacher, but she was unable to maintain order among her pupils and was not successful in that branch.'
>
> Inspector Duprez asked, 'Why shouldn't she be allowed to go where she likes?'
>
> The mother superior replied, 'We cannot allow her to go away to people we do not know anything about. We are responsible to her parents for her.'
>
> Mother Clare added, 'Any sister is free to leave, and Sister Liguori could have left in a proper way.'
>
> Mother Stanislaus said, 'If Sister Liguori were to return I will send her to her parents. We will provide for her and her parents could take charge of her. Under the circumstances, even if she wished to stay we could not keep her.'

Dr Tivey remarked, 'My wife is in want of a maid. We will take her.'

Mother Stanislaus replied, 'I could not allow that.' She inquired, 'Is Sister Liguori insane?'

Inspector Duprez said, 'Dr Tivey believes she is quite sane.'

Mother Stanislaus responded, 'I do not know how she could be quite sane when she left the convent in her nightdress the way she did. If she wanted to leave, she could have done so properly.'

Tivey asked, 'Hasn't she vows?'

Mother Stanislaus said, 'Yes, but our bishop could arrange all that.'

Mother Clare added, 'Anyone of us can leave if we wish and be nicely provided for.'

Dr Tivey asked, 'Did Dr Leahy ever suggest Sister Liguori was of unsound mind and needed watching?'

Mother Stanislaus said, 'No, he had not.'

Dr Tivey asked, 'After her return to the convent, did Dr Leahy mention anything about unsound mind?'

Mother Stanislaus replied, 'No.'

Tivey said, 'Well, I have been unable to detect any evidence of unsoundness of mind or insanity, and the matter is, therefore, out of my hands. I can do nothing further with the case, as it has now become a legal matter, and her physical condition does not seem to call for treatment at present, as far as I can see.'

The visitors then left. That afternoon, Mother Stanislaus requested Father Barry to deliver two letters, one to Mrs Thompson and the other to Sister Liguori, and to take some clothing for Sister Liguori. When he arrived at the Thompson house, Mrs Thompson told him that Inspector Duprez had ordered that no one was permitted to see the nun. (When Dr Leahy later mentioned this to Inspector Duprez, the policeman denied that he had issued any such instruction.) Father Barry gave to Mrs Thompson the letter addressed to them but, being unable to deliver the other letter to Sister Liguori, he retained it. The letter to the Thompsons read:

> Just a line to say I am grateful to hear that our dear sister had the shelter of your home last night. We have been very grieved over her actions. I am sending over a few articles of clothing, and anything she needs will be supplied. With best wishes, dear Mr and Mrs Thompson.

Mrs Thompson refused to take the clothing, saying she would supply all of the sister's wants in that regard. Mrs Thompson said that the nun had written a letter to the bishop which she handed to Father Barry. The letter to the bishop read:

> I, Sister M. Liguori, was not treated at Wagga Wagga Convent as I ought. I tried to do my duty the same as the rest of the sisters, but my health was broken down. I asked for medicine. The doctor gave me poison to end my life, and I fled from the convent. I do not wish on any account to again go back to Mount Erin. I am going for a little holiday. My death bed was fixed for me at Mount Erin. I got into it—just like me. I drank poison—just like me. The hand of God sustained me. I fled to the protection of a stranger, who is giving me a holiday. I'll ask to return to another order I wish; then I'll ask your permission to stay with friends otherwise.

At the trial Sister Liguori would claim that although she at first believed the mixture had been administered with the intention of killing her, she had come to the view, after a few months, that she had been drugged so that she could be punished for running away by being subjected to ill treatment while she was semi-conscious so as not to disturb the boarders. However, she admitted she did not mention to Mrs Burgess, Dr Tivey, or the police her suspicions as to the plot to murder her. She claimed, however, to have told Mrs Thompson. When the letter was shown to Dr Leahy, it confirmed his opinion that Sister Liguori was suffering from delusions of persecution and was of unsound mind, notwithstanding Dr Tivey's opposite opinion, which had been made known to him.

Throughout the day, a watch was kept on the Thompson house in case the Thompsons should try to spirit Sister Liguori away. Clearly there existed between the Thompsons and the watchers a mutual mistrust as to the other's motives and intentions regarding Sister Liguori. This mistrust was the product of years of conditioning. Often educated separately and segregated in their social pursuits, Protestants and Catholics had grown up hearing absurd stories of the beliefs and practices of the other. As we have seen, lurid accounts of the cruelty of convent life and of 'escaped' nuns were common in the nineteenth and early twentieth centuries. To the Thompsons and their Protestant friends Bridget Partridge was a refugee from an evil system that subordinated the freedom of the individual to the wishes of Rome. To Ferry and his Catholic friends, Sister Liguori was being held a prisoner by enemies of Sister Liguori's faith and of their own in order to further their campaign against the Catholic Church and its convents.

Suspicions do not always indicate paranoia. And, in this case, the Catholic watchers' suspicion that the Thompsons might try to spirit Sister Liguori away proved correct. In a statement to the press some months later, Grand Master Robert Barton described what happened:

> During the day many people came about Thompson's house and many of them made some very threatening remarks, and it was then decided by her many friends who had come to her aid that it would be wise to remove her. Accordingly, arrangements were made to remove her from Wagga. In carrying out this idea it was necessary to arrange a 'surprise party' to visit Mr Thompson's house, and accordingly many young people arrived in the early hours of the evening, and after playing and singing a move was made to get Miss Partridge out of the house.[2]

The extraction was done using 'sleight of hand', with Sister Liguori, who now preferred to be called Bridget Partridge, emerging from

---
[2] *Watchman*, 7 October 1920, p. 3.

the house arm-in-arm with a young man and appearing to be one of the partygoers. She was wearing a dress belonging to Mary Thompson and a coat and hat belonging to her sister Ethel Heathwood. As Mrs Thompson later explained:

> Her escape was quite open. She went out the front door on the arm of a friend. I went out the back. We walked past the pickets down the road, across a paddock, into Turvey's Park, where we stood under a tree conversing for fully 20 minutes, when a motor car came along, picked her up, and dashed off to Adelong, 40 miles away, where my sister took charge of her. We were a happy little party, and no one guessed that the nun's flight had commenced.[3]

In addition to Bridget and Mrs Thompson, the party included George Edney, the Worshipful Master of Wagga Wagga's No Surrender Loyal Orange Lodge. They drove to a farm at Mount Pleasant, 20 kilometres from Adelong, an old gold mining town at the gateway to the Snowy Mountains, 80 kilometres south-west of Wagga Wagga. As the travellers approached the farm, the car met with an accident and they had to proceed the rest of the way on foot. At 11.30 pm they eventually arrived and were greeted by Letitia Howell, Mrs Thompson's 45-year-old sister, whose husband Frank was a grazier in the district. Once Bridget had settled in and they had eaten supper, her escort left Mount Pleasant and drove back to Wagga Wagga. Bridget would remain at the Howells' farm for four nights.

In spiriting Bridget out of Wagga Wagga and refusing thereafter to tell anyone, including the police of her whereabouts, the Thompsons made their second fateful decision. This followed on from their decision the night before to lie to the police about her presence in their house. While the Thompsons' suspicion of Catholics was explicable in terms of the years of conditioning mentioned above, their decision to keep the police in the dark as to Bridget's

---

[3] *Sun*, 13 August 1920, p. 5; *Daily Telegraph*, 12 August 1920, p. 6; *Sydney Morning Herald*, 14 August 1920, p. 13.

whereabouts is curious. As we have seen the police stationed in Wagga Wagga were a mix of Protestants and Catholics, with the two most senior officers, Inspector Duprez and Sergeant Gallaher, being freemasons. It is possible, of course, that Inspector Duprez was informed of her whereabouts. However, he reported to his superiors that he did not know where the nun was and he gave evidence on oath that those who knew had refused to tell him. As a result of the Thompsons' decision not to tell, the police were as unaware of Bridget's well-being as Bishop Dwyer and Mother Stanislaus and therefore could not put their minds at rest. This secrecy contributed significantly to the escalation of the affair into a full-blown controversy. As the person ultimately responsible for Sister Liguori's welfare until she could be returned to her family, the bishop could not simply wash his hands of the matter.

Having covertly removed Bridget from Wagga Wagga, the Thompsons sent a messenger to Sydney to call on Grand Master Barton. According to Barton:

> Our people in Wagga thought it would be better to send to Sydney to see what could be done to assist this young woman, and accordingly they, knowing that you cannot with safety send a wire, a telephone message, or even a letter, without Rome knowing something about what is going on decided to send a messenger direct. The messenger came to me at 5.30 on Wednesday, 28th July, and advised me that Miss Partridge had run away from the convent and asked me to go to Wagga to make all the necessary inquiry and see what could be done as to maintaining her liberty. I accordingly left Sydney that evening by the Albury mail, arriving in Wagga next morning. It was very amusing to watch the agents of Rome at every station along the line, scrutinising every compartment of the train to see if they could find the young lady.[4]

It seems it was not only the Catholics who were showing signs of paranoia. In this case, however, Barton's fears seem far-fetched, es-

---

[4] *Watchman*, 7 October 1920, p. 3.

pecially his reference to 'agents of Rome' scrutinising every compartment of his train. If the Catholics believed Partridge was on the move, surely they would be searching for her travelling away from Wagga Wagga, not towards it. A feature of the affair, once it became public, is the way Barton frequently claimed that vigilante groups, some armed, were harassing Bridget and her guardians.

In inviting Grand Master Barton to intervene, the Thompsons had made their third fateful decision. It was one that would take the matter out of their hands and place it into the hands of the Loyal Orange Institution. When the LOI's involvement became public ten days later, it provoked a reaction from militant Catholics who interpreted that involvement as proof the LOI intended to use Sister Liguori's flight from Mount Erin to attack the Catholic Church and its system of convents. This transformed Bridget's personal travails into a clash between 'them and us'.

Monday, 26 July

At 5.30 pm on the Monday evening, Bishop Dwyer returned from Albury. For him it was supposed to have been a pleasant weekend blessing additions to the convent of the Sisters of Mercy and joining in the jubilee celebrations of the Albury Hibernian Society.[5] However, his reverie had been interrupted on Sunday when Father Barry telephoned him to tell him that Sister Liguori had fled the convent. The priest now briefed him in detail as to what had happened.

Meanwhile, groups of Catholics continued their vigil around the Thompson house, unaware that Sister Liguori had slipped through the net. According to Mrs Thompson, 'One man spent three days and nights up a tree watching the house.'[6]

Tuesday, 27 July

The next morning the bishop requested Mr William Walsh, a local solicitor who had sometimes done work for him, to draft a letter

---

[5] *Catholic Press*, 29 July 1920, p. 19.
[6] *Sun*, 13 August 1920, p. 5.

to Mr and Mrs Thompson. The bishop then sent Father Barry to the Thompson house armed with the letter plus another letter addressed to Sister Liguori replying to her letter to him. The first letter was in the following terms:

> Dear Sir and Madam,
>
> On my return from Albury last evening, I was put into possession of full particulars of the departure of Sister M. Liguori and of her being cared for at your home. Whilst endorsing the thanks already expressed to you by the Rev. Mother for the accommodation extended by you to Sister Liguori, I feel in duty bound to express the opinion that you have erred in two respects—firstly, in failing to at once disclose on Saturday evening to the Rev. Mother or the priest in charge at the Bishop's house or to the friends who were searching for the sister that she was with you and thus saving all concerned a most anxious and distressing night. Instead of giving such information, I am advised that the sister's presence under your roof was denied. Secondly, in refusing Father Barry an interview with the sister on Sunday last, or to receive clothing sent to her by the convent authorities, I am also impelled from consideration for Sister Liguori herself and her people, for the sisters of Mt Erin, and for the Catholic community and myself, to call upon you personally to seek an interview with Sister Liguori in the presence of yourselves, if you so wish, and one or two gentlemen I may bring with me, to ascertain from the sister personally why she came away from the convent, and what her complaints may be; what her condition of health is, and to invite her to return to the convent, to inform her she is most welcome to return if she so desires, and knowing her act to have arisen from some temporary hallucination, to ensure she is most readily forgiven by her superior and myself. Also, that if she insists on remaining away from the convent for some little time there are several highly respectable Catholic families who have informed me they will only be too pleased to make her comfortable and at home. That if she will not return to conventual life then the convent authorities will provide

her reasonable expenses for comforts and passage to her own people. May I also say that I deem it to be your duty to exercise every influence you may have to induce her to return to her duties and dissuade her from taking any ill-advised action which may be to her discredit.

Should Sister Liguori refuse to return and persist in remaining on your hands, then you must recognise you are taking upon yourselves a very great responsibility, for which you alone must answer.

Yours truly,

J.W. Dwyer

Bishop of Wagga Wagga

The letter to Sister Liguori read:

Dear Sister,

I have just returned from Albury and received the letter you sent to Father Barry. I regret the course you have taken without consulting me, but I am willing to see you if you wish me to do so. I am writing to the people who have sheltered you. I enclose a copy of the letter I have sent to them.

When Father Barry arrived at the house, the Thompsons refused to accept the letters.

That afternoon, Bishop Dwyer called at the police station and spoke with Inspector Duprez. He told him of Sister Liguori's letter and that the Thompsons had refused to allow Father Barry to deliver his reply to the nun. He added, 'I suppose they won't let me see her either. Would you let one of your constables go with me for protection.' Duprez said he would accompany the bishop himself. He also related to the bishop how he had come to know of the case, telling him that he personally could not see any signs of insanity about the young woman, and that she appeared to him to be perfectly sane.

When Duprez and the bishop arrived at the Thompson house, Mrs Thompson was standing on the veranda. Inspector Duprez said to Mrs Thompson,

'Does Sister Liguori want to see the bishop? She has asked him for some directions in a letter which she wrote to him.'

The bishop said, 'I want to see Sister Liguori.'

Mrs Thompson said to Duprez, 'I know a letter was written—she would have seen him on Saturday. She won't see him now.'

The bishop said, 'I have written a letter to her in reply to the one she wrote to me. I want Sister Liguori to read it and give me a reply, yes or no.'

Mrs Thompson again said, 'She won't see you.'

The Bishop said, 'Bring her to the door so that I can hand it to her through the door.'

She said, 'No, she won't see you.'

The bishop asked, 'May the inspector deliver it to her personally and report to me her answer?'

Mrs Thompson replied, 'Yes.'

Dwyer then handed Duprez the letter. 'Give it to the sister and see that she reads it. And bring back her reply.'

Duprez accompanied Mrs Thompson along the veranda towards the side of the house and through a side door. Mrs Thompson turned to him and said, 'She is not here.' Duprez asked why she had not told this to the bishop instead of making a fool of both of them. The inspector returned to the bishop and reported that Mrs Thompson had told him Sister Liguori was not there. The bishop asked,

> 'When did she go away?'
>
> Mrs Thompson replied, 'On Sunday evening.'
>
> The bishop retorted, 'I do not believe it; she was seen here this morning.'
>
> Mrs Thompson said, 'You can believe it or not. She has not been here since Sunday night.'
>
> The bishop said, 'I have it on the best authority that she has been seen here this morning walking about the yard.'
>
> Mrs Thompson said, 'You can search the place if you like.'

Dwyer declined but Duprez conducted a search and concluded that Bridget Partridge was not there. Duprez and the bishop withdrew, the letters still undelivered.

Later that afternoon, Bishop Dwyer again called in at the police station. He asked Sergeant Gallaher whether he would be good enough to take the two letters to the Thompsons' house. Dwyer still believed that Sister Liguori was there. The sergeant did as requested but the Thompsons refused to accept the letter addressed to Sister Liguori. At the trial, Bridget said she never received the bishop's letter nor did she see its enclosure, the copy of the bishop's letter to the Thompsons.

That night Bishop Dwyer went to see Mother Stanislaus, who filled him in on Sister Liguori's family background and circumstances.

Wednesday, 28 July

The next day, still unconvinced that Sister Liguori had left the Thompson house, Bishop Dwyer arranged for John Joseph Byrnes, a local stock and station agent, to deliver to the nun the letter he had written her. At the bishop's suggestion, Sergeant Gallaher accompanied Byrnes. After Mrs Thompson told them that Sister Liguori was not there, Archdeacon Joseph Pike emerged from a room in the house. English-born Pike was a senior member of the Church of England in the Anglican diocese of Goulburn. He had been ordained in 1894, the same year as Bishop Dwyer, and in 1914 had been appointed to the Church of England parish at Wagga Wagga. He said to Byrnes,

> 'Are you a relative of the girl?'
> Byrnes said, 'No. Do you know where she is?'
> 'Yes,' he replied, 'She is in another town and is all right. I give you my word, Sister Liguori is not here.'

With Mrs Thompson's permission, Byrnes and Gallaher searched the house, without finding the nun. During a conversation in the yard, Mrs Thompson said to the sergeant,

'We have been pestered by these people, and we want police protection.'

The sergeant replied, 'You can have all the police protection you want.'

Looking at Byrnes, Pike then said to Gallaher, 'Remove this man from the premises, sergeant, these people are in a state of collapse.'

Byrnes retorted, 'You need not bother. We are going away now.'

Byrnes and Gallaher then left, bringing back the letter that Byrnes had been unable to deliver.

Byrnes, with two other men, then went to see James Patrick Sheekey, a solicitor who had been in practice at Wagga Wagga since returning from the war. The two other men were Mr Toohey, perhaps James Francis Toohey, Byrnes' soon to be partner in Shaw, Byrnes & Toohey, and Mr Walsh, said to be a farmer, so not the solicitor William Walsh previously mentioned. The purpose of the visit is unclear. Presumably, Byrnes wished to seek Sheekey's advice as to what could be done under the law to get Sister Liguori back. This is borne out by the fact that later that afternoon Sheekey met with Dr Leahy, who Byrnes had approached to see if he would give a certificate as to the nun's mental condition. Sheekey took instructions from Leahy and then drafted an affidavit for the purpose of the *Lunacy Act 1898*.

At the trial Bishop Dwyer denied he had requested Byrnes to consult Sheekey and said he had been told by Father Barry that some in the searching party had approached Dr Leahy and asked him to prepare a statement as to his knowledge of Sister Liguori's condition. Sheekey told the court that the bishop had never been his client and that he only told him what had transpired between himself and Byrnes and Leahy when he met with the bishop the following Saturday, 31 July.

Unlike Leahy, who remained convinced Sister Liguori was in Wagga Wagga, Dwyer now suspected she had left the town, though he was still unsure. Rather than pursuing a local remedy as Byrnes and Leahy were doing, Dwyer's thinking led him to decide to go to Sydney to discuss the matter with Attorney General Edward McTiernan, a leading Catholic and member of the Catholic Federation, who was known to the bishop through church circles. McTiernan was also reputed to have a brilliant legal mind. At 28 years of age, he was the youngest attorney general the state had ever had and ten years later he would be appointed a justice of the High Court of Australia, a position he would hold until 1976.

Before leaving for Sydney, Dwyer wanted to be sure of Sister Liguori's fragile mental state. He wanted to see Dr Leahy but was told the doctor was visiting a patient at Mount Peter, 40 kilometres away. So, he telephoned the patient's house. The bishop said to Dr Leahy,

'I believe you have expressed the opinion that Sister Liguori is of unsound mind?'

'Yes,' replied the doctor.

'Will you give a certificate to that effect?'

'Yes. I will do it tomorrow'.

That evening, Bishop Dwyer took the overnight train to Sydney, the Sister Liguori problem at the forefront of his mind. Ironically, as he made his way north towards the metropolis, Grand Master Barton was on his way south to Wagga Wagga, also with Sister Liguori on his mind. At some point along the track their paths crossed – like trains passing in the night, literally.

Thursday, 29 July

After arriving in Sydney, Bishop Dwyer went to see the attorney general. He related to him the facts of the case and showed him the letter he had received from Sister Liguori. Dwyer asked the attorney what could be done. McTiernan replied that he could do nothing as it did not concern his department at this stage. It was a matter for the police. He advised the bishop to see the chief secretary, the government minister responsible for the police. The chief secretary, James Dooley, was away and Bishop Dwyer saw the under-secretary, Edward Burns Harkness, who promised to make an appointment for him with Inspector General of Police James Mitchell. Born in Scotland in 1865, Mitchell came to Australia in 1884 and joined the New South Wales Police Force. His title would be changed in 1926 to Commissioner of Police. He was a Protestant and a freemason. Dwyer related to Mitchell the facts as he knew them and showed him Sister Liguori's letter. Mitchell said, 'This letter does not seem to be written by a person of normal mind.' The inspector general said he would contact the inspector in Wagga Wagga and ask him to locate the nun. While the bishop was in his office, Mitchell sent a cable to Inspector Duprez:

> Has Sister Liguori been located? When located, cannot arrangements be made for her medical examination, with a view to ascertaining her mental condition, and restoration to her friends? Dr Dwyer says Father Barry will attend to Sister Liguori's comfort and see that she is properly attended to. Understand Dr Leahy is of opinion that Sister Liguori is temporarily mentally affected, and in need of medical attention. Wire details promptly of action taken.

Mitchell suggested that Dwyer stay overnight and he would send a message to his hotel once he received an answer from Wagga Wagga as to the result of his inquiries.

Meanwhile, that afternoon, James Sheekey and Dr Leahy visited the office of William George Hazell, the clerk of petty sessions at Wagga Wagga. Hazell had only just arrived in town, having been appointed to the position on 21 June. What occurred would be the subject of contention at the trial. According to Bridget Partridge's counsel, Sheekey and Leahy, on instructions from Bishop Dwyer, asked Mr Hazell for an arrest order under section 4 of the *Lunacy Act* and that Hazell refused to do so. According to Bishop Dwyer's counsel, Sheekey, on instructions from Mr Byrnes and unbeknown to the bishop, called on Hazell to take steps to have Sister Liguori examined under section 5 of the *Lunacy Act*.

The *Lunacy Act*, which has since been repealed, provided in section 4 that upon information on oath before a justice that a person deemed to be insane was without sufficient means of support, the justice might make an order for the person to be apprehended and brought before the court. Section 5, on the other hand, provided that where someone informs a justice of the peace on oath that a person deemed to be insane is not under proper care and control, then the justice should either visit and examine that person personally or make inquiries and arrange for a medical practitioner to do so and report to the justice. While a section 4 order issued in Sydney would ultimately be used to have Sister Liguori arrested, Sheekey denied he ever sought such an order from Hazell.

According to Sheekey, he showed Hazell a draft affidavit to be sworn by Leahy in which the doctor would depose that he believed Sister Liguori 'is at present at a certain private dwelling-house in Wagga Wagga and, if such is the case, I am of the opinion that she would not receive the proper control that her mental condition requires'. When Hazell questioned Leahy as to where he believed Sister Liguori was staying, the doctor said he believed she was at the Thompson house. Hazell said, 'Is not Thompson a reputable man?' Leahy agreed. Hazell then said that if she were staying with the Thompsons, there might be some doubt that she was not 'under proper care and control' as required by section 5. Leahy said he would have to consider the doubt that Hazell had raised. Hazell added, 'In any case, I will not act unless my personal safety is guaranteed.' When asked what he meant, Hazell told Sheekey he thought Thompson might attack him and do him some personal injury.

Earlier in the day Grand Master Barton had arrived in Wagga Wagga and, after being briefed on the matter, was driven in the evening to Adelong. When Bridget had first arrived at Mount Pleasant, she had asked Mrs Howell to give her protection and not to give her away to anyone who came asking for her. She told Mrs Howell she was afraid the convent authorities would send for her. Although Mrs Howell considered Bridget to be sane, she also thought she appeared to be frightened. Bridget went for a walk each day, but not alone, and she slept with Mrs Howell. On the Monday Bridget had written a letter to her brother Joseph and another on the Tuesday, both of which Mrs Howell had posted.

Bridget was not feeling well. According to Mrs Howell, she was suffering with a menstrual problem. In the afternoon Mrs Howell decided to take her to the hospital. In a car driven by a neighbour, Mr Smith, the two women, accompanied by two men, Mr Craig and Mr Prowse, drove into Adelong. After dropping Bridget at the hospital, Mrs Howell remained in town at a place a few doors away.

Friday, 30 July

Just after midnight, Mrs Howell, who had already gone to bed, received a message from Mr Prowse that Grand Master Barton wanted to see her as the grand master was about to take Bridget to Sydney. Mrs Howell went with Prowse and was introduced to Barton, whom she had not met before. Bridget was present, as was George Edney, with whom Bridget had travelled from Wagga Wagga. Barton told Mrs Howell that Edney would take charge of the young woman and that they would accompany her to Sydney as she wanted to get away and go somewhere she would be safe.

The party left for Cootamundra, 94 kilometres away, at about 1 am intending to catch the morning train to Sydney, which was due to depart at 7 am. However, the poor condition of the road delayed their progress. In those days, unsealed roads were common between country towns and the recent heavy rain had damaged the surface. Travelling through mud and slush and having to ford small creeks, the car broke down and a replacement had to be found. They eventually arrived at Cootamundra, where they stayed with friends of the Thompsons until it was time to catch the overnight express from Melbourne, which arrived in Sydney at 11.30 on Saturday morning.[7]

---

[7] *Daily Telegraph*, 9 August 1920, p. 5; *Sun* 30 June 1921, p. 7.

While Bridget was making her way to Cootamundra with Barton and Edney, Bishop Dwyer, still in Sydney, was reading through a letter he had received from Inspector General Mitchell:

> Dear Bishop Dwyer,
>
> I am in receipt of a wire from Inspector Duprez to the effect that Archdeacon Pike refuses to say where Sister Liguori is at present, but states that she is not in Wagga, but is well cared for. When seen by Inspector Duprez on July 25 Sister Liguori appeared perfectly sane and rational, and stated that she would not go back to the convent. Dr Tivey, of Wagga, also saw Sister Liguori on July 25, at the request of Mr Thompson. The doctor afterwards stated to Mr Thompson and the Mother Superior that he could find no indication of insanity and that she was perfectly normal. The local police have been directed to make renewed inquiries to locate Sister Liguori and inform you at Wagga Wagga of the result.
>
> Faithfully yours,
>
> JAMES MITCHELL,
>
> Inspector-General of Police.

That evening Dwyer took the night train back to Wagga Wagga. Once again, like a French farce, the train carrying Bishop Dwyer south crossed with the train bearing Grand Master Barton and the missing nun north.

Saturday, 31 July

After Bridget and her escort arrived at Sydney's Central railway station, they headed to Chapel Street in Kogarah, a suburb about 12 kilometres south of the city. There Barton introduced Bridget to Reverend William Touchell, the minister in charge of the Kogarah Congregational parish, and his wife Laura. Born in 1869 at Wangalere, northeast of Adelaide, South Australia, Touchell had begun his ministry at Southern Cross, a town in the eastern goldfields of Western Australia. In 1910 he transferred from the goldfields to the Congregational church at Kogarah. He was a fervent temperance campaigner and an active supporter of the Protestant Federation. Touchell personally established several branches of the federation in several country towns.[8] Laura (née Marsh), also from South Australia, was born in 1871 at Evandale, a suburb of Adelaide. She and William married in Perth in 1900.

Meanwhile, Bishop Dwyer, on returning to Wagga Wagga, telephoned Inspector Duprez. At the trial Dwyer and Duprez would give slightly different accounts of the conversation, but on both versions it was clearly very tense. According to Duprez it began with the bishop saying,

> 'Have you got that woman yet?'
> To which Duprez replied, 'No.'
> Dwyer then said, 'Well, you will have to arrest her.'
> To which Duprez replied, 'I have nothing to arrest her for and I don't know where she is.'

According to the bishop, the conversation started by his asking,

> 'Have you located Sister Liguori yet?'
> To which Duprez replied, 'No'.

It is common ground that Duprez then said,

> 'Archdeacon Pike told me he knew where she is and that she is well and happy and in good hands, but he refused to tell me where she is. If you see him, perhaps he will tell you.'
> Dwyer said, 'I would not go within a mile of him with the crowd he has with him.'

Dwyer's comment reflects the poor state of relations between the Catholic and Anglican hierarchies in Wagga Wagga at the time. Both men were plain-spoken. An obituary for Pike after his death in February 1947 described him 'as a man of strong opinions and one who was never afraid to voice his views, even at the risk of incurring the displeasure of his friends'. An obituary for Dwyer,

---

[8] *Watchman*, 7 October 1920, p. 3.

following his death in October 1939, was not dissimilar. It stated that he 'did not hesitate to express himself plainly and forcibly on occasion'.[9] Even so, in peremptorily rejecting Duprez's suggestion, Dwyer turned down an opportunity to talk with Pike, clergyman to clergyman. It might have made no difference. After all, the Thompsons had not been forthcoming. But, approached in the right way, the archdeacon might have been prepared to act as a conduit between the bishop and Sister Liguori. That way Dwyer might have been able to learn more about the woman for whose welfare he was responsible, at least about her condition if not her whereabouts.

> The conversation continued with Dwyer saying to Duprez,
> 'Are you acting on Dr Tivey's certificate?'
> Duprez said, 'I've not seen a certificate from him.'
> Dwyer said, 'Then why did you report to the Inspector General what Tivey said if you did not have a written certificate to that effect?'
> Duprez replied, 'All I know is that Dr Tivey said she was not insane.'
> Dwyer said, 'You will have to get a certificate from him.'
> Duprez said, 'Dr Tivey will not give me a certificate. I don't know that it has anything to do with me. Why don't you ask him for one?'
> Dwyer said, 'No, you will get a certificate even if I have to go through the Inspector General to get it.'
> Duprez said, 'If the inspector general orders me to get a certificate I will get one. Who is going to pay for it?'
> Dwyer said, 'I will.'
> Duprez said, 'I will see the doctor and see what he says.'
> According to Duprez, Dwyer then said, 'You have let this woman slip through your fingers.'
> To which Duprez retorted, 'I never had her in my fingers to let her slip through.'

At the trial Dwyer denied saying this. He claimed he did not charge

---

[9] *Daily Advertiser*, 21 February 1947, p. 2; *Goulburn Evening Penny Post*, 12 October 1939, p. 7.

Duprez with purposely letting Sister Liguori slip through his fingers but believed the police were negligent in not locating her. Dwyer was aware that at that stage the police had no power to arrest the nun but he thought they should have been doing more to locate her and considered they would make a greater effort if directed by the inspector general. The conversation ended with Dwyer saying, 'You will hear more about this.'

Duprez was shaken by this conversation. Dwyer had accused him of not doing his duty and had gone over his head to speak to the inspector general about the matter. The two men would not speak to each other again.

The next day Duprez did ask Dr Tivey for a certificate but Tivey refused to give him one, saying he would give one to the bishop if he asked for it. Presumably, Tivey agreed with Duprez that the police had no business asking for such a certificate whereas it was appropriate to give Dwyer one because he was responsible for the nun's welfare. Duprez reported to Father Barry what Tivey had said.

Despite being aware of what Tivey told Duprez, Dwyer did not ask the doctor for a certificate. Once again, Dwyer turned down an opportunity to learn more about Sister Liguori's condition. Perhaps he considered Tivey to be a co-conspirator with the Thompsons. Yet, as with his refusal to approach Archdeacon Pike, Dwyer was unwilling to ask the question. Perhaps Dwyer was beginning to see the affair through a Manichean lens as part of the ongoing struggle between 'them and us', Catholicism versus Protestantism.

Later that Saturday, Father Barry reported to Bishop Dwyer on the recent activities of Byrnes, Sheekey, and Leahy. He showed him Leahy's affidavit in which the doctor had sworn that Sister Liguori was of unsound mind. Dwyer then rang Sheekey and requested he call on him. When Sheekey arrived, he told the bishop of the consultation he had had with Byrnes and of his visit the next day to the clerk of petty sessions, Mr Hazell. He informed Dwyer that Hazell appeared unwilling to act in the matter and did not want to get mixed up with it. He discussed with the bishop the provisions of the *Lunacy Act*, in particular section 5, to which Dr Leahy's affidavit was directed. When he spoke to the bishop about an order under section 4, Sheekey said it would be advisable to take the matter to Sydney and see the inspector general rather than apply to the local authorities. As Dwyer later explained to the court, he believed an order issued in Sydney was likely to have more impact than one from Wagga Wagga, where the local police had failed to locate Sister Liguori.

Dwyer was clearly frustrated. On his watch, a nun, for whose welfare he was responsible, had left the convent in circumstances that suggested she was not of sound mind and had vanished without trace. Not even the police knew where she was. And neither he nor they could be sure she was safe and well. As Inspector Duprez later told the court, 'I had no more idea where she was than the man in the moon', agreeing with the proposition that 'she had disappeared as though swallowed up'. It is possible that Duprez was lying and that he did know Sister Liguori's whereabouts, but there is no evidence to suggest that was the case. Nevertheless, it is likely the thought crossed Dwyer's mind. After all, Duprez was a freemason. Perhaps he was party to a conspiracy with the Thompsons to spirit the nun away.

As far as Dwyer was concerned, his options were now limited. He could not just wash his hands of the affair and accept that Sister Liguori had decided to leave the convent. Under Canon Law, she was considered 'an apostate from a religious institute' and he was obliged to inquire after her and to 'take care cautiously for [her] return'.[10] Apart from his canonical obligations, how was he supposed to respond if her parents inquired as to her whereabouts and her welfare? A local solution no longer seemed feasible, particularly if Duprez was in league with the Thompsons. Sister Liguori could be anywhere in the state, or even interstate. As he saw it, his best chance to locate her, to ensure she was safe and well, and then to arrange for her return to her family, was to go to Sydney and request the authorities there to take the necessary steps under section 4 of the *Lunacy Act*.

---

[10] Canons 644 and 645 of the 1917 *Code of Canon Law*.

3
Arrest

Sunday 1 August

On Sunday afternoon, James Sheekey called on Bishop Dwyer and the two men discussed what needed to be done to obtain an order under section 4 of the *Lunacy Act*. Sheekey advised the bishop that Dr Leahy's existing affidavit was not sufficient as it did not mention that Sister Liguori was without visible means of support. That was a requirement of section 4 but not of section 5. Sheekey told Dwyer he had spoken to Leahy that morning after 10 o'clock mass and the doctor was prepared to add that to his affidavit. In the bishop's library, Sheekey redrafted Leahy's affidavit adding the necessary clause and another one stating that Leahy was the government medical officer. Dwyer had suggested that amendment when he saw Sheekey the day before, presumably because he thought it would add weight to Leahy's opinion regarding Sister Liguori's mental condition. Sheekey then typed up the revised affidavit in the bishop's library and left it with him. The redrafted affidavit read:

> On the first day of August 1920, William Leahy of Wagga Wagga in the State of New South Wales, medical practitioner, being duly sworn, makes oath and says as follows:
>
> 1. I am a duly qualified medical practitioner residing at Wagga Wagga in the State aforesaid.
>
> 2. I know and am well acquainted with Bridget Partridge, a member of the religious Order of the Presentation Nuns, residing at Wagga, and known in religion as Sister Mary Liguori.
>
> 3 I have been attending the said Sister Mary Liguori for the past six or eight weeks.
>
> 4. I am of the opinion that she is of unsound mind, and that she should be placed under proper care and control.

5. I am informed, and verily believe the same to be true, that she is at present at a certain private dwelling-house in Wagga Wagga aforesaid, and, if such is the case, I am of the opinion that she would not receive the proper care and control that her mental condition requires. Further, I am of the opinion that she should be placed in a hospital for the insane for treatment and observation.

6. I am informed, and verily believe the same to be true, that the said Sister Mary Liguori is without sufficient means of support.

7. I am the Government Medical Officer stationed at Wagga Wagga aforesaid.

....

W. LEAHY

Apart from the newly added clauses 6 and 7, the draft was in the same terms as the affidavit Dr Leahy had sworn previously, including clause 5, which, though superfluous for section 4 of the *Lunacy Act*, reflected its genesis as an affidavit for the purposes of section 5.

Meanwhile, in Sydney, Bridget had settled into her new accommodation with the Touchells. On the afternoon of her arrival Mrs Touchell had obtained some clothes for her and arranged to return to Mrs Thompson the clothes she came in. To those not in the know, Bridget was referred to as Miss Jones. That evening Bridget attended the church service conducted by Rev. Touchell in the Congregational church.[1]

Monday, 2 August

The next day Dr Leahy and Bishop Dwyer met in the street, whether by arrangement or accident is unclear. The bishop produced the draft of the revised affidavit and showed it to Leahy, who agreed to sign it. The two men then walked to the office of Mr J.K. O'Reilly, a justice of the peace, where Leahy went inside and swore the affidavit. When he came out, he handed the sworn affidavit to Dwyer.

---

[1] *Daily Express*, 14 August 1920, p. 1.

None of the three men noticed that the affidavit bore the date 1 August, being the date Sheekey had typed when drafting it the day before. This would cause a little confusion at the trial when Dwyer, Leahy, and Sheekey were being questioned as to the sequence of events.

Leahy would also be questioned as to his assertion in clause 5 that Sister Liguori was at a certain private dwelling-house in Wagga Wagga. He might have believed that when he swore his first affidavit but it is incredible he still held that belief when he swore the second, particularly as Sheekey and the bishop were now working on the assumption the nun had left the Thompson house and, indeed, the town. Nevertheless, at the trial Leahy maintained that it was his belief when he swore the second affidavit.

Tuesday, 3 August

Armed with Dr Leahy's new affidavit, Bishop Dwyer returned to Sydney, where he again met with Inspector General Mitchell, who confirmed what the bishop already knew. Mitchell had received a wire, presumably from Inspector Duprez, reporting that nothing had been learned of Sister Liguori's whereabouts despite an exhaustive search. After Dwyer showed Mitchell Dr Leahy's affidavit, the inspector general said he would ring Mr Camphin, the clerk of petty sessions and chamber magistrate at the Central Police Court, who, Mitchell said, 'knew a lot about these matters'. Born in Sydney in 1867, William Joseph Camphin was well regarded among the legal fraternity. According to Sydney's *Truth*, 'A kindly smile and a benevolent outlook on all mankind are the outstanding characteristics of William J. Camphin'.[2] He was also a Catholic.

After Mitchell finished speaking with Camphin, he told Dwyer that Camphin was of the opinion he could issue a warrant on the information the bishop had in his possession. Mitchell suggested, however, that Dwyer should go and see the attorney general, just to make sure. The inspector general rang McTiernan's office but was

---

[2] *Truth* 18 April 1926, p. 10.

told the attorney was in Newcastle. Mitchell then suggested trying the solicitor general. In those days the office of solicitor general was held by a government MP and was not a public service appointment as it is today. The incumbent was 39-year-old Robert Sproule, who had been appointed to the position in April at the same time as he was appointed a member of the Legislative Council. Born in County Tyrone, Ireland, Sproule was a Presbyterian. Mitchell rang him and said the bishop wished to see him and made an appointment.

When Dwyer arrived at the solicitor general's chambers, Sproule agreed to hear what he had to say. Dwyer then recounted the story of Sister Liguori's departure from the convent and her subsequent disappearance. He showed him Dr Leahy's affidavit and told him of Dr Tivey's opinion and of Mitchell's conversation with Camphin. The bishop asked Sproule's opinion. Sproule said that if he had the power, he would issue a warrant on that information but it was a matter for a magistrate. About to leave his chambers, Sproule offered to drive the bishop in his car to the Central Police Court. There he introduced the bishop to Mr Camphin. Camphin was quite busy at the time but when he became free he heard the bishop's story. Dwyer once more related the facts of the case. He also told Camphin that he had been informed that Dr Tivey said she was normal while Dr Leahy claimed she was of unsound mind, as stated in his affidavit. The bishop then showed Camphin the letter which Sister Liguori had written him claiming she had been given poison. Dwyer told Camphin that he wanted to get Sister Liguori out of the hands of 'the extremists'. At the trial he said that by 'extremists' he meant members of the Orange order. Mr Camphin said he would make an order under section 4 of the *Lunacy Act* if the bishop would swear that he deemed Bridget Partridge to be of unsound mind and without means of support. When Dwyer did so, Camphin issued the order for Bridget Partridge's apprehension.

That afternoon Inspector General Mitchell sent a cable to Inspector Duprez informing him of the making of the order and containing the following instructions:

> Interview Mr Thompson and Archdeacon Pike and inform them of issue of warrant and necessity for the Sister to receive medical attention without delay. They may if possible arrange for the Sister to be handed over to you. You can arrange to send a nurse or female attendant with Sister Liguori from Wagga to Sydney when arrested. No necessity for her to be detained in police custody except to wait for the first train. Wire me any developments.[3]

Wednesday, 4 August

While police stations across New South Wales were being informed of the order for Bridget Partridge's apprehension, the young woman was hiding in plain sight at the home of Mr and Mrs Touchell. This was possible because there had been no reports in the press of her disappearance let alone her whereabouts. Bridget took the time to write a letter to Mrs Thompson, which she signed "Mavourneen":

> Accept my little letter as a token of gratitude for your kindness. I am all there, thanks be to God, with all the policemen. I am more than grateful for all the kindnesses, and it will not be repaid with ingratitude. The present year has done me good. I have had a rest, but not yet under the soil. I am getting my green dress, if you understand, which I mean when God calls me. But I will never aid anyone to commit a murder for me.

When questioned at the trial about this letter and its strange wording, particularly the final sentence, Bridget said she did not recall writing it.

In Wagga Wagga, Sergeant Gallaher interviewed George Edney, who informed him that Sister Liguori had left the Thompsons' house in a motor car on 25 July and had travelled to Mount Pleasant, where she was left with Mr and Mrs Howell. Edney told Gallaher

---

[3] Typed copy of a cable dated 3 August 1920 from the Inspector General of Police to Inspector Duprez, Wagga Wagga Diocesan Archives.

that he last saw the missing nun that night at the Howells' residence and that he had not seen her since.[4] That was untrue. According to Mrs Howell's evidence at the trial, Edney had returned the following Thursday and took charge of Bridget, telling Mrs Howell that 'he brought her [to Adelong] and he would take her'.[5] But Inspector Duprez already knew, from information he had received, that Bridget was in Sydney and he reported that fact to Mitchell.[6]

It seems clear that Barton was aware of the issue of the section 4 order and was taking steps to meet it. During the day Bridget met with Charles Harold Stocker, grand secretary of the Loyal Orange Institution. Born in 1865 in Yorkshire, England, Stocker emigrated as a young man to Australia, where he joined the LOI. In 1913 he was elected as grand secretary, a position he held until his retirement in 1936. Stocker was also a justice of the peace and, in that capacity, he witnessed Bridget's signature on a statutory declaration setting out in detail the reasons for her sudden departure from the convent:

> On account of being dissatisfied with conventual life I resolved on the morning of the 24th ult., there being confusion over something to which I was a stranger, though, from questions asked by the sisters suspicion seemed to centre on me. I resolved to run to a house nearby, intending to wait there until order had been restored. From this house I rang up the Bishop, but he was not in. My intention was to inform him where I was staying and explain the incident.
>
> Then three of the mothers came from the convent, and I returned with them. They said they were glad to get me back.
>
> In about half an hour I was ordered to appear before Dr. Leahy in the presence of the Rev. Mother. I was not ill,

---

[4] Typed copy of a report dated 4 August 1920 Sergeant 1/c S. Gallaher, Wagga Wagga Diocesan Archives.
[5] *Truth*, 10 July 1921, p. 11.
[6] Typed copy of a cable dated 4 August 1920 from Inspector Duprez to the Inspector General of Police, Wagga Wagga Diocesan Archives.

though very much run down in health. The doctor said, 'So you are run down, sister.' I said, 'Yes, doctor.' I was asked to put out my tongue. No further questions were asked about my health, and no examination was made. He then said goodbye.

I was sent to bed which had been prepared for me, and holy water sprinkled about the room and on the bed. Sister M. Brendan gave me something in a cup which she called oil. I really thought it was poison. This conviction is based on the agonising look on the doctor's face during the Angelus. The Rev. Mother could not look at me at all. There was certainly oil in the cup, but to a very small degree, and something else which had a very dead taste. Sister M. Brendan told me to lie quite still and not to move, and that I would sleep for six months. Other things were said about death to convince me I was to die.

Taking advantage of an opportunity I swallowed three cupfuls of soapy water from my wash basin, went to a lavatory, and brought up the dose as best I could. Sister M. Brendan begged me to come out and get to bed at once. I was only in my nightdress and bare feet.

While Sister M. Brendan had gone downstairs sto get a hot-water bag I made my escape.

My reason for thinking a deliberate attempt had been made on my life answers the question why I escaped from the convent and from conventual life.

Fortunately, I received protection, and at the earliest possible moment resigned from the convent and the life of a nun.

I am now resolved never again to submit to the care of those who professing religion and Christian charity, practise it so sparingly.

Presumably, the statutory declaration was to be given to the Lunacy Court as and when required but that proved unnecessary. Although made on 4 August, it was not released to the press until a month later.[7] That night Bridget had another visitor, Dr William Binns. He was the Touchells' general practitioner and had been asked to examine Miss Partridge, not for any physical ailment but to see if he could find anything mentally wrong with her. His visit at this time for no other reason, suggests Bridget's guardians wanted an up-to-date mental assessment they could rely on if and when the police came calling.

Binns's immediate impression was that Bridget seemed perfectly self-possessed, though a little restrained and a little reserved. He examined the young woman for about 35 to 40 minutes. After satisfying himself that her heart and lungs were sound and her temperature was normal, he questioned her to ascertain if there had been any mental or neurotic trouble in her family. She said there had not been and that she had never suffered with mental trouble. He then asked her the usual questions to test her cognitive ability and her memory, which she answered correctly. Next he questioned her about her life at the convent and the circumstances of her leaving. Finally, he asked questions as to her state of mind, whether she dreamed much or heard voices or had visions. She said she did not. When he asked if she had any suspicions against anybody, she answered that she did not have up till that time and that she had been on good terms with everybody in the convent. She said she had no reason to suspect any of them of being spiteful towards her. She also told him she had no intention or inclination to change her religious beliefs and she did not consider she had been acted upon by any external agency. When Binns remarked that her determination to leave the convent had been sudden, she admitted that it had been so, but said that for a couple of months before she had been tired of convent life. Bridget told him that to support herself she would like to teach. At the end of the examination, Binns concluded that Bridget was a rather reserved, unsophisticated, mentally normal person – certainly not insane.

---

[7] *Daily Telegraph*, 3 September 1920, p. 6. As then published it contained some gaps that were later filled in when it was republished in the *Watchman*, 7 October 1920, p. 2.

Thursday, 5 August

As dawn broke on the twelfth day of Bridget's flight from her convent, the press had still not reported the story. But that was about to change. In the days before the internet and social media, a syndicated cable news service would pick up on a local news item in a town's newspaper and, if newsworthy enough, distribute it to its city and regional subscribers. Within hours the story would be appearing in newspapers across Australia. In this case, the silence of the press was not because the story was unnewsworthy, it was because there had been no local news item to pick up on.

Why neither of Wagga Wagga's newspapers reported Sister Liguori's disappearance as and when it occurred is one of the unexplained mysteries of the Sister Liguori affair. The story of Wagga Wagga's own 'escaped' nun was big news, as the later publicity attests. Furthermore, it is not as if her departure from the convent had gone unnoticed. Several of the townsfolk, including the police, had been out all night and into the next day searching for the missing nun; several others had been involved in keeping her whereabouts hidden. It would have been the talk of the town. After all, Wagga Wagga's top policeman and its Catholic bishop were deeply involved. The local reporters who did the police rounds would have been quickly tipped off. The two newspapers must have made a deliberate editorial decision, perhaps in collusion, to suppress the story. This is evidenced by the fact that on 25 July a reporter from the *Daily Express* interviewed Dr Tivey about his examination of Bridget Partridge.[8] Perhaps the newspapers remained silent to avoid upsetting the precarious peace and harmony of a community already divided over the war in Ireland and the recently concluded war in Europe, including over how the district's dead should be remembered. Whatever the reason, the story was about to break.

---

[8] *Daily Express*, 7 August 1920, p. 2. Referring to events on Sunday, 25 July 1920, the article reports: 'Dr Tivey stated to a 'Daily Express' representative <u>that evening</u> that he was called by Mrs Thompson to medically examine Miss Bridget Partridge ...' [emphasis added].

That Thursday morning, Sydney's *Daily Telegraph* carried a report on Bridget's disappearance under the headline 'Nun Disappears'. The article, datelined 'Wagga, Wednesday', began:

> Much excitement has been created here owing to the disappearance of a nun, Sister Liguori, from the Mount Erin Convent, Wagga.
>
> Miss Bridget Partridge (28) is a native of England [sic], and came to Australia nine years ago, and entered the convent, taking up the name Sister Ligouri [sic].
>
> On Saturday night, July 24, she left the convent in a night dress, was sheltered at a neighbouring house for the night, and has since disappeared.[9]

The report quoted Inspector Duprez as saying that the police in Wagga Wagga had no knowledge of the nun's whereabouts.

That afternoon, another Sydney newspaper, the *Sun*, under a four-line headline, 'Sister of Mercy [sic]/Leaves Wagga Convent/Allegation of Insanity/Information Laid by Bishop', reported:

> Following upon the sworn information of Bishop Dwyer of Wagga, Mr Camphin, the chamber magistrate at the Central Court, has issued a warrant for the arrest of Bridget Partridge, otherwise Sister Mary Ligouri [sic] of the Wagga Convent.
>
> The information of Bishop Dwyer was that Sister Ligouri [sic], who recently left the convent, is of unsound mind.
>
> The warrant has been handed to the police for execution, and it directs the attendance of the accused at the Sydney Lunacy Court.[10]

Throughout the day the story travelled across Australia. By the weekend, newspapers in every state carried one or other or both of those reports. Within a week, the story had appeared in newspapers in New Zealand and England, including the *Times*.[11] Curi-

---

[9] *Daily Telegraph*, 5 August 1920, p. 6. The misspelling 'Ligouri' is common in press reports, even later during the trial.
[10] *Sun*, 5 August 1920, p. 7.
[11] *Auckland Star*, 10 August 1920, p. 5; *Times* (London) 11 August 1920, p. 9.

ously, people in Perth were able to read of the affair before readers of Wagga Wagga's *Daily Advertiser*, which did not report the story until Friday morning. The *Daily Express*, however, did run the 'Much excitement …' story that day. Given the dateline of the *Daily Telegraph* report, it is likely that the *Express* had been the one to break the embargo and was the original source that fed that story through the cable news services.[12]

Friday, 6 August

The *Daily Advertiser*'s report of the affair on the Friday morning led with an article datelined 'Sydney Thursday' that reported on the issue of the 'warrant' similar to the *Sun*'s report. But it also carried two detailed reports of what occurred on the weekend of 24/25 July and on Tuesday 27 July after Bishop Dwyer had returned from Albury.[13] The amount of detail in those two reports suggests that the *Advertiser*'s reporters had already investigated the matter well before the story broke. Either that or they had worked at a very fast pace to put the story together overnight. The *Express* carried a short piece on the issue of the section 4 order.[14] It did not provide a detailed report of the affair until the next day.

Saturday, 7 August

The *Express*'s Saturday edition included articles informing readers of the police search and explaining the procedures under the *Lunacy Act*. It also gave a history of the affair, complete with comments from Mrs Thompson, Archdeacon Pike, and Dr Tivey.[15] The *Advertiser*'s Saturday edition followed up with just a short piece on what the police were doing to find Sister Liguori, which included the dramatic disclosure that 'The police have organised search forces

---

[12] *Daily Express*, 5 August 1920, p. 2. Newspapers that carried both stories reported the 'Nun disappears' story before the one relating to the issue of the warrant, which was included among late cables.

[13] *Daily Advertiser*, 6 August 1920, p. 2.

[14] *Daily Express*, 6 August 1920, p. 1.

[15] *Daily Express*, 7 August 1920, p. 2.

to pay attention to the city with special eyes on the inter-State and foreign shipping'.[16]

Once the story became public, it was only a matter of time before the police would learn of Bridget Partridge's whereabouts. It is likely the breakthrough came from a tip-off by a close neighbour of the Touchells. On Saturday night, Detective Sergeant James Farley and Sergeant Harrowsmith knocked on the door of the Touchell house. According to Rev. Touchell, he refused them entry to his home as they did not have a warrant, leading him to suspect it was a bluff to get Bridget out of his hands. After a long argument, the police withdrew, leaving a constable to guard the door.[17] An hour later, just before midnight, Detective Farley returned armed with a copy of the order. Upon reading it, Touchell allowed him to enter. Bridget appeared and Touchell said, 'This is the lady in question. Have a talk to her yourself and see if you think she is insane.' He then turned to Bridget and said, 'This is Detective Farley who has a warrant for your arrest.' Addressing Farley he added, 'You have anticipated me by a little more than a day. I have had the girl medically examined. We were intending to take her to the Reception House on Monday morning to let her surrender herself.' Sergeant Farley then said to Bridget,

> 'I have a warrant for your arrest and I want you to come to the Darlinghurst Reception House.'
>
> She said, 'Could you not possibly leave it until Monday. It's my intention to surrender myself to the authorities at 9 o'clock Monday morning.'
>
> Farley replied, 'I can't do that. The order compels me to take you to the Reception House immediately.'
>
> She said, 'I've sent my resignation to Bishop Dwyer. Why is he making all this fuss?'
>
> Farley said, 'I can't say.'

---

[16] *Daily Advertiser,* 7 August 1920, p. 5.

[17] *Watchman,* 12 August 1920, p. 5. At the trial Detective Farley did not mention this part of the arrest.

Sergeant Farley then interviewed Miss Partridge about her family and the circumstances of her leaving the convent. She said that she had left the convent on the Saturday afternoon to try to get the bishop on the telephone and that when she returned to the convent something happened which determined her to leave. She did not elaborate but acknowledged that had she communicated with the bishop things would probably have been all right. She then asked, 'Can I bring a friend?' He said, 'Yes, but I can't guarantee she will be able to remain there.' Accompanied by Mrs Touchell, Bridget was then driven to the Darlinghurst Reception House. According to press reports, during the drive she chatted to the police about her flight from Wagga Wagga and told them she was sick and tired of convent life and would not put up with it any longer: 'It was like a prison, and I will not go back on any consideration. I would sooner be in the hands of the police than back there.'[18]

After arriving at the Reception House at about 1.15 am, Bridget's admission was processed. She then shook hands with Detective Farley and, accompanied by Mrs Touchell, retired to her room.

Sunday, 8 August

On Sunday, Grand Master Barton began a campaign to rally Protestants to the cause of Bridget Partridge's liberty. That afternoon he addressed the annual religious service of the Loyal Orange Lodges at Balmain Town Hall. After telling his audience of his visit to Wagga Wagga and his bringing Bridget to Sydney, he said:

> The young woman is now in a reception-house at Darlinghurst. I have secured counsel on her behalf, and acting on advice I instructed two specialists to examine the young woman. Tomorrow she is to come before the court. I have made all arrangements. I shall be there. I have received a letter from a gentleman who is prepared to form a committee to raise £1000 towards the cost. I am sure and satisfied that the Protestant people of New South Wales are going to

---

[18] *Newcastle Morning Herald*, 9 August 1920, p. 4.

assist and fight to the end. We are going to gain the young lady her liberty.

But Bridget's liberty was not all that Barton was interested in defending. Bigger issues were at stake:

> Rome is not going to have her way today. I am determined to fight. It is Rome versus the Orange Institution in this matter. I want the Protestants of New South Wales to stand behind the institution. We want your moral and financial support. …
>
> It is time that the convents were inspected to see what is behind the walls. We are not going to tolerate this thing in a free country like Australia.[19]

Barton's message soon filtered down to the Protestant grass roots. At the close of a service at the Methodist church in Haberfield that evening, a meeting was held that passed a resolution requesting the government to see that Miss Partridge, 'the escaped nun', 'be given a full and impartial inquiry … and that her liberties as a British subject be safeguarded'.[20]

If Barton was throwing down the gauntlet, the Catholic authorities were slow to pick it up. According to the *Sunday Times*, they were disinclined to discuss the matter: 'Their attitude is that an unfortunate incident is being investigated in the right way, and that any attempt to make a scandal of it is gratuitous and dishonest'. A priest explained that convents were responsible to the law like any other house and as open to investigation by the officers of the law. Pointing out that a bishop is responsible for the wellbeing of a nun without family nearby, he said that in this case Bishop Dwyer had taken certain action in the regular and appointed way.[21] But some individual Catholics were more than willing to join battle with Barton and the Loyal Orange Institution. One of them was Patrick Joseph Minahan.

---

[19] *Daily Telegraph*, 9 August 1920, p. 5.
[20] *Sydney Morning Herald*, 9 August 1920, p. 9.
[21] *Sunday Times*, 8 August 1920, p. 1.

A native of County Clare who came to Australia in 1878 as a 12-year-old boy, Minahan was a successful businessman and well connected politically. He joined the Labor Party and became a member of the executive in 1907, vice-president in 1909, and president in 1910. He contributed much to the organising and financing of the party's victories at the 1910 state and federal elections. Elected as the member for Belmore in the New South Wales Legislative Assembly in 1910, he was defeated at the 1917 elections when he contested Cootamundra against the premier William Holman. In March 1920 he was elected to the seat of Sydney. Minahan was also experienced in Catholic lay organisation, having been one of the founders in 1909 of the Catholic Club, an association of Catholic laymen, and its first president from 1909 to 1923. He was also one of the promoters of the Catholic Federation and exercised a strong influence over its administration. In addition, he was instrumental in the establishment in 1919 of the Knights of the Southern Cross, sometimes described as the Catholic equivalent of the freemasons, which assisted Catholics find employment and resist discrimination.[22]

Minahan and his wife Elizabeth visited Bridget Partridge at the Darlinghurst Reception House. Their visit would provoke a question in the New South Wales Legislative Assembly from an opposition member, Thomas Henley. Born in England in 1860 and having emigrated to Australia at age 24, Henley was a member of the LOI, who regularly spoke out against the Catholic church. He demanded to know whether Mr and Mrs Minahan had been permitted to visit Miss Partridge by order of the Crown Law Department. Attorney General McTiernan played a straight bat, replying that they had no order from him. Minahan, on the other hand, when it was his turn to speak, answered Henley's question flippantly: 'there was a very amiable gentleman in charge ... and after I had had some short conversation with him I whistled eight bars of "Boyne Water" and

---

[22] Bede Nairn, 'Patrick Joseph (Paddy) Minahan (1866–1933)' *Australian Dictionary of Biography*.

he let me in'.²³ Having posed his question, Henley went on to claim that during Mr and Mrs Minahan's visit to Bridget Partridge, Minahan had snatched from Bridget's hand a book called *Let There Be Light* and said 'What a dreadful book'.²⁴

The book, whose subtitle is 'Why I Withdrew from the Church of My Fathers' had been written by John Enright, a Presbyterian minister, who was formerly a Catholic priest known as Father Andrew. Born in Dublin in 1863, Enright emigrated in 1888 to Australia, where he worked as a teacher until 1891 when he joined the Congregation of the Passion of Jesus Christ, known as the Passionists. Ordained in 1896, he soon became dissatisfied with the Catholic church for both personal and theological reasons, eventually leaving the church in 1907. He immediately married and became a Congregational minister in Perth before becoming a Presbyterian. In 1919 he transferred to Cootamundra in New South Wales where he wrote *Let there be Light* before moving in February 1920 to Bondi, where he wrote another book, *Breaking the Fetters: How I Left the Church of My Fathers: The Romance of a Monk and a Maid*, a more personal story than his first volume. The foreword to this book was written by Rev. William Touchell.²⁵ If Henley's claim is right, and Minahan did not deny it, Bridget would have been given *Let there be Light* by the Touchells or Grand Master Barton, a fact that would have confirmed in Minahan's mind that she was being proselytized by people Minahan believed were her captors. According to Minahan, when he and Mrs Minahan visited the reception centre, Bridget said to them,

> 'You are the first Catholic friends who have come to see me.'
> Minahan said, 'While many anti-Catholics could interview

---

[23] NSWPD, 25 August 1920, p. 422; 31 August 1920, p. 535. 'Boyne Water' is a martial air popular among Orangemen to celebrate the victory of William of Orange at the Battle of the Boyne in 1690.

[24] *Sun*, 26 August 1920, p. 4. NSWPD, 25 August 1920, p. 421.

[25] Malcolm Prentis, 'The Formation of a Passionist Presbyterian: John Enright in Ireland and Australasia', *Journal of the Australian Catholic Historical Society*, Vol. 27, 2006, pp. 17-29.

you at Wagga, no decent Catholic was permitted to see you?'

Bridget said, 'That is what the newspapers say.' She then said, 'I will not go back to the convent. I will lead a good Catholic life in the world and seek employment.'

Minahan said, 'The convent people will not take you back; you need not go back; you are perfectly free. All the convent people require of those who desire to leave is that they shall leave the place in a decent manner. You can come with us. Mrs Minahan will take you as a companion at a substantial salary.'

'I would like that. But first I want to spend a few days with friends.'[26]

Minahan told the house that he 'took compassion upon the poor creature, because of the hands into which the poor girl had landed herself'. It is clear he did not have a high opinion of Bridget's capacity to know her own mind. He told his fellow MPs: 'There is no doubt that, whilst she is a woman in years, she has the mind of a child. She is a simple, irresponsible young woman. She has had it put all over her, the poor child, by those contemptible … '. His words were cut off by an interjection demanding to know who they were. Minahan continued with a diatribe that included personal attacks on various unnamed Protestants, saying they were typical of their countrymen in Ulster, which, he said, had the highest rates of crime and illiteracy in the United Kingdom.[27]

With the intervention of sectarian warriors, such as Barton, Henley, and Minahan, Bridget Partridge was no longer a young woman with personal issues to be resolved in a quiet and caring manner. She was now an object in the centuries-old apocalyptic struggle between Protestantism and Roman Catholicism, a trophy to be fought over in a conflict which Barton had described in his Balmain speech as a fight to the end.

---

[26] NSWPD 31 August 1920, p. 539; *Daily Advertiser*, 16 August 1920, p. 2; *Daily Express*, 16 August 1920, p. 2.
[27] NSWPD, 31 August 1920, p. 535-536.

4
Release

Monday, 9 August

The Darlinghurst Reception House was ill-prepared for the invasion of press and people that descended on it that Monday morning. Built in 1868 the two-story sandstone building in Forbes Street, opposite Darlinghurst Gaol, was designed to temporarily house persons believed to be insane in order to determine the nature of their illness, if any. Court proceedings were held in a small room with only twenty seats for the public. Among those occupying the seats were Grand Master Robert Barton and Mrs Barton, Past Grand Master James Robinson, Mr and Mrs Touchell, Rev. John Enright, and parliamentary members of the Protestant Federation, Dr Richard Arthur MLA and Mr Tom Hoskins MLA. Close by were Mr and Mrs Minahan. Also filling the room were barristers, solicitors, doctors, and officials concerned in the inquiry plus representatives of the press. A large crowd gathered outside in the yard. The presiding officer was 60-year-old Charles Henry Gale, an experienced and highly regarded jurist, who had served as a police magistrate in country New South Wales for more than 20 years before being appointed in December 1919 as a stipendiary magistrate at Parramatta and three months later at Sydney.

On taking his seat at 9 o'clock, Mr Gale looked at the list of that day's inquiries and called the first name: Bridget Partridge. As if it were derby day at Ascot, the reporter for the *Daily Telegraph* described the scene as Bridget made her appearance:

> Entering with a nurse and her legal friends, she carried the impression of a woman of no mean culture. Of average height, her deportment was virile, her demeanor was demure, and there was a natural appearance of nervousness.

> But her bright blue eyes lighted up as she modestly acknowledged the quiet greetings of those whom she looked upon as friends in her troubles—and especially as they met the wholesome smile of Mrs. Touchell. She is an attractive woman, not what one would describe in the common phraseology of "pretty," but in face, deportment, and demeanor a woman of fine character. Her cropped hair was neatly brushed. The brown golfer coat and the grey gabardine costume that she wore became her well and combined with her demeanor to give her a dignity, as she faced the Court, that impressed those who crowded the comparatively small room. ... Mrs Touchell sat with her from the outset. Later on Mrs P.J. Minahan sat on the other side of her.[1]

Reports in other newspapers contained similar descriptions of the young woman, commenting on her looks, her demeanour, and her clothes. The *Evening News* even had a sub-headline that read, 'Nun has Buster-Brown Haircut', referencing the comic strip character created in 1902 by Richard Felton Outcault. As with the sectarian warriors arrayed in the court room, the press too had begun to regard Bridget as an object, one for the delectation of its readers. When the young woman had taken her seat, Mr Boyce, barrister, stood and announced that he appeared for Bridget Partridge instructed by Messrs J.W. Maund and Christie.[2]

Born in New South Wales in 1872, Francis Stewart Boyce was the son of a prominent Church of England archdeacon, the English-born Francis Bertie Boyce. Admitted to the bar in 1897, he would be appointed King's Counsel in 1924 and Attorney General in 1927 in the Nationalist government of Thomas Bavin. During the war Boyce was a member of the executive of the Universal Service League, a pro-conscription organisation. He was a leading freema-

---

[1] *Daily Telegraph*, 10 August 1920, p. 5.
[2] The narrative of what transpired at the hearing is derived from reports in several newspapers: *Sun* 9 August 1920, p. 7; *Evening News*, 9 August 1920, p. 1; *Daily Telegraph*, 10 August 1920, p. 5; *Sydney Morning Herald*, 10 August 1920, p. 7.

son, serving as grand registrar of the United Grand Lodge of New South Wales and as deputy grand master.

Next, the information was read, alleging that Bridget Partridge was a person deemed to be insane and without sufficient means of support. Then Detective Sergeant Farley gave evidence of Bridget's arrest. After Farley had concluded his evidence in chief, Mr Ryan K.C. announced that, on instructions from Messrs Collins and Mulholland, he appeared with Mr Power for Mr and Mrs Minahan, as friends of Miss Partridge, and also for Miss Partridge.

Religiously, ethnically, and politically, Ryan was the polar opposite of Boyce, reflecting the ethno-religious conflict that the Sister Liguori affair had become. Born in 1876 in Victoria to Irish Catholic immigrant parents, Thomas Joseph Ryan had served as Labor premier of Queensland from 1915 to 1919. He was now a member of the House of Representatives, representing the electorate of West Sydney. During the war, he had been the only state premier to oppose conscription. Along with Archbishop Mannix, he was regarded by militant Protestants as disloyal to the Empire for his opposition to conscription and support for Irish self-government. After Ryan announced his appearance, Boyce interjected,

> 'I object strongly to Mr Ryan appearing on behalf of Mr and Mrs Minahan. And, so far as he says he appears for Miss Partridge, I am instructed to emphatically protest, as she is well able to instruct me as counsel.
>
> Ryan replied, 'That is beside the question. The question is whether she is capable of instructing anyone.'
>
> Boyd retorted, 'If she is not capable of instructing anyone, she is not capable of instructing you!'
>
> Ryan continued, 'Last evening, I understand, Miss Partridge expressed a desire to go to Mrs. Minahan, so Mr. Minahan was informed.'

Bridget was heard to whisper to Mr Boyce that Mrs Minahan had called on her on Sunday and offered friendship.

With the magistrate's consent, Boyce proceeded to cross examine Farley. In answer to his questions, the policeman said that he had spoken with Miss Partridge on various topics and had not detected the slightest signs of insanity, adding that she was quite normal in her conversation, rational in her statements, and gave no trouble. When Boyce had finished his cross examination, Mr Gale said to Ryan,

> 'Before you go any further, I will have to be satisfied why you are here. Where does Mr Minahan come into it?'
>
> Ryan replied, 'He is a friend of Miss Partridge, and there is a section of the Act ....'
>
> Boyce cut him off, 'Well, I would like to cross-examine Mr Minahan on the point. I suggest he has never seen the lady until this morning.'

Ryan then quoted from subsection (5) of section 6 of the *Lunacy Act*: 'Any relative or friend may retain or take such person under his own care, if he satisfies the Justices before whom such person is brought that such person will be properly taken care of'.

> Gale said, 'I have to be thoroughly satisfied. I understood it is only a matter for remand. It is not a case to be rushed.'
>
> Ryan said, 'I am not suggesting it should be rushed, but the inquiry may so develop that subsection 6(5) will come into operation.'
>
> Gale said, 'Possibly it may, at a later stage.'
>
> Ryan said, 'At present we do not know what the position is – whether the lady can instruct anyone.'
>
> Gale said, 'It is a matter for medical examination at present.'
>
> Ryan said, 'The medical gentlemen are unable to give any opinion at present, yet counsel say they are instructed by her.'
>
> Boyce said, 'Including you.'

The reception house had two government medical officers. One was Dr Chisholm Ross. Born at Inverell, New South Wales in 1857, Ross was of Scottish Presbyterian heritage. He was an early practitioner of psychiatry, having studied medicine at the University of Edinburgh. From 1883 he held appointments in New South Wales at several hospitals for the insane before going into private practice in 1903. In 1909 he was appointed a visiting medical officer at the Darlinghurst Reception House. Although considered one of the State's most eminent psychiatrists, some of his decisions were marred by controversy. The second medical officer, Dr Alexander Gibbes, was a general practitioner employed by the state department of health. When Dr Ross requested a remand for seven days, Gale said,

> 'That is usual. You want an opportunity to further examine the young woman. If in the meantime the case is called on, the parties will be notified.'
>
> Ryan said, 'I have no objection to that course.'
>
> Boyce said, 'I ask, at Miss Partridge's request, that she should not be visited by any person during the remand whom she does not wish to see. Yesterday Mrs Minahan visited her, and Miss Partridge had never seen her in her life before yesterday. Miss Partridge does not wish her to visit her.'
>
> Gale said, 'I don't know whether I have the power to make such an order. I think not. The position will be governed by the ordinary rules and procedure.'
>
> Dr Ross said, 'It is really a matter for the medical officers.'
>
> Ryan said, 'I take it then that no order has been made prohibiting Mrs Minahan visiting her?'
>
> Gale replied, 'No. It will be left to the medical officers who her visitors should be.'

Mr Gale then granted a remand for seven days for the medical observation of the patient. Bridget then left the room accompanied by the uniformed nurse with whom she had entered. As she was going through the door, Mrs Touchell gave her a kiss.

At the same time as the Lunacy Court was conducting its proceeding in Sydney, in Melbourne the Victorian Protestant Federation was holding its annual convention. Its guest speaker was Alderman John Ness, who assured the delegates that the federation in New South Wales would move heaven and earth to give Bridget Partridge the protection she deserved. Declaring that this incident might be the starting point for the opening of all convents, he added that he recognised only one prison system.[3] That night, the church committee of St Luke's Anglican church, Clovelly passed a resolution requesting the government 'to see that Miss Partridge (the escaped nun) be given a full and impartial inquiry ... and that her liberties as a British subject be safeguarded'. The committee also called for the abolition or inspection of religious houses of communal character.[4]

Tuesday, 10 August

From Tuesday, advertisements began appearing in the Sydney metropolitan dailies appealing for donations 'from the Protestant public for the defence of Miss Bridget M. Partridge (ex-Sister Ligouri [sic])'. Signed by Grand Master Barton and Grand Secretary Stocker, these LOI advertisements declared, 'Counsel has been briefed to watch her case, and money is needed to see that she has a square deal.' The Protestant Federation also appealed for donations 'to help us to defend Miss Partridge, THE ESCAPED NUN' but it broadened its appeal by adding 'and to help her in her new sphere of life'.[5]

Meanwhile, that morning Bishop Dwyer arrived in Sydney by the overnight mail train from Wagga Wagga, accompanied by two sisters from Mount Erin convent.[6] At the trial, Bishop Dwyer would deny any involvement in Patrick Minahan's engaging counsel to appear for Miss Partridge in the Lunacy Court. His absence from the court to witness Ryan in action, in contrast to the line-up of militant Protestants who came to watch Boyce, is evidence of the truth

---

[3] *Argus*, 10 August 1920, p. 7.
[4] *Sydney Morning Herald*, 12 August 1920, p. 7.
[5] *Sydney Morning Herald*, 10 August 1920, p. 3; 11 August 1920, p. 10; *Daily Telegraph*, 10 August 1920, p. 7; 11 August 1920, p. 8.
[6] *Daily Telegraph*, 10 August 1920, p. 5.

of his denial. In fact, armed with the news of Bridget's remand, Dwyer had come up with a different idea as to how to bring the matter to an end without the confrontation to which Minahan seemed willing to resort. He would visit Miss Partridge at the reception house and speak to her in person. Unfortunately for the bishop, Dr Chisholm Ross refused to allow him to visit her. In fact, no one was permitted to visit her that day.[7] What was worse was that Bridget was not told that the bishop had called, reinforcing her growing belief he had no interest in her welfare. She did not learn of his visit until much later.[8]

Wednesday, 11 August

Bridget Partridge received her first visitors on Wednesday afternoon. According to press reports they included Patrick Minahan and his solicitor Neil Collins as well as John Maund, the solicitor instructing Francis Boyce. However, it is not known what was discussed. A visitor not mentioned in the press was Dorothea Walsh, a sister of Nurse Harriet Bridgefoot who had been assigned to look after Bridget during her stay at the reception house. Born in 1879, Dorothea was the eldest of the nine children of John and Annie Bridgefoot. Harriet, born in 1883, was the fourth child. They were members of a prominent Catholic family from Parramatta. In conversation with Dorothea, Bridget said she wished to publish a contradiction of some of the claims being made in the newspapers about her and convent life. She then sat down and wrote a statement, which read:

> Having bidden adieu to conventual life of my own free will, I wish to thank my former friends for all kindnesses shown me. I hold convent life in my highest estimation, and on no account would wish anyone to speak against it. Visitors can at any time visit Mt Erin Convent and will be most cordially received. There is no cruelty shown to members

---

[7] *Daily Telegraph*, 11 August 1920, p. 10.
[8] *Truth*, 3 July 1921, p. 10.

of the community. At any position in life, one meets with crosses for ourselves. I am proud of my religion as an R.C. and of my country as an Irish girl. Freedom and justice are mine and should any member of a community wish to leave they are perfectly free to do so. In our position in life, one meets with crosses and sometimes we make crosses for ourselves.[9]

At the trial, Bridget said that what she wrote was her composition and she had not acted on any suggestion. She also gave Mrs Walsh a letter addressed to Bishop Dwyer in which she wrote, 'My Lord, it is in your power to grant me a dispensation from my vows. I ask you to call and see me on Friday.' The return address on the letter was the General Post Office.[10]

That night a Protestant rally was held at Newtown. The main speaker was Rev. John Enright, who told the audience that Protestantism had been asleep too long but now its fighting spirit had been aroused. He complained that with the election of a Labor government in March the whole of the New South Wales administrative system was almost in the grasp of 'the Roman Catholic menace', declaring amidst uproar: 'I tell you that unless you arouse yourselves speedily you will find yourselves saluting the Sinn Féin flag.' After referring to 'the poor little Irish girl who had committed no greater crime than wanting her liberty', he concluded with an impassioned appeal to Protestants to band together and make a firm stand against the Roman menace. Enright was followed by Grand Master Barton who told of his part in the rescue of Sister Liguori. Alluding to the poem 'Lochinvar' by Sir Walter Scott, he said, 'It was reminiscent of young Lochinvar and the lost bride of Netherby'. The meeting concluded with an appeal for funds to pay for legal assistance 'to prove that Sister Liguori is perfectly sane and to combat the efforts of Rome to prove by legal argument that she is insane'.[11]

---

[9] *Truth*, 10 July 1921, p. 13; *Watchman*, 7 July 1921, p. 8.
[10] *Truth*, 3 July 1921, p. 10.
[11] *Sun*, 12 August 1920, p. 7.

Thursday, 12 August

Although the hearing in the Lunacy Court had been adjourned until Monday, Dr Ross and Dr Gibbes did not require the full seven days to complete their observations of Bridget Partridge. The court informed the parties and the press that the matter would be listed for further hearing the next day, Friday 13 August.

On Thursday Nurse Bridgefoot called at the presbytery of St Mary's Cathedral looking for Bishop Dwyer in order to hand to him the statement and letter Bridget had written the previous evening. At the trial Dwyer would say he had not known of Nurse Bridgefoot before then and only knew she was at the presbytery because a Mr Finn met him in the street and told him she was waiting for him.[12] This was probably Alexander Donald Finn, secretary of the Parramatta branch of the Catholic Federation. Although Bridget had written the statement to contradict errors in the newspapers, a search of Trove, the National Library of Australia's online newspaper database, has failed to find any newspaper report in which it was published.

In the meantime, Bridget received a visit from an old friend, Miss Kathleen Cooney. Born in 1895, Kathleen had been a boarder at Mount Erin when Bridget was in the novitiate there. They had become friendly and had remained friends. The Cooney family lived at Ganmain, where Bridget taught after taking her vows. Kathleen's father Lawrence owned the Ganmain Hotel. When Bridget was asked at the reception house whether she had any friends in Sydney, she mentioned Miss Cooney. During their talk, the young woman told Bridget that Bishop Dwyer wished to speak with her and that, if she was agreeable, the meeting could take place at her house in Avoca Street, Randwick. Bridget agreed, telling Miss Cooney that when the court proceedings concluded the next day, she would go with her to meet with the bishop.[13]

---

[12] Some newspaper reports of the evidence indicate it was Nurse Bridgefoot's sister or both of them who had called at the presbytery.
[13] *Sun*, 17 August 1920, p. 7; 1 July 1921, p. 7.

However, Bridget seems to have had second thoughts about her arrangement with Miss Cooney. That same day she wrote to the bishop:

> Your Lordship,
>
> Accept a few lines to thank you for the kind offer in my regard. Why not visit me here when it is all over? I don't blame you in the least for the false statement made. Worse has been said and proved otherwise. Father Barry was brought into it, too. I will explain later. I am too full of it. I have had a trying experience. All is well that ends well. Pray for your sincere child.
>
> Bridget[14]

That day she also wrote to Mrs Touchell:

> My Dear Mrs Touchell,
>
> Accept my little letter in acknowledgment of your many kindnesses to me. Friends are multiplying every day, also letters, telegrams, and gifts. So, you see time is being wiled away for me.
>
> I am as happy as the day is long—and 'plenty more day'. Please God, everything will be soon fixed up for the better. I would like you to send on my white hat, as the remark was in the paper last time that I had no hat on. I am almost finished my sewing.
>
> But never mind now—I hope before another week is over to be quite settled again. Thank all kind friends for me for their letters, etc. Hoping to see you soon.
>
> P.S. I wish to spend a few days more with you before I leave Australia.[15]

The postscript refers to what Bridget had told Mrs Touchell before her arrest, that she wished to return to her people in Ireland once her brother Joseph had arrived from China.[16] The body of the letter, however, indicates she was not expecting to return to the Touchell

---

[14] *Catholic Press*, 7 July 1921, p. 17.
[15] *Daily Telegraph*, 14 August 1920, p. 11.
[16] Ibid., p. 1.

home immediately after her release but makes no reference to the arrangement she had made with Miss Cooney. Clearly, something else was planned. Four days later Bridget would write in a letter to the bishop, 'I asked you to call and see me when the crowd had dispersed on Friday last. I was too ill to go visiting that day'.[17] In view of events that occurred the next day and in light of her evidence at the trial, Bridget was less than truthful in suggesting illness was the reason she reneged on the arrangement she had made with Miss Cooney. She was also disingenuous when she added, 'They are all Catholics round here, and some from Ireland', as if she were living among her co-religionists. As she admitted at the trial, she never met or spoke with any Catholics after leaving the reception house.

Friday, 13 August

On Friday morning, the small room at the Darlinghurst Reception House was crowded long before 9 o'clock, the appointed hour for the resumed hearing. According to Thomas Henley MLA, Father Peter Murphy, administrator of St Mary's Cathedral, visited Bridget at 7.30 that morning to confirm the arrangements for Bridget to go with Miss Cooney after she was released.[18] When the resumed hearing began, it terminated with dramatic suddenness. Upon Mr Boyce announcing that he appeared for Miss Partridge, Mr Gale SM said,

> 'I don't think your duties will be very arduous. Dr Chisholm Ross has recommended Miss Partridge's release. That being so, my duty is to discharge her.'
>
> Looking around the courtroom Mr Boyce said, 'Where's Ryan?'

But Tom Ryan KC was not there. He was in Melbourne. The solicitor, Neil Collins, appeared in his stead. In an interview with the *Evening News*, Ryan later explained that he had left Sydney after the first hearing to attend federal parliament, which in those days

---

[17] *Catholic Press*, 7 July 1921, p. 17.
[18] NSWPD, 25 August 1920, p. 422.

sat in Melbourne, and that it had been impossible for him to return on short notice. That is likely true as the federal parliament sat that week on Wednesday, Thursday, and Friday during which Ryan took part in debates on several bills. He told the reporter that he had initially been brought into the case at the last minute to watch the proceedings with a view to having Miss Partridge given over to Minahan's custody if the evidence justified such a course. He denied any part in initiating the proceedings or having acted for the Catholic church or the convent authorities.[19]

Boyce said, 'I did not think he would be here. Is there no apology? Nothing to soothe the feelings of this injured girl? Her place has been picketed and her feelings have been lacerated. She has been hounded down. Is there no …' Mr Gale interrupted him saying, 'If this lady has suffered any wrong, she has her remedy.' He then closed the court.[20] According to the *Sun*:

> The sudden ending stupefied the spectators, who sat looking at one another. The voice of an official, 'Those who have no further business here leave the court,' brought them to a realisation of what had happened, and they filed out eagerly discussing the situation.[21]

Those who had been in the courtroom mingled with the larger crowd assembled in the yard, watched on from the street by those who had not been able to get into the yard. One newspaper reported, 'In the crowd were members of parliament, clergymen, priests, members of the Loyal Orange Institution, and many women'.[22] One of the women was Mrs Thompson from Wagga Wagga.

Rev. John Enright proclaimed to anyone who would listen his belief that those who wish to leave a convent should be free to do so. Catching sight of Patrick Minahan he said,

---

[19] *Evening News*, 16 August 1920, p. 1.
[20] A copy of Bridget Partridge's case record is in the NSW state archives at MHNSW-StAC: NRS-905 Colonial Secretary Correspondence [5/8254] Item 34342.
[21] *Sun*, 13 August 1920, p. 5.
[22] *Sydney Morning Herald*, 14 August 1920, p. 13.

'You didn't get her after all. We have beaten you today and we will beat you again. We will beat you every time.'

Minahan said, 'Where are you taking her?'

Enright said with a laugh, 'You'll hear all about it afterwards.'

Enright's gloating confirmed that for some Protestants the Sister Liguori affair was about much more than the problems of an individual young woman, it was the latest battlefield in the continuing war between enlightened Protestantism and obscurantist Roman Catholicism.

As the crowd dispersed, several members of the press and public remained to await Bridget's emergence from the reception house. When Mr Gale had announced she was discharged, a nurse had hustled her out of the courtroom and into the reception house, preventing anyone following. Among those waiting out the front of the building was Miss Cooney. But Bridget did not appear. As had happened in Wagga Wagga a fortnight before, she was spirited away, leaving the reception house by the back door in the company of Inspector General Mitchell, Sergeant Farley, Grand Master Barton, and Mr Maund, thus pre-empting the proposed dialogue between her and Bishop Dwyer. At the trial, Bridget would say that it was her wish not to go with Miss Cooney as she did not want to be taken back to the convent. Although Bridget would agree she had no reason to distrust Miss Cooney's honesty, she said she thought she might be forcibly taken back to the convent if she went with her.

Despite Bridget's denial that anybody had suggested she break her arrangement with Miss Cooney, there can be no doubt she would have been strongly advised of the risk of going with her Catholic friend to see the bishop. Ever since his involvement in the affair, Barton had adopted the 'cloak and dagger' approach, making allegations of pickets and search parties on trains and in cars racing about the countryside in pursuit of their prey. One does not have to be too cynical to see that a rapprochement between Bridget and her bishop would derail Barton's grand plan: 'Rome is not going to have her way today. I am determined to fight. It is Rome versus the Orange Institution in this matter'. And so far Barton's plan had played out well. Bridget was convinced by his scaremongering. She wrote to Mrs Thompson, 'I was hunted like a cat after a mouse all along the line'.[23] The newspapers, too, were on side, adopting the 'escaped' nun trope in their headlines and their articles which published Barton's narrative of events in their news reports. The *Catholic Press* reacted to the obsequiousness of the press. Referring to what it called the *Daily Telegraph*'s 'dirty campaign about poor Sister Liguori' it complained:

> Three of its valuable columns were devoted to free advertisement of philanthropists, renegades, and suburban aldermen, and to long drawn-out irrelevancies and time-dishonoured sectarianism. It is many years since we experienced such a pitiful exposition of low journalism.[24]

Some Protestants, conditioned by years of anti-Catholic propaganda, might honestly have believed Bridget was at risk of being abducted and forcibly returned to Mount Erin convent. Statements by Protestant leaders, such as this one from Alderman John Ness, would have confirmed such opinions:

> As it has been disclosed that this young woman was locked up against her will it now becomes a question for the authorities to say whether action should be taken to have these places inspected by non-interested persons, to ensure that any others are not restrained in their wish for liberty.[25]

However, most Protestants, including Barton, would have realised that the law of the land prevented such a scenario from occurring. For Barton, the real danger lay in the issue being resolved amicably, with Bridget being dispensed from her vows and returned to her family in Ireland. That having been said, it emerged at the trial

---

[23] *Daily Express*, 26 August 1920, p. 2.
[24] *Catholic Press*, 19 August 1920, p. 22.
[25] *Sun*, 15 August 1920, p. 2.

that John Maund had made an offer to Bishop Dwyer in which he proposed an interview with Bridget Partridge at his office, an offer the bishop turned down. Instead, Dwyer had required the meeting be held at St Mary's Cathedral.[26] As with his refusal to discuss the matter with Archdeacon Pike and with Dr Tivey, Dwyer exhibited a stubbornness that was unproductive.

After Bridget left the reception house, Sergeant Farley, under instructions from the inspector general, drove her and Mr and Mrs Barton to the Barton house in Burwood, where she would stay for four days before going to Berry on the New South Wales south coast for a holiday. That afternoon she received a visit from Mary Thompson, in whose home she had taken refuge an eventful three weeks before. The visit was short as Mrs Thompson was due to return to Wagga Wagga on the evening train. She told the *Daily Telegraph*:

> I am glad to say she was happy and contented but looked drawn and tired. A rest is what she wants and she is going away for a brief trip into the country very shortly. Where, I cannot say, but she will be among friends who will treat her kindly and considerately. My only regret is that I am not taking the dear little girl home with me.[27]

---

[26] *Truth*, 10 July 1921, p. 13.
[27] *Daily Express*, 14 August 1920, p. 1; *Daily Telegraph*, 14 August 1920, p. 11.

A montage of Bridget Partridge's family including her parents, her sisters, Bridget, and her brother Joseph (*People*, 11 August 1954, p. 9)

Top: Mount Erin Convent 1916 (Wikipedia); lower left: Bridget Partridge c. 1921 (*People*, 11 August 1954, p. 7); lower right: Bishop Joseph Dwyer (Author's collection)

Top left: Grand Master Robert Barton (*SMH*, 12 January 1921, p. 12); top right: Banner of the Loyal Orange Institution of NSW (Author's collection); lower: An example of the 'escaped nun' literary genre

Top left: Joseph Partridge c. 1921 (Author's collection); top right: Attorney General Edward McTiernan (Wikipedia); lower left: Patrick Joseph Minahan (Parliament of NSW); lower right: Lunacy Court finds Bridget Partridge to be sane (*SMH*, 13 August 1920, p. 9)

5
CRUSADE

'This business is not finished with'

One might have thought that, once the Lunacy Court had determined that Bridget Partridge was not insane and was therefore free to go where she liked, the Sister Liguori affair would be at an end. Having invoked the *Lunacy Act* to ascertain Bridget's whereabouts and welfare, Bishop Dwyer ought now to be satisfied she was safe and well. As she had freely expressed her wish not to return to convent life, his obligation under canon law to inquire after her and to 'take care cautiously for [her] return' had been satisfied. He was neither obliged nor entitled to force her to return to the convent pending finalisation of the paperwork dispensing her from her vows. Equally, one would have thought that Grand Master Barton and Mr and Mrs Touchell would have been satisfied with the decision of the court and, apart from offering her their continuing hospitality, they ought now to let the matter fade into obscurity, pending her brother's arrival to take her home. But such thoughts would have been naïve. To quote Barton's former partner Alderman John Ness: 'This business is not finished with'.

Following the Lunacy Court's decision, Alderman Ness had spoken to the *Daily Telegraph*. His message was less about Miss Partridge's welfare and more about the coming showdown with the Catholic church over its system of convents:

> I know where she is but I have undertaken not to divulge the secret. Miss Partridge needs sanctuary temporarily, and we are going to provide it. … But this business is not finished with. We are going to fight for Miss Partridge, if needs be, and for any other unfortunate, irrespective of creed, who may be submitted to such cruel persecution as

> has Miss Partridge. We are out to protect her freedom and the freedom of all others similarly situated.
>
> We have come to a time when a proper and complete investigation should be made of a system which threatens the individual liberty of any person. We are going to get that investigation. We must take up a firm and aggressive stand – and now.
>
> …
>
> You should have seen the Protestant demonstrations in this suburb last night. They were wonderful. … The enthusiasm was intense. The case of Miss Partridge has brought things to a head. … It is a fight. We have had to put up with the insults of these people too long.[1]

Past Grand Master James Robinson also spoke with the *Telegraph*. In an even more sinister tone, he said:

> It is sincerely hoped that this exposure of convent life will lead the citizens of Australia to force the hands of the legislators not to subject convents to Government inspection but to absolutely close them.

He showed his disdain for those who chose convent life by saying:

> I would not accept it as proof of insanity when a nun wants to run away from a convent; rather might I doubt the sanity of a healthy young girl who allows herself to be shut up in such a place.

In his long statement Robinson used martial language, speaking of the Loyal Orange Institution 'having won such a victory' and of Ryan's absence showing that the Catholic church 'was afraid to cross swords with the worthy sons of the worthy sires who fought for victory'. Referring to the papacy as 'a foreign power', he declared, 'Truly this failure on the part of Rome is the handwriting on the wall, showing the utter downfall of Rome's attempted supremacy!'[2]

Meetings of Orange lodges, Protestant Federation branches, and

---

[1] *Daily Telegraph,* 14 August 1920, p. 11.
[2] Ibid.

Protestant churches around Australia passed resolutions congratulating the LOI and the Touchells on their success in securing the liberty of Bridget Partridge and urging the government to inquire into the convent system. Letters pages in the newspapers echoed such sentiments.³ Rev. Touchell told the *Evening News*, 'The whole country seems to have been aroused over this matter. Letters of congratulations are pouring in from all over Australia. … It is impossible for us to answer all these letters. We are doing so only in cases where money is sent'.⁴ The Touchells also claimed to have received anonymous and abusive letters, examples of which they made available to the press. Rev. Touchell told the *Daily Telegraph*, 'These and similar letters are useful as showing the type of mind Roman Catholic theology and practice produces'.⁵

Responding to calls for an inquiry into convents, Chief Secretary James Dooley said if he knew of any nuns being detained against their will in any convents he would take steps to get them out but he knew no such thing: 'As far as I know, no nun is kept against her will.' He then outlined the procedure for a nun to relinquish her vows, adding, 'This is the regular way. Of course, if a nun goes away in her nightdress, no one can blame the Bishop, who has the responsibility of her oversight, for taking steps to see that she is safe'.⁶

Barton hit back by making public the statutory declaration which Miss Partridge had made on 4 August when she was staying with the Touchells, the text of which is set out in chapter 4. He also released a supplementary statement by Bridget about the taste and smell of the mixture she had been given. The declaration and statement added little to the corpus of facts then known. However, their

---

³ See, for example, *Sydney Morning Herald*, 14 August 1920, p. 13; 18 September 1920, p. 14; *Daily Telegraph*, 16 August 1920, p. 6; *Sun*, 16 August 1920, pp. 6-7; 24 August 1920, p. 2.
⁴ *Evening News*, 14 August 1920, p. 1.
⁵ *Daily Telegraph*, 3 September 1920, p. 6.
⁶ *Evening News*, 30 August 1920, p. 4.

release was intended to boost the LOI's anti-convent campaign, as Barton made clear to the press:

> In view of the facts which have been revealed in the statements made to the press by Miss Partridge, I claim on behalf of the Protestants of this State, that a Royal Commission should be appointed with all the powers to call any person and obtain any evidence required, regarding the management of convents.[7]

Initial Catholic response to the campaign was subdued. The *Freeman's Journal* criticised the daily papers 'which give Orange ranters publicity and print every anti-Catholic libel' and which had adopted the 'escaped' nun narrative with 'their screaming scare lines' repeating the sensational claims of 'sectarian-mongers and the hangers-on of Orangeism':

> The editors of our daily papers are well aware the religious life is a voluntary one, and that there are neither chains nor dungeons there and so the fact that they have suppressed that knowledge to give colour to a flimsy Maria Monk sort of story is the best evidence that more than bigotry is at the bottom of the newspaper uproar.[8]

The *Freeman's Journal* also appealed to Protestant rationality in relation to the good works of the sisters who devoted themselves to convent life:

> Surely, only demoniacal spirits could blind them to the obvious fact that the priests and nuns they have been insidiously assailing are foremost in every work of charity in our midst and that in these convents, which they slyly hold up to execration, those devoted souls are trained who are seen ministering to the sick, the aged and the helpless in a host of charitable institutions, who fought the deadly plague in the poorest slums, and who have gathered the little orphaned children by thousands to their mothering knees.[9]

---

[7] *Daily Telegraph*, 3 September 1920, p. 6; 4 September 1920, p. 11.
[8] *Freeman's Journal*, 12 August 1920, p. 22; 19 August 1920, p. 26; 2 September 1920, p. 23.
[9] *Freeman's Journal*, 19 August 1920, pp. 22, 26.

The *Catholic Press* also criticised the press, particularly the *Daily Telegraph*, which it accused of giving two columns to 'the vapourings of frothy Orangemen, though falsehood and insincerity was conspicuous in every line'.[10] In Brisbane, the Catholic archbishop, James Duhig, spoke out on the affair:

> Sister Liguori had been well treated at the convent and must have been in a queer mental mood to leave the convent attired as she did and undertake a journey of 70 miles with any man, even though he was Grand Master of the Orange Lodge. But the most patent thing of all is that Sister Liguori has been taken up by those people, not so much out of sympathy for herself, as out of a deep-seated hatred of the Catholic Church and its nuns.[11]

In Melbourne, Father Paul Cullen, provincial of the Vincentian Fathers, told a gathering at Fitzroy that a wave of bigotry was passing over the land and Catholic people should not submit tamely: 'Base insinuations are being made against convents by a certain section, which is urging that steps should be taken to pry into the inner life of the nuns. ... The Catholic section should stand by the nuns and assist them generously as possible'.[12]

The gunmen of Berry and the wreckers of Mount Erin convent

The LOI's propaganda took a more sensational and sinister tone at the end of August when Grand Secretary Charles Stocker declared that 'those who were persecuting Miss Partridge had traced her to the place where she was resting'. This was the residence of Thomas Newing at 'Westbury', a dairy farm near Berry. He said that while she was holidaying there with Grand Master Barton and his married daughter, they were being spied upon and annoyed. He said Barton had told him that the house had been surrounded for the past three nights and that:

> This morning at an early hour Mr. Barton and those with

---

[10] *Catholic Press*, 12 August 1920, p. 20; 19 August 1920, p. 22.
[11] *Daily Express*, 17 August 1920, p. 2.
[12] *Daily Telegraph*, 20 September 1920, p. 6.

> him discovered a party of spies in a gully within 100 yards of the house. They were armed with rifles. Mr. Barton also informed me that it was generally believed in the Berry district that there was a reward of £100 offered for the girl, dead or alive.

He quoted Barton as saying, somewhat cryptically, 'Seeing that these people have gone to such extreme measures everything will be now told to the public.' Stocker added:

> I also had a communication from Wagga that feeling there over the treatment of the girl was running so high that unless the persecution of Miss Partridge was discontinued the returned soldiers of the district and their Protestant friends would wreck the Roman Catholic Convent at Wagga.[13]

On reading the press coverage of Barton's and Stocker's allegations, Chief Secretary James Dooley called for reports of the incidents from the police. When the reports were in hand, he informed the press that the Berry police had advised:

> Some strangers had been seen hanging about the neighbourhood of the house where Miss Partridge had been staying. A young man, armed with a rifle had been seen planted behind a log below the house at night-time. It is a common thing for young men from the town to go out shooting foxes on moonlight nights, and the police opinion is that it was one of these young men who was seen out the night in question.

Dooley added that the Wagga police had reported that representatives of the returned soldiers and the Orange Lodge had denied that an attack on the Wagga convent was contemplated.[14] This he based on advice from Inspector Duprez that 'there is no indication of excitement at Wagga. There is no likelihood of the destruction of property. Sectarian feeling is not running high'.[15] The president

---

[13] *Sun*, 29 August 1920, p. 4
[14] *Sydney Morning Herald*, 1 September 1920, p. 12.
[15] *Daily Advertiser*, 1 September 1920, p. 2.

of the Wagga Wagga branch of the Returned Soldiers' League also issued a denial of Stocker's allegation:

> I wish to deny the allegation coming from Sydney that the returned soldiers of this district intended to interfere in any way with the Roman Catholic Convent at Wagga. Such a statement could only emanate in the first place from an enemy of this organisation, which is strictly non-sectarian and non-partisan in relation to party politics.[16]

Barton responded to the Berry police report by denying the men were fox hunting: 'People do not go out after foxes in the daytime and the fact that several shots were exchanged between the spies and those responsible for the protection of Miss Partridge is a contradiction of the alleged police report.' He demanded that a proper and authentic report be submitted of what did actually occur.[17] In another statement, Barton said that the men guarding Miss Partridge discovered three armed men in a gully near the house, two of whom ran away, while the third remained: 'I suppose this was because he noticed our men were not armed, they having left their revolvers and rifles at the house'.[18] In yet another statement a month later, Barton spoke of three incidents, in two of which he claimed shots were fired, yet none of the alleged incidents is consistent with his previous statements. One of those incidents was said to be on 28 August 'at 5.30 am (just daylight)'.[19] Sunrise is at 6.36 am in Wagga Wagga on 28 August. Neither 'daytime' nor 'just daylight' as Barton claimed; more like 'night' as the police report stated or perhaps 'pre-dawn', which is considered a good time for hunting foxes.

Dooley answered Barton's criticisms of the Berry police report by saying that while he had released only truncated versions of the two police reports, the full reports were available for inspection by the press and the LOI. He said, 'Mr Barton is undoubtedly suffering a severe mental strain. I would recommend him to have a little

---

[16] *Daily Advertiser*, 4 September 1920, p. 4.
[17] *Daily Telegraph*, 3 September 1920, p. 6; 4 September 1920, p. 11.
[18] *Evening News*, 2 September 1920, p. 7.
[19] *Watchman*, 7 October 1920, p. 2.

peace and quietness in order that he might gain strength for further efforts.' He added that the inspector general had assured him that responsible officers had 'declared emphatically that all statements about shooting, capturing, the likelihood of onslaught, and various other things of an alarmist nature were not true, and Mr Barton and others had no substantial grounds or reasons for inferring that the police were shirking their duty'.[20]

Despite Barton's claim to represent the Protestants of New South Wales, not all were on his side. Under the penname 'Non-Catholic', one wrote to the *Sun*:

> Families may go homeless, scantily clad and underfed, yet this simple case of a girl who became dissatisfied with and ran away from a calling which she voluntarily elected to follow, must, in the light of some, have the whole public view focussed on it, must receive the whole attention of Parliament, and the whole energies of the police force must be employed in unravelling the 'myths of Berry', searching logs and chasing armed murderers, who exist only in the vicious imagination of those in search of fetid matter.
>
> After passing through the troublous years of war, and the trying period of drought, this, our fair land, is sorely in need of rest from the turbulence of every kind. ... Now when we should be reverting to a state of peace, why allow a hot-headed few to stir up strife.[21]

The *Freeman's Journal* responded to the Berry allegations in a similar fashion to its response to the attack on the convents by criticising the press for 'so freely opening their columns to palpable slanders on the Catholic community'. It observed that Bridget Partridge's movements 'are not occasioning the slightest flutter in Catholic circles', adding, 'But they print the sensational and creepy fiction for the plain and malicious purpose of discrediting Catho-

---

[20] *Daily Telegraph*, 4 September 1920, p. 11; *Daily Advertiser*, 4 September 1920, p. 4. The police reports are in the NSW state archives at MHNSW-StAC: NRS-905 Colonial Secretary Correspondence [5/8254] Item 34326.
[21] *Sun*, 9 September 1920, p. 8.

lics in credulous non-Catholic circles'.[22] The paper doubled down on its criticism after Dooley's release of the police reports, claiming that they 'should make even our anti-Catholic dailies more careful in the future about publishing cock-and-bull stories from prejudiced sources'. The *Freeman's Journal* had a point: the charges were unsubstantiated yet the dailies reported them as fact; their sources were the partisans Barton and Stocker yet the dailies made no attempt to verify their claims; Barton's various allegations were inconsistent yet the dailies repeated them without question. A phone call to the RSL and LOI in Wagga Wagga would have given the lie to Stocker's assertion, while Barton's inconsistencies should have raised a red flag in the mind of any competent journalist.

Nevertheless, the LOI's relentless campaign was having an effect even among ordinary Protestants—after all, as the proverb says, 'where there is smoke there is fire'. In a letter to the *Daily Telegraph*, M. Moore wrote that it was 'a pity so much sectarian capital has been made out of Miss Partridge's case.' But then proceeded:

> At the same time, one cannot help wondering why, if nuns (or lay sisters) are free to leave convents when they wish there was so much apprehension on Dr Dwyer's part, why the warrant was not issued in Wagga, and why such strenuous efforts were made to recapture her.[23]

Clearly the Catholics were losing the propaganda war. Then the Catholic Federation entered the fray with a statement by its general secretary Charles Lawlor. Referring to Barton's claims about armed spies at Berry, which he called 'absolute twaddle', Lawlor said:

> Since the day Sister Liguori left the Central [sic – Lunacy Court?], no Catholic has ever sought to ascertain her whereabouts, nor has made any effort to remove her from her present surroundings excepting the letters written to the press by Mr Justice Heydon.[24]

---

[22] *Freeman's Journal*, 2 September 1920, p. 23.
[23] *Daily Telegraph*, 17 August 1920, p. 5.
[24] *Sun*, 30 August 1920, p. 5.

Enter Charles Heydon

The letters to which Lawlor referred were letters which Charles Heydon wrote to the press inviting Bridget Partridge to stay with him and his wife.[25] Born in Sydney in 1845 to English parents, his father being a recent convert to Catholicism, Heydon was a retired justice of the Industrial Court who had received notoriety in 1917 when he and other leading Catholics had strongly criticised Archbishop Daniel Mannix for his outspokenness about Ireland, conscription, and the war, declaring that Mannix had 'shown himself to be not only disloyal as a man, but untrue to the teachings of the Church of which, by his office, he should be the guardian'. Pro-conscriptionists and empire loyalists, mostly Protestant, loudly endorsed Heydon's sentiments, while Irish nationalists and Catholic anti-conscriptionists unleashed a howl of protest at his treachery.

Three years on, with conscription and the war no longer issues, Heydon directed his criticism at those who had earlier praised his stand against Mannix. Referring to Bridget Partridge's discharge by the Lunacy Court, Heydon wrote:

> I see that Miss Partridge, who does not give the impression of being very much her own mistress, has been taken away by people who say that her address is to be kept secret. Consequently, no influences are to be admitted except such as these people desire.

He then invited Bridget to come to his home to stay as a guest until her brother came. He asked that he be informed of her address so that his wife might visit her, adding, 'If this is refused, it will be evident that Miss Partridge, whether or not she was an "escaped nun", is now a captured nun, and is to be kept under exclusive influences for as long as suits her capturers'. He then referred to his two deceased sisters who were nuns. One was a Sister of Charity who, he said, died thankful she had adopted the religious life. The other, a Benedictine, decided after several years that she no longer had a

---

[25] *Daily Telegraph,* 16 August 1920, p. 6; *Sydney Morning Herald,* 16 August 1920, p. 8.

vocation to religious life. Without difficulty, she left the order and married. Heydon concluded his letter with a lament:

> Between Catholic Sinn Féiners instilling national hatred and anti-Catholic bigots instilling religious hatred (each of these hatreds unfortunately blowing up the other to a white heat), a poor, ordinary Catholic, who wishes to be true to both the Empire and his Church – to fear God and honour the King – is in somewhat of a cleft stick.

Rev. Touchell wrote to the press in reply to Heydon's letter declaring that those caring for her 'stand for liberty for every individual within the limits of the laws of our own country'. He wrote that Bridget had asked to be taken away to a quiet place to rest and that 'Judge Heydon's request to know where she is will be granted just when she herself thinks fit'. Heydon responded with a letter in reply saying he offered a home that was free and open to visitors: 'What Mr Touchell prefers to this is a secret home to which no one can go except those whom he chooses to admit'. After listing some of the restrictions Touchell had outlined in his letter, Heydon concluded:

> Many people will become thoroughly convinced that he is keeping the girl practically a prisoner, and using influences to turn her from her faith, or to make her go on to the platform as an "escaped nun"—an example of the horrors of which (I am sure he believes) Rome encourages within Convent walls.

Heydon's correspondence must have hit a nerve as a letter appeared in the press signed 'Miss B.M. Partridge', saying that she noticed Heydon's offer of a home, for which she thanked him, but 'I already have a good home, with every comfort, and all my requirements are well supplied. Best of all, I have no worry. I am not hidden away; I am only having a quiet and complete rest'.[26]

Yet, this would not be the end of the matter. The following week Rev. Touchell told a rally at Bexley to promote the Protestant Fed-

---

[26] *Daily Telegraph*, 19 August 1920, p. 3; 20 August 1920, p. 9; *Sydney Morning Herald*, 25 August 1920, p. 11.

eration that he thought Bridget Partridge would take legal action against Bishop Dwyer and Dr Leahy. At the rally, William Bagnall MLA spoke of the need for organisation among the Protestant churches to combat the evil forces of the Roman Catholic church. He said he was opposed to sectarianism, but this struggle was one of patriotism: 'The Church of Rome had done its best to destroy the Empire by bringing about disintegration within the countries that formed it. All through the war the Vatican had been hand-in-glove with the enemy.'[27] Once again, Bridget Partridge's personal situation was linked with the wider sectarian conflict, the focus of which would now shift to the New South Wales parliament.

A 'fistic encounter' in Parliament

When the Sister Liguori affair first came to public notice, parliament was in recess. But on its resumption, it became the new location for the LOI's campaign against Catholic convents, resulting in a potent mix of sectarianism and party politics.[28]

Following the elections on 20 March 1920 the new parliament sat on 27 April 1920 for the election of the Speaker and the swearing in of members. It was prorogued the next day and did not return until 10 August. The elections had been conducted under a new electoral system involving proportional representation with multi-members constituencies. The Labor Party under John Storey had won 42 out of the 90 seats in the Legislative Assembly, the Nationalist Party and the Progressives together had won 43, and independents five. The Catholic Federation, which had run candidates under the banner of the Democratic Party, did not win a seat. The Nationalists and Progressives failed to form a coalition, and Daniel Levy, Nationalist Speaker in the old Parliament, agreed to continue in that role, thereby enabling the Labor Party, with the support of

---

[27] *Sydney Morning Herald*, 27 August 1920, p. 9.
[28] NSWPD, 30 November 1920, pp. 2902-2913; 7 December 1920, pp. 3215-3222; 21 December 1920, pp. 3971-3974; *Daily Telegraph*, 1 December 1920, p. 9; 8 December 1920, p. 9; 22 December 1920, p. 8; *Sydney Morning Herald*, 8 December 1920, p. 14.

a Socialist Party member and two Independent Labor members, to form a minority government. Of the two independent Labor members, one was Patrick Minahan, who had been disendorsed just before the elections.

Contrary to the wishes of the party executive, Minahan had signed a pledge that he would support the unconditional release from prison of members of the Industrial Workers of the World (IWW), a revolutionary organisation that had opposed the war. In 1916 twelve of its members had been convicted and imprisoned on charges of conspiracy to commit arson and excite sedition. The correctness of their convictions and long prison sentences had come into doubt and sections of the labour movement had been agitating for their release. When the new government took office it appointed a royal commission to investigate the matter. On the recommendation of the royal commissioner, ten of the men were released in early August 1920. Although disendorsed, Minahan always voted with the Labor government and in October was admitted to the Labor caucus.[29]

Despite the existence of a sectional Catholic party, the elections resulted in Catholics under the Labor banner entering the parliament and the Cabinet in record numbers. Of the 43 members who would constitute the Labor caucus, 25 were Catholics, and in the cabinet, five of the 13 ministers were Catholics. The presence of so many Catholics in the Labor government alarmed Protestants, particularly those elected to the new parliament with the endorsement of the LOI.

The first item of business when the parliament met on 10 August was the governor's speech setting out the government's proposed legislative program. This was followed by debate on the parliament's address in reply to that speech and a censure motion moved by the leader of the opposition criticising the government's handling of the IWW royal commission. The address-in-reply debate, which continued until 2 September, gave members freedom to range over

---

[29] *Sydney Morning Herald*, 10 March 1920, p. 11; 12 October 1920, p. 10.

subjects of interest to them. Although the Sister Liguori affair had come to public notice in early August, it was not mentioned by any of the speakers during the first two weeks of the debate. However, on 25 August, opposition member and Orangeman Thomas Henley raised it for the first time. As discussed in chapter 3, Henley demanded to know who gave Mr and Mrs Minahan, Mr Collins, and Father Murphy permission to visit Miss Partridge in the Darlinghurst Reception House. But Henley went on to link the affair to the opposition's censure motion regarding the IWW. Incensed by what he saw as double standards, Henley told his fellow MPs:

> I want the country to understand that during the past few months we saw the whole of the legal fraternity in our law department straining to get men whom a jury said were guilty out of gaol, and we also saw the same department straining all its energies to capture an innocent woman and have her put back into a convent gaol. ... I want to know why Mr Sproule, the Solicitor-General, interested himself on behalf of Bishop Dwyer to get a warrant for the arrest of this young lady. ... What I want to know is why we should be so anxious about the IWW criminals, and give no heed to persons who are locked up in convents and such places? ... The liberty of the subject is at stake owing to the policy they [i.e., government members] advocate—a policy of letting criminals out and keeping innocent persons in gaol-like places such as convents.[30]

When Patrick Minahan rose to speak in the debate, he dealt with Henley's inquiry as to his visit to the Darlinghurst Reception House, as set out in chapter 3. But like Henley, he also put the affair in a wider context: 'The general public are getting tired of these Dr Mannix hunters, of these Father Jerger hunters, and of all this stuff about the poor girl whom they captured at the reception house at Darlinghurst.' Opposition member Tom Hoskins, a prominent member of the Protestant Federation who had attended the first hearing in the Lunacy Court, interjected, 'You tried hard to capture her!'[31]

---

[30] NSWPD, 25 August 1920, pp. 420-423.
[31] NSWPD, 31 August 1920, p. 539.

Thomas Henley returned to the issue in mid-September, asking the premier on notice whether the government would appoint a royal commission to inquire regarding women in convents. This echoed Grand Master Barton's call for a royal commission regarding the management of convents. The premier's response was, 'The Government does not propose to take any such action'.[32] The next move came in November when the newly knighted Sir Thomas Henley sought leave to introduce a bill 'to provide security against detention of persons against their will, in any institutions, or by any persons.' He disingenuously argued that the *Unlawful Detention Bill* was not directed against any section of the community. When pressed for examples of the need for such legislation, he said:

> Several cases have come under notice lately. Take the case of Sylvia Thomas. Did not certain people try to restrain her from coming out of an institution and did they not try to get her back again? And did they not also try to get Sister Liguori back? If the hon. member wants to know what institutions are affected he can ascertain them.[33]

Sylvia Thomas was the subject of an application for a writ of habeas corpus made to the Supreme Court on 7 September 1920 by her paternal aunt Helen Duval. Sylvia was a 16-year-old orphan, whose mother had died when she was 14 and whose father had died in April. Sylvia's parents had been baptised as Catholics, as had Sylvia, but the family had not been practising. When the father died, Mrs Duval had looked after Sylvia and her siblings but eventually she had to give them up as she was unable to care for them. She had taken them to Ormond House, Paddington, a government-run reception house and shelter for children. Sylvia's maternal aunt Lydia Smith, a Catholic, then arranged for the children to be placed in Catholic orphanages. Sylvia was sent to St Magdalene's Retreat at Tempe, run by the Good Samaritan sisters. Mrs Duval claimed that her brother had expressed to her his wish that the children be brought

---

[32] NSWPD, 15 September 1920, pp. 807-808; *Daily Telegraph* 4 September 1920, p. 11.
[33] NSWPD 30 November 1920, p. 2904.

up in the Church of England. So, she arranged for the removal of the children to Protestant orphanages, but the sisters at Tempe refused to allow her to take Sylvia. At the hearing, counsel for the mother superior of the convent said his client did not oppose the court's ordering Sylvia's release but requested an order that she be brought up in the Catholic faith of her father. In the end, the case was determined on the basis of child welfare considerations, with Justice Sir Charles Wade releasing her unconditionally, saying that because Sylvia was 16, she could legally determine with whom she wished to live and what religion she wished to practice.[34]

The Sylvia Thomas case illustrates the strength of feeling over religious identification in early twentieth-century Australia, particularly with regard to the raising of children. Proselytisation in institutions was a concern of both Catholics and Protestants, hence the existence of denominational orphanages. But the case had little to do with the Sister Liguori affair. As Patrick Minahan told parliament, 'We know that this young woman, a Catholic, was placed in a Catholic institution by her Catholic aunt [and] the sisters merely carried out the instructions of the aunt'.[35] Ironically, the Sylvia Thomas case served to undermine rather than assist Henley's argument for it showed that the existing law was adequate to deal with such situations in a practical and sensible manner. For the most part Catholic MPs responded with derision to Henley's thinly disguised attack on the convent system. However, at times the debate became quite heated, with Patrick Minahan declaring that if Henley and other members 'were in any way to interfere with these Catholic institutions … there would be a "mess-up" here as bad as anything that occurred on the plains of Flanders'.[36] At the close of one of the debates, after the Speaker had left the chair, members had to intervene to prevent physical violence between Henley and a Catholic Labor member, Carlo Camillo Lazzarini:

---

[34] *Sun*, 8 September 1920, p. 3; 9 September 1920, p. 7; 14 September 1920, p. 7; 16 September 1920, p. 7; 21 September 1920, p. 7.
[35] NSWPD, 7 December 1920, p. 3216.
[36] Ibid., p. 3218.

Few members were in the Chamber at the moment, but enough were there to prevent what looked like the possibility of a fistic encounter. Mr Lazzarini suddenly made round the table towards Sir Thomas but was intercepted by Mr Fitzpatrick and another member, who used their persuasive influence on the antagonists successfully.[37]

When the parliament was prorogued on 5 January 1921 the motion lapsed before a vote was taken.

---

[37] *Daily Telegraph*, 8 December 1920, p. 9.

6

Reunion

Arrival of Joseph Partridge

The *Daily Telegraph*'s report of the arrival in Sydney of Bridget Partridge's brother Joseph started with the prediction that the 'now familiar case of Miss Bridget Partridge … has entered its final stage'.[1] Sadly, the *Telegraph*'s optimism was misplaced.

Bridget's younger brother Joseph was born on 30 April 1897 at Burtonwood, Warrington in Lancashire, England, where the family had moved following Edward Partridge's discharge from the army in 1891. When Edward re-enlisted ten years later, the family moved back to County Kildare, where Bridget had been born in 1890. Educated by the Patrician brothers at Tullow, County Carlow from 1910, Joseph entered the novitiate of the order in 1913 but left two years later before taking his final vows. His oldest sister, Susan, had also entered religious life, taking the veil in a French convent, only to leave the order when she decided it was not the life for her. Like Joseph, she left religious life without a problem. Another sister, Elizabeth, had contemplated entering the convent but decided against it after discussing her intentions with a priest.

On leaving the brothers, Joseph attempted to enlist in the British Army but was rejected as being underage. He then took a position in the ordnance office at the Curragh military camp, resigning in September 1915 to begin teacher training at Marlborough Training College, Dublin. On graduation he was appointed to St Thomas's College, Newbridge, County Kildare, where he taught mathematics, commercial subjects, and French. In 1919 he left teaching and went to London to take up a position as a shipping clerk with William Powell Ltd, a firm of outfitters, furnishers, and drapers that

---

[1] *Daily Telegraph,* 8 September 1920, p. 8.

operated in China. When offered a position in Hong Kong, he accepted it. On 11 February 1920 at Newbridge, he married Evelyn Johnson whom he had met in Dublin when he was at Marlborough College. Their honeymoon was short, for on 28 February 1920 Joseph sailed from London on the *Mishima Maru*, leaving his new wife at home. He would be in the job only a few months before he received cables from Australia requesting he come to the aid of his sister Bridget. According to Grand Master Barton, one of the cables was from Mother Stanislaus which read, 'Come at once. Your sister has gone mad'.[2] Resigning his position, Joseph took the first ship heading to Sydney, the *Aki Maru*, which left Hong Kong on 19 August.[3]

On 3 September the Loyal Orange Institution issued a statement advising it had received information that Joseph was expected to arrive in Sydney the following week. The statement noted, 'It has been arranged for Mr Partridge to be taken immediately to see his sister and it then remains for them to decide upon their future movements'.[4] When the *Aki Maru* arrived in Sydney at 4.30 am on Tuesday 7 September, Joseph was not among the passengers who disembarked. He had left the ship at Brisbane on Saturday 4 September and had taken the mail train to Sydney on Monday night, arriving at Central station about three hours after the *Aki Maru* docked at Dawes Point.[5] This change in Joseph's itinerary was adopted as a precaution against the possibility of a member of the LOI boarding the ship at Brisbane and intercepting him on the final leg of his voyage to Sydney. After arriving in Sydney, Joseph rested before contacting Grand Master Barton that afternoon.

Despite the LOI's statement that Joseph would be taken immediately to see his sister, Grand Master Barton and Grand Secretary

---

[2] *Tweed Daily*, 15 August 1921, p. 2.
[3] *Evening News*, 9 August 1920, p. 1; *Daily Telegraph*, 17 September 1920, p. 6; MyHeritage Family Trees.
[4] *Sydney Morning Herald*, 4 September 1920, p. 13.
[5] *Sydney Morning Herald*, 6 September 1920, p. 10; *Sydney Morning Herald*, 22 November 1921, p. 11.

Stocker imposed several conditions on his gaining access to her: when Joseph wished to see Bridget he had to approach them 'as only they could enable him to do so'; he 'must not be accompanied by bishops, priests, or Roman Catholic laymen'; he must first meet Mr Maund, solicitor for the LOI; and he had to be interviewed by Barton and Stocker at the offices of the LOI at the Protestant Hall. After Joseph satisfied those conditions, Barton drove him to his Burwood home, where he met with Bridget, who filled him in on what had led her to leave the convent. Joseph stayed overnight. The next day, Wednesday, Barton travelled with him into the city. There Joseph met with Bishop Dwyer and heard the bishop's side of the story.[6]

What happened after this is contested. In a detailed statement that Joseph issued to the press the following Sunday night, he said that when he met with Bridget at Barton's house on Tuesday she had expressed a wish to come away from there as soon as Joseph could make arrangements for her.[7] He claimed that, when he returned to Barton's on Thursday morning to collect his sister, he was prevented from seeing her for an hour while Barton tried to dissuade him from taking Bridget away. When he eventually saw Bridget she told him of a Catholic family in the neighbourhood with whom she would like to stay. When he left the house to look for that family, he was intercepted in the street by Barton, who was in the company of Mr and Mrs Touchell, whom Joseph had not yet met. According to Joseph, they requested that he guarantee he would not allow Bridget to come under Catholic influence, saying the 'Romish' church was her enemy. He told the press that this conversation was most offensive to him as a Catholic, which confirmed his desire to remove Bridget from that atmosphere. According to Joseph, when he saw Bridget privately that day, she promised to go with him the next day. When Joseph arrived at Barton's house on Friday, Barton

---

[6] *Daily Telegraph*, 8 September 1920, p. 8; *Sydney Morning Herald*, 13 September 1920, p. 7.
[7] *Sydney Morning Herald*, 13 September 1920, p. 7.

told him he would not be allowed to see Bridget as she was ill and receiving medical attention. After arguing the point, Joseph left but returned that evening with a doctor and a Catholic friend, who had offered them his house. However, he was once again refused permission to see his sister and eventually told 'to get'.

Grand Master Barton also issued a detailed statement describing these events.[8] In his statement Barton said that Joseph and Bridget spoke for about two hours on the Tuesday night and again the next morning up until lunchtime, after which Barton talked to him for two hours explaining his role in the affair. Barton claimed he understood Joseph was going to Wagga Wagga the next day to investigate the matter. This might have been a misunderstanding in that Barton might not have realised Joseph had arranged to see Dwyer in Sydney not Wagga Wagga. In any event, it became a point of contention, for Barton added he was surprised that Joseph turned up on Thursday morning as he was supposed to be on his way to Wagga Wagga. Barton claimed that Joseph saw Bridget without delay in his presence. According to Barton, Joseph told her he had arranged a car to take her to a place in Randwick. However, Bridget said she could not leave immediately as she had arranged to meet friends. Barton persuaded Joseph to let her see her friends and the young man stayed at Barton's house during the afternoon awaiting his sister.

According to his statement, Barton meanwhile left the house to meet Mr and Mrs Touchell at Burwood station. On their way back to the house they encountered Joseph in the street. Upon being introduced, Mr Touchell remarked that it was a very serious thing that had been done to his sister in the convent. Joseph replied, 'I don't believe a word of it.' Barton claimed in his statement: 'That was the first intimation that I had that he was not playing the game with his sister.' What the 'game' was is not clear. Barton said he advised Joseph he should go to Wagga Wagga and speak with those who had helped Bridget. Joseph stayed at Barton's house until 6

---

[8] *Sydney Morning Herald,* 13 September 1920, p. 7.

o'clock and had 'a private interview' with Bridget and left. Afterwards, according to the statement, Bridget told Barton that Joseph had said he would stand no more nonsense from her. Barton's statement continued that Joseph returned on Friday morning wanting to see Bridget but Barton said he could not as she was ill because of his behaviour the day before. When Joseph said he wanted to take her away, Barton refused and ordered him out of the house. That night Joseph returned with four men and again demanded to see Bridget. Barton again refused, saying the doctor had given orders that nobody was to see her. Barton concluded his statement: 'On the Thursday evening Miss Partridge was reluctant to see her brother, but after her interview with him that night she expressed a definite desire not to see him and has since expressed her determination not to go anywhere with him'.

Rev. Touchell also issued a statement to the press denying Bridget was being held against her will. He claimed that he and Mrs Touchell plus two others were present on Friday when Bridget asked her brother to allow her to remain with her Protestant friends until the time came to leave the country and that Joseph had agreed.[9] In a letter to the *Sydney Morning Herald*, Touchell denied that he and his wife had asked Joseph to give a guarantee that he would not allow Bridget to come under Catholic influence, or that his church was spoken of as the 'Romish' church, or that it was said to be his sister's enemy. He claimed that Joseph said he would go to Wagga Wagga to investigate the matter and that Bridget could remain with Barton until he returned from the country. Instead, he turned up next morning demanding to take her away. He accused Joseph of not being his own master, alleging that he had left the ship in Brisbane in the company of two priests and another man, who had boarded at Townsville, before taking the train to Sydney. Touchell claimed that Joseph did not come with an open mind and knew what he was going to do even before speaking with Bridget:

---

[9] *Daily Telegraph*, 11 September 1920, p. 10.

'Naturally enough she is afraid to trust him since he does not believe her and has failed already to keep his promise to her'.[10]

The next day the *Sydney Morning Herald* published a letter from a correspondent, J.F.D. O'Keeffe, who refuted Touchell's assertion that Joseph had left the ship in Brisbane in the company of two priests and another man. He said there had been one priest on board who had been met on arrival by another priest and that the two priests and himself had left together in a car and Joseph was not with them.[11] The priest who disembarked would have been Father John Blowick, superior general of the Irish Mission to China, who was travelling to Australia on the *Aki Maru* on his way home to Ireland. The other priest was probably Monsignor Edward Maguire, a member of the Irish Mission to China who was based in Australia to raise funds for the mission. Blowick and Maguire stayed a few days in Brisbane with Dr James Duhig, the Catholic archbishop of Brisbane, before heading to Sydney.[12]

Joseph also issued a statement refuting Rev. Touchell's claims. In it he said the ship did not call at Townsville. This was not true. The *Aki Maru* docked there at 3 am on 2 September 1920 and left the same morning at 7 am.[13] Perhaps Joseph was asleep and did not know this, but he was being less than candid. O'Keeffe, who joined at Townsville, stated in his letter, 'I enjoyed the closest association with Mr Partridge, and was frequently seen in his company'.

Although Touchell's intelligence was not accurate, it was close to the mark. On 26 August Archbishop Duhig had written to Bishop Dwyer advising of his concern that the Sydney LOI would probably notify their Brisbane counterparts of Joseph's impending arrival. Duhig told Dwyer he wanted to forestall them by intercepting Partridge at Townsville, adding that he had sent particulars to Monsignor Thomas Bourke, the parish priest there. Father Peter Murphy,

---

[10] *Sydney Morning Herald*, 14 September 1920, p. 8.
[11] *Sydney Morning Herald*, 15 September 1920, p. 11.
[12] *Southern Cross*, 24 September 1920, p. 21.
[13] *Sun*, 14 September 1920, p. 7; *Daily Commercial News*, 3 September 1920, p. 4.

administrator of Sydney's St Mary's cathedral, had previously sent a telegram to Duhig requesting him to send someone to Townsville to meet the ship and persuade Joseph to come to Sydney by land. Presumably O'Keeffe was assigned the task of passing on instructions, though not to accompany him to Sydney. Joseph's escort on the final leg is likely to have been a member of the Catholic Federation of New South Wales, if not Charles Lawlor himself. We know this because six years later the federation was sued for non-payment of a debt. In his statement of claim, the plaintiff, Alphonsus Kennedy, alleged he lent the federation £55: 'Lawlor ... explained that owing to the Liguori Case expenses were very heavy on the Federation and informed me that one of the expenses was going to Brisbane to meet Mr Partridge'.[14]

Dwyer was kept informed of Joseph's journey south by a series of telegrams written in Latin, Italian, and coded English. One, dated 5 September and signed 'Maguire' (probably Monsignor Edward Maguire), reported that everything was right with the travellers. Another dated 6 September referred to the progress of the 'consignment' and the expected arrival of the 'Perdriau tyre ... splendid condition'. That same day Duhig cabled Dwyer in Italian that the 'traveller' had been put on the overnight train and that he was 'well disposed'. Another cable suggests that Joseph had been vetted before being sent on his way. In that cable Father Barry informed Bishop Dwyer that 'Lane' (probably Father Maurice Lane, administrator of St Stephen's Cathedral, Brisbane) had reported that a 'firm most trustworthy' had examined the balance sheet carefully and that it showed a 'big dividend'.[15]

Not content to rely solely on his and Touchell's accounts of their dealings with Joseph Partridge, Grand Master Barton released a statement by Bridget Partridge dated 14 September which, he assured the press was in her own handwriting and was written without

---

[14] The correspondence and Kennedy's statement are in the Wagga Wagga Diocesan Archives.
[15] The cables are in the Wagga Wagga Diocesan Archives.

any prompting from others. In the statement, Bridget complained that Joseph 'looked upon the charge of lunacy brought against me as a mere nothing and my being hunted from one house to another as of no consequence. This plainly shows others have interfered for their own interests.' She said she had a good home and wished to stay as long as she pleased: 'I did promise to go with my brother to another house but, seeing what undermined his motives for taking me there, I refused to go'. She said she was run down in health and wished to be left alone to regain her strength. She finished with: 'I have known all along who the friends were into whose hands, thank God, I had fallen'.[16]

That night Barton addressed a Protestant rally at Leichhardt in which he claimed that when Bridget had said she would not go with him, Joseph produced a revolver, saying 'he would have no more of it.' Barton continued to control the narrative, issuing another statement to the press in which he claimed Joseph was picketing his house and that the young man had said he did not believe Bridget had written the statement under her name. He also claimed that Joseph had said to him, 'I am a Sinn Feiner and proud of it … and have done my bit for Ireland'.[17] Joseph responded by telling the press, 'I am not endeavouring to take my sister back to the convent. I know they will not allow her to re-enter the convent, any convent. I have been childishly accused of being in league with Bishop Dwyer. The accusation is ridiculous. My interest in my sister arises in the fact that I am her brother'.[18]

No doubt increasingly frustrated by the ability of the older and more experienced Barton to spin the story his way, the 23-year-old Joseph decided to confront Barton at his house, this time in the presence of the press. When Joseph and his entourage of reporters arrived at Barton's house on Saturday 18 September, Barton was sitting on the front veranda with his son. As Joseph moved to put his arm over the front gate to open it, Barton said,

---

[16] *Sydney Morning Herald*, 15 September 1920, p. 11.
[17] *Sydney Morning Herald*, 18 September 1920, p. 14.
[18] *Daily Advertiser*, 17 September 1920, p. 3.

'Keep out. I don't want any more of you about here.'

Joseph replied, 'I would like a message delivered to my sister.'

Barton said, 'You know very well that your sister told you that she does not wish to see you.'

Joseph countered, 'I have not once been told by my sister that she has no wish to see me. It is you who has, on each occasion, told me so. I ask you again to deliver, personally, to my sister a message from me.'

Barton said, 'Write the message on a piece of paper.'

Joseph replied, 'I have no paper. I ask you as a favour to deliver the message for me.'

Barton said, 'Very well, what is the message?'

Joseph said, 'I want you to ask her if she will go to mass with me tomorrow?'

Barton laughed and, turning to his son, said, 'Fancy she will go to mass?'

Raising his voice, Joseph replied, 'Never mind about your remarks.'

Barton said, 'I will not worry your sister by delivering such a message to her.'

Joseph then asked Barton to come out on to the footpath and speak to him there. But Barton did not move. Joseph turned from the gateway and said, 'I will have my say yet. You can depend on that.'

Barton answered, 'You can go your hardest and do your level best.'

The conversation over, Joseph left. As he was walking back to the station he met Mrs Barton in the street and asked her to deliver his message to Bridget as he wanted to reassure their parents in Ireland. She promised she would do so. When Joseph said he was very anxious for Bridget, Mrs Barton said, 'I am very sorry for the poor girl. She is not well'.[19]

The following Tuesday, Bridget gave separate interviews to a

---

[19] *Sun*, 19 September 1920, p. 2; *Daily Telegraph*, 20 September 1920, p. 6.

reporter from each of the *Sydney Morning Herald* and the *Daily Telegraph*, telling them she wished to be left alone: 'Sister Liguori is dead,' she told the *Herald* reporter. 'She died when I sent my resignation to the Bishop of Wagga. I am now a free girl in a free country. Why can't they let me have the rest that I so much need'. Who 'they' were she did not say. Later in the interview she said she had told Joseph 'that he was a fool not to see that he was being made a tool of for the purpose of getting me into their power again'. Once again she did not say who was wanting her in their power. In the interview with the *Telegraph* reporter, she said she wished to be an ordinary citizen 'free from the curiosity of strangers'. She then accused Joseph of 'working in the interests of others as against myself'. Who the 'others' were and what their interests might be was again unspoken. However, at the end of the interview with the *Herald* reporter, she said, 'The Bishop and the Mother Superior have said I was free to resign and go where I will. I have resigned, and now all I want is peace and quietness and liberty to go where I wish unmolested'.[20]

Armageddon

The LOI had been running the line that they had only intervened in the Sister Liguori affair to preserve the liberty of a young woman who had escaped from imprisonment in the Mount Erin convent and had been hunted down and persecuted by the agents of Rome who wished to imprison her once again. The metropolitan dailies had willingly adopted that dramatic narrative in their reporting of the affair. And the interview with the two Sydney dailies indicates that Bridget had also adopted the LOI's narrative. This is not surprising, given that for the past two months Bridget had been under the influence of Barton, whose constant carping about the use of pickets and pursuers, spies and gunmen, and the posting of rewards to force her back into the convent cannot have failed to have

---

[20] *Sydney Morning Herald*, 22 September 1920, p. 11; *Daily Telegraph*, 22 September 1920, p. 9.

had an influence on her. The term 'gaslighting' might be of recent origin but the phenomenon is not new.

The Catholic newspapers ran a more prosaic line.[21] Bridget Partridge was a nun who, having decided she no longer wished to remain in the convent, had left in circumstances that suggested mental instability and had then vanished. The Catholic authorities responsible for her welfare invoked the processes of the law to locate her and have her mental capacity assessed. That having been done and her safety and sanity established she was free to live with whom she wished or return to Ireland with her brother. End of story. But, as we have seen, that is not what happened, for the LOI had a goal that extended beyond the person of Bridget Partridge: abolition of the cruel convent system that had imprisoned her. As Grand Master Barton had earlier declared: 'It is Rome versus the Orange Institution'.

With the sectarian warriors of the LOI already 'assembled for battle on the great day of God the Almighty … at the place called Armageddon',[22] their counterparts, militant Catholics, now began arriving on the field. One of the first was Patrick Minahan, whose engagement of the high-profile lawyer politician Tom Ryan KC guaranteed that the legal processes, ordinarily straightforward, would be sensationalised. The stated aim of the militant Catholics was the mirror image of the LOI's – we will fight for this young woman's liberty, but also for the convents and the honour of all women who choose the religious life.

On 16 September Charles Lawlor, the general secretary of the Catholic Federation, announced:

> All lovers of liberty will be interested in the effort of Mr Joseph Partridge, who came speedily from Hong Kong to rescue his sister, who had fallen into the hands of the enemies of our faith. … In order to enable Mr Partridge to

---
[21] *Freeman's Journal*, 16 September 1920, p. 22; *Catholic Press*, 16 September 1920, p. 26.
[22] Revelation 16:14, 16:16.

use every possible legal means to free his sister from people who deliberately lay themselves out to ruin her soul, and afterwards to help him take her to their relatives in Ireland, a sum of money is needed. We believe that everybody who professes Christian freedom will contribute to a fund with this worthy object. ... The processes of the law may be costly, but those who would protect our devoted Sisterhoods from wanton insult, and who resent an impudent outrage on a nerve-wracked girl, will, we are sure, add their tributes.[23]

In a separate note the federation declared, 'This will be an opportunity to test the loyalty of Australian democracy to the true principles of liberty'.[24] The *Catholic Press* reinforced the federation's message with the publication of Joseph's initial statement and a lengthy editorial in which it referred to Bridget's current situation in the hands of the 'unscrupulous enemies of her faith':

> Sister Liguori is in the same condition as when she left the convent. Instead of recovering, as they claimed she would, she has grown worse under the steady mental persecution which they inflict upon her. Her disturbed mind is terrified by the dreadful terrors with which they threaten her. As she stated to her brother, if she is not removed from her present surroundings, she will certainly be driven insane. ... While she is in the hands of her present enemies, her distracted mind will never be allowed to form a clear decision.[25]

Charles Heydon had coined the term 'captured nun' in response to the LOI's 'escaped nun' slogan.[26] Support for his scepticism emerged at the trial when it was revealed that, pursuant to an arrangement suggested by Barton, letters to Bridget had to be addressed to the post office box of the Protestant Federation. Barton

---

[23] *Catholic Press*, 16 September 1920, p. 20.
[24] Ibid., p. 11.
[25] Ibid., p. 26.
[26] *Sydney Morning Herald*, 16 August 1920, p. 8; *Southern Cross*, 3 September 1920, p. 10.

would collect the mail and bring it to her. After opening the letters Bridget would send them on to the LOI's solicitor. To conceal her whereabouts Bridget would write letters headed with the name of a town she had not been in.[27] Under the rubric of the 'captured nun', the Catholic Federation claimed it was right and just for Joseph to rescue his sister, just as the LOI, under the rubric of the 'escaped nun', claimed it was right and just for Protestants to shield her from her brother and his masters. A certain mutuality emerged with each side proclaiming itself to be Bridget's guardian and the other side her gaoler. Ironically, the more self-righteous the rhetoric, the more it reinforced the animosity of the other side.

On 13 October 1920 Joseph Partridge travelled to Wagga Wagga, where he spent the day interviewing various persons regarding his sister's flight from the Mount Erin convent.[28] Having heard the convent's side of the story, he wrote to Bridget on his return. In her reply she rejected his suggestion that she had misunderstood what had happened the night she ran away: 'You can't maybe believe what we already know as to the dose. I was dosed because I ran away. ... I have learned many lessons since. I know what the dose was so they can't deny it.'[29] Joseph showed the letter to Charles Lawlor who sent a copy to Bishop Dwyer, observing in the covering letter, 'Our friend [Bridget] is evidently coming under their influence. The enclosed conveys that impression.' Other letters Bridget wrote to her brother would confirm Lawlor's impression. In one she sent him the following February, Bridget wrote:

> Don't think for a moment that I am blaming you, Joe. All I say is that as a brother and I am sure it was at the time your wish to see me first on landing. If I had the cables which were sent to you, I would be most anxious to find out if it were true and then believe myself. But I was made aware of everything just as it happened and in consequence must

---

[27] *Truth*, 3 July 1921, p. 7, 10; *Cootamundra Herald*, 4 July 1921, p. 3.
[28] *Daily Advertiser*, 14 October 1920, p. 2.
[29] Letter, 17 October 1920, Bridget Partridge to Joseph Partridge, Wagga Wagga Diocesan Archives.

be firm, and grateful for the protection I am receiving. I have heard enough to what has happened to others who have run away and when appealing for a dispensation have never been seen or heard of again. There is hardly anyone who has not got a story to tell.[30]

Frustrated that he had been beaten at every turn by Barton and the Touchells and convinced they were keeping Bridget under duress, Joseph determined to stay in Australia until he had persuaded his sister to go with him – however long it took.

'A veritable hurricane of sectarian strife'

As 1920 drew to a close, many would look back in dismay at the sectarian carnage that littered the year. The Catholic archbishop of Sydney, Michael Kelly had been out of the country from 15 February to 7 December and thus had been absent when the peace and harmony of the community had been disturbed by a series of incidents: the deportation of Father Charles Jerger; the dramatic departure of Sister Liguori from her convent at Wagga Wagga; the British navy's arrest of Archbishop Mannix on his way to Ireland; and the expulsion of Hugh Mahon from the federal parliament for speaking out against British rule in Ireland. The cumulative effect of these events had stretched to breaking point the social fabric of Australian society.[31] At the annual speech day of Marist Brothers' High School, Darlinghurst attended by the archbishop, Attorney General McTiernan said:

> I am very sorry to have to report that during the time your Grace has been away, we have passed through a veritable hurricane of sectarian strife in this fair land. Catholics have been accused of every sinister ambition. Even the Church itself was embraced in this attack.[32]

---

[30] Letter, 4 February 1921, Bridget Partridge to Joseph Partridge, Wagga Wagga Diocesan Archives.
[31] Jeff Kildea, "'A veritable hurricane of sectarianism": The Year 1920 and Ethno-Religious Conflict in Australia' in Colin Barr and Hilary M. Carey (eds), *Religion and Greater Ireland: Christianity and Irish Global Networks, 1750- 1950*, McGill-Queen's University Press, Montreal, 2015, pp. 363-382.
[32] *Catholic Press*, 16 December 1920, p. 17.

But they had not yet passed through the hurricane, at least so far as the Sister Liguori affair was concerned. They were merely resting in the calm of its eye. Soon the year 1921 would see the return of battering sectarian winds, their locus shifting to the Supreme Court of New South Wales.

7

TRIAL – PART ONE

Writ of Summons

The day after the Lunacy Court discharged Bridget Partridge, the Loyal Orange Institution issued a statement:

> If Miss Partridge gives her consent, we will issue a writ claiming at least £5000 damages for malicious prosecution and wrongful arrest. All legal formalities have been completed and we are awaiting the ex-nun's commands. We decided not to trouble the young woman until she had had a complete rest. We have the sinews of war, the money will come in freely, and a firm of solicitors is preparing the necessary documents. If Miss Partridge says 'Go' no time will be lost in our endeavour to secure for her that measure of justice which we and a great section of the public think she is entitled to.[1]

Apart from the martial language—'the sinews of war'—which was increasingly common in utterances by the LOI regarding the Sister Liguori affair, the statement is notable in two respects. First, it makes clear that it was the LOI's idea to commence legal proceedings and, second, it indicates that the LOI had already instructed solicitors to prepare the necessary documents before obtaining the putative plaintiff's consent. It was not until 28 October 1920, more than two months later, that a writ of summons was filed, suggesting that Bridget had been less than keen to give that consent. After the case was over, Joseph claimed in a written statement he made following a meeting with his sister in August 1921, that Bridget had told him: 'She did not suggest a case. She did not want it. She "fought till she was black in the face against it for two days" – her own words'.[2]

---

[1] *Daily Express*, 16 August 1920, p. 2.
[2] Undated hand-written Statement by Joseph Partridge in Wagga Wagga Diocesan Archives.

The case of *Partridge v Dwyer* was a civil action in which Bridget Partridge was claiming damages of £5000 (about $400,000 in today's money) by way of compensation against Bishop Dwyer. It was not a criminal prosecution, though some of the reporting gives the impression that Bishop Dwyer was on trial for an offence. The declaration filed on Bridget's behalf setting out her cause of action alleged:

1. that Dwyer had falsely and maliciously and without reasonable or probable cause informed a justice of the peace on oath that she was a person deemed to be insane and was without sufficient means of support; and
2. that he had falsely and maliciously and without reasonable or probable cause caused and procured the justice to grant and issue a warrant for her apprehension.

It further alleged that, by virtue of the warrant, Dwyer had caused and procured Bridget to be arrested and to be imprisoned for a long time with the result that she had been injured in her reputation and suffered great pain of body and mind and was prevented from attending to her affairs and business and had incurred various medical and legal expenses in obtaining her release.

Bishop Dwyer's solicitors filed a plea in defence of the action in which the bishop gave a general denial of the allegations, adding a specific denial to the allegation that he caused or procured Bridget to be arrested and imprisoned. This specific defence was based on the fact that Bridget's arrest and imprisonment were the consequence of a judicial officer making an independent decision to order Bridget's apprehension under section 4 of the *Lunacy Act*.

The build-up to the trial

The delay in filing the writ meant that the case could not be heard before the end of the year. In January 1921, the press predicted a hearing date in March but in mid-April it was reported that, owing to congestion in the court lists, it would not be heard until the

June-July sittings.³ The case was in what is called a running list, that is, it was not allocated a specific hearing date but took its place in a queue of matters awaiting hearing. As those cases were determined or settled, Bridget's case edged closer to the front of the queue. With the June-July sittings approaching, anticipation grew. The *Evening News* reported that because the case had excited such widespread interest, special arrangements were being made to accommodate 'a small army of Press reporters'. In addition to the city papers, it was expected that several country and interstate journals would engage special representatives to report the case.⁴ According to the *Sun*, Solicitor General Sproule was interesting himself in the question of the accommodation at the trial, while several 'well-dressed ladies' had called at the court and asked court attendants if tickets were being issued for reserved seats: 'Madam,' a court official was heard to say, 'these are courts of justice, not theatres'.⁵

A fortnight before the hearing, the focus briefly returned to Wagga Wagga which, according to the *Adelong and Tumut Express*, was 'stirred to high tension' when Rev. William Touchell and Alderman John Ness visited the town. They had come to Wagga Wagga to hold Protestant rallies and to establish there a branch of the Protestant Federation:

> Meetings were held on Saturday and Sunday and concluded on Monday night with a gathering in the Great Southern Hall, unprecedented in Wagga. The building was unable to accommodate the crowd. The speakers confined themselves to solid criticism of the methods of the Irish priesthood in Australia ... An unorganised gang of disturbers found themselves lost in the huge meeting.⁶

That same weekend, Wagga Wagga's Catholics met at St. Joseph's

---

³ *Watchman*, 4 November 1920, p. 5; *Sun*, 13 January 1921, p. 8; *Sun*, 11 April 1921, p. 5.
⁴ *Evening News*, 9 June 1921, p. 6.
⁵ *Sun*, 13 June 1921, p. 7; 21 June 1921, p. 7; 23 June 1921, p. 9.
⁶ *Adelong and Tumut Express*, 24 June 1921, p. 3.

Hall after 10 o'clock mass. Mr. William Walsh, the solicitor whom Bishop Dwyer had first consulted, presided over the meeting which passed two resolutions:

> That this meeting of the congregation of St. Michael's Catholic parish at Wagga confidently voicing the opinions and feelings of the whole of the Catholic body in this diocese in connection with the recent departure of ex-Sister Liguori from Wagga, expresses complete appreciation of the efforts made by our beloved Bishop, Dr. Dwyer, to discover her whereabouts and ascertain her mental condition, knowing as we do that his actions were prompted and directed by the purest motives and the highest sense of duty.
>
> That the foregoing resolution be tendered to his Lordship, Dr. Dwyer, on our behalf, by the diocesan administrator, Father Ryan, with an intimation that we sincerely regret worry cast upon him by his being called upon to answer an action at law for his prompt performance of a manifest obligation, and with an assurance that he has our complete and manifest support in every way and in all circumstances.[7]

In the final week of June, *Dwyer v Partridge* made it to second place in the queue behind an action for damages against Waverley Council, expected to finish that week. One of the problems of a running list is that the parties, particularly the plaintiff, need to have their witnesses ready in case the matter is called on. It is especially difficult for country cases as the parties and the witnesses cannot be summoned at short notice by telephone. Consequently, at the start of the week Bishop Dwyer and some of the Wagga Wagga witnesses along with several country and interstate reporters had already come to Sydney. But the case against Waverley Council was taking longer to conclude than first thought.[8] Then, just as the parties, the press, and the witnesses were resigning themselves to having to come back the following week, the list cleared and the parties were

---

[7] *Freeman's Journal*, 30 June 1921, p. 26.
[8] *Daily Examiner*, 27 June 1921, p. 5.

informed that *Partridge v Dwyer* would start on Thursday morning 30 June.

Dramatis personae

The judge allocated to hear the case was Justice David Gilbert Ferguson, a 59-year-old native of Muswellbrook, New South Wales. He was the son of a Scots Presbyterian father, John, and an Australian-born mother, Elizabeth. To finance his studies at Sydney University, Ferguson had worked as a reporter for the *Sydney Morning Herald*, the *Daily Telegraph*, and *Hansard*. He was admitted as a barrister in 1890. While practising at the bar, he was also a Challis lecturer at Sydney University's Law School, where he taught the law of procedure, evidence, and pleading. In 1911 he was appointed an acting judge of the Supreme Court and in March 1912 he was confirmed in that office. During the First World War his second son, Arthur, was killed in action in France. Ferguson would serve as acting chief justice in 1929 before retiring from the bench in 1931.

The two legal teams briefed to represent the parties included some of the state's finest courtroom advocates. *Truth* would later claim:

> The case will go down to history as one of the most remarkable that have ever engaged the attention of a Supreme Court Judge in this State, not only by reason of the degree to which public interest was excited, but for the exacting, thorough, and searching cross-examination to which each of the witnesses was subjected by counsel on both sides.[9]

Appearing for Bridget Partridge were Messrs A.B. Shand KC, F.S. Boyce, and P.R. Higgins instructed by Walter Hill of D. M. Myers and Hill, solicitors. Alexander Barclay Shand was born in 1865 at Ulladulla on the New South Wales south coast, to a Scots Presbyterian father, John, and his wife, Mary. Admitted to the bar in 1887, he took silk in 1906. He was a former Crown prosecutor and a leading member of the bar, having served on the Bar Council, the

---
[9] *Truth*, 10 July 1921, p. 7.

governing body for barristers. He was the first of three generations of outstanding common lawyers, followed by his son Jack Shand KC and his grandson and namesake Alec Shand QC. Shand was assisted by two junior counsel. Francis Stewart Boyce had appeared for Bridget Partridge in the Lunacy Court. His biographical details are set out in chapter 4. Percy Reginald Higgins was born at Armidale, New South Wales in 1872. He was admitted to the bar in 1895 before transferring to the roll of solicitors in 1901. He practised as a solicitor in Wagga Wagga until 1920 when he returned to the Sydney bar.

Appearing for Bishop Joseph Dwyer were Messrs J.L. Campbell KC, G.E. Flannery KC, and A.V. Maxwell instructed by Thomas Purcell of T.J. Purcell and McCarthy, solicitors. James Lang Campbell was born in Scotland in 1858 and emigrated to Australia at age seven. Like Justice Ferguson and Shand KC, he was from a Scots Presbyterian family. Called to the bar in 1886, Campbell practised mainly in common law before taking silk in 1910. He, too, was a leading member of the bar, serving on the Bar Council from 1911 to 1920. In September 1922 he would be appointed as a judge of the Supreme Court. Campbell was assisted by senior and junior counsel. George Ernest Flannery KC was born in 1872 at Albury to Irish immigrant parents, and educated at Sydney High School, St Ignatius College, Riverview, and the University of Sydney. He graduated in law with first-class honours and was awarded the University Medal. Admitted to the bar in 1894, he served as secretary to Prime Minister Edmund Barton from 1901 and as associate to Justice Richard O'Connor of the High Court of Australia from 1903. Returning to the bar in 1904 he practised mainly in appellate law. He was appointed a king's counsel on 5 May 1920. Alan Victor Maxwell was born at Balmain in 1887 and was admitted to the bar in 1913, where he practised mainly in the common law jurisdiction. He would serve as a Supreme Court judge from 1934 to 1955.

Day 1: Thursday, 30 June

Two hours before the gates to the Supreme Court opened, a crowd of about 50 people were queued in drizzling rain in King Street, hoping to secure a seat in No. 3 Jury Court where *Partridge v Dwyer* was to be heard. An hour later the line had swollen to 150 and by 10 o'clock it numbered several hundred, stretching along King street. A large force of police and sheriff's officers guarded the entrances to the courthouse, keeping the waiting crowd in line, and preventing gawkers from blocking the footpath. Across the road, crowds sheltered under verandas, watching the scene with interest. When the gates opened only a small portion of the waiting crowd were allowed in as space was limited. Some of the disappointed continued to wait in the rain in the hope of being admitted at lunch time. Inside, the public was confined to the gallery, which held 40 persons seated and 20 standing. The body of the court was reserved for the parties, their legal teams and close friends, as well as members of the legal profession, parliamentarians, and the press. Between thirty and forty reporters would be engaged on this case, working in relays. According to *Truth*, 'Never in recent times were so many reporters engaged on one case'.[10]

When Bridget Partridge entered the courtroom, accompanied by Mrs Touchell and Grand Master Barton, all eyes turned towards her. The *Daily Advertiser* provided a description of the plaintiff in the manner of a gossip column:

> Dressed in a navy-blue coat frock, brightened with trimmings of henna, which suited her slight figure, and wearing a hat to tone, she looked more like 19 years of age than 28. … She wore glasses and looked quite composed.[11]

The *Advertiser* did not run the same ruler over the bishop, perhaps because he was well known to its readers. The *Watchman*, on the other hand, described both parties. Having said of Miss Partridge,

---

[10] *Truth*, 3 July 1921, p. 7.
[11] *Daily Advertiser*, 1 July 1921, p. 2.

'She seemed just an ordinary sort of woman, and was modestly dressed, and had a hat and veil and wore spectacles,' it continued, 'The Bishop is a robust man, with good, clear-cut features'.[12]

A few minutes after 10 o'clock the chattering crowd inside the courtroom hushed and then stood as Justice Ferguson entered. He nodded to the barristers arrayed along the bar table, who gave a short bow in return, and then took his seat at the bench. As if the legal gods were determined to torment the expectant audience, his associate announced not the Partridge case but another matter, an undefended jury action, which the judge dealt with in a short time, and then after that another matter, similarly despatched. During the progress of these cases a hubbub of chitchat in the gallery could be heard. When, at last, *Partridge v Dwyer* was announced, it was 10.30 am. The impatient crowd fell silent and the business of empanelling the jury began.

Counsel had been provided with a list of the names, addresses and occupations of the eight members of the jury panel from which four were to be chosen. Apart from physical demeanour, that was the only guidance the lawyers had as to how the potential jurors might decide this case. With each side permitted two objections, the jury of four eventually emerged: Frederick Sigismund Adams, customs agent of 7 Wharf Road, Balmain; John William Smith, builder of Railway Street, Rockdale; Frederick Matthews JP, insurance superintendent of 65 Lyons Road, Drummoyne; and James Joseph Reilly, independent means of Herbert Street, Dulwich Hill. According to the *Daily Express*:

> All were apparently over middle age; two were silver-haired; one had a generous sprinkling of grey in a well-thatched head; and the fourth, the youngest of the lot, was showing signs of approaching baldness.[13]

Although the barristers were given only limited information, today, with the aid of modern genealogical resources, we can ascertain

---

[12] *Watchman*, 7 July 1921, p. 4.
[13] *Daily Express*, 1 July 1921, p. 2.

much more. Three of the jurymen were Protestants, reflecting by chance the proportion of Protestants in the state's population. They were Adams, who was born in 1856 at Balmain in Sydney; Smith, born in 1863 at Deeping Gate, Northamptonshire, England; and Matthews, born in 1874 at Stoke Newington, London, England. The fourth juror, Reilly, was a Catholic who was born in 1855 in County Cavan, Ireland. Had Bishop Dwyer known Reilly was a Catholic, he could not have taken much comfort from that fact. Even if Reilly were prepared to put loyalty to the church above his duty as a juror, it could not have prevented a verdict for the plaintiff unless at least one of the Protestants joined him, as the law then governing civil juries permitted a majority verdict.

Not remarked upon in the press was the fact that the jurors were all men, for it was not until 1947 that women were permitted to serve on juries in New South Wales. Looking around No. 3 Jury Court that morning, it must have dawned on Bridget Partridge that the fate of her action against Bishop Dwyer rested solely in the hands of men, for the judge, the jury, and the legal representatives were all men, a situation that would remain the norm for decades to come. It was not until June 1924 that Sibyl Morrison became the first woman barrister to practise in New South Wales. Three years before, Ada Evans had been admitted as the first female barrister but she did not practise. The year 1924 also saw Marie Byles admitted to practise as the first woman solicitor in the state. Another 56 years would pass before Jane Matthews would be appointed to the District Court in 1980 as the state's first woman judge. In 1987 she would be appointed the first female Supreme Court judge. As if to acknowledge the fact that litigation was then firmly considered to be men's business, the *Sydney Morning Herald* saw fit to remark, as if it were newsworthy, that 'Women were as strongly in evidence as men among the spectators'.[14]

Once the jurors had taken their seats in the jury box, Mr Shand opened the case for the plaintiff with an address that proved a dis-

---

[14] *Sydney Morning Herald*, 1 July 1921, p. 9.

appointment for those who had come to court expecting to hear salacious tales of the mysteries of convent life. After telling the jury that it was a case that had excited a great deal of interest in the community, he dampened the mood in the courtroom by adding, 'You won't be concerned with that. It is simply an ordinary case between two citizens who are supposed to be enjoying the same privileges of the law'. He then framed the question to be determined:

> Whether the defendant acted within his rights, which are given to him by the law, or whether he has abused those rights, and taken advantage of his position in the community, especially in the community where this young lady was?

He then recited in an anodyne manner the facts of the case: Bridget's background, her history after joining the Presentation order, her demotion, her growing dissatisfaction with religious life, and her decision to leave the convent, the first time after the dispute over the broom, and then again when she formed the belief that serious harm was to come to her. He then referred to her seeking refuge with the Thompsons and the exchanges that took place in Wagga Wagga between them and the police and the bishop before Dwyer went to Sydney and sought an order under the *Lunacy Act*. He made no reference to bizarre practices in the convent or to acts of cruelty inflicted upon Bridget or her fellow nuns. The wrong the plaintiff had suffered and for which she sought redress he summarised as follows:

> [T]he Bishop ... comes to Sydney and swears an information that the girl is deemed to be insane and is without means of support.
>
> These two statements were false and were false to the Bishop's knowledge. Every person in this community who is capable of working has means of support, and every person who is in the care of people who are willing to care for them is in possession of lawful means of support.
>
> When the Bishop was informed that the girl was well and

happy, and being properly looked after, he knew that she was not in the condition which the Legislature in the *Lunacy Act* had described as insane. The *Lunacy Act* in New South Wales was intended for the protection of the public, and an insane person, or a person who was 'deemed to be insane'.

...

But the Bishop was not concerned about the welfare of this young woman. What he really wanted was to get her out of the hands of the heretics, into whose hands he believed she had fallen. He desired to get her under those influences which would work in the direction of getting her back into the convent. This Miss Partridge was unwilling to do and the Bishop knew it.

He concluded by telling the jury that money was not Bridget's object: 'She wants to clear her character from the stigma which had been cast on it by the proceedings in lunacy. ... If the bishop will apologise now for putting the law in motion and admit that he had no justification for it and pay costs, we will withdraw now.' This was not the first time such an offer had been made. Several months previously, Rev. Touchell had told Joseph Partridge that the case need not go to court and a lot of dirty linen need not be washed if he could persuade Bishop Dwyer to apologise to Bridget and pay the costs to date. Touchell suggested that in writing the apology the bishop need not humble his dignity too much.[15]

As his first witness, Mr Shand called Bridget Partridge. Miss Partridge answered his questions in a calm soft voice relating the facts of the case. Again, there were no allegations of cruel treatment. Moreover, during her cross examination by Mr Campbell she admitted she was on friendly terms with the mother superior and the other nuns, that they had been kind to her, and that none had wished her any harm. She also admitted that she knew she could leave convent life at any time by asking for a dispensation. *Truth*

---

[15] Note by Joseph Partridge of a conversation between Rev. Touchell and himself at Blackheath on 7 December 1920, Wagga Wagga Diocesan Archives.

expressed the letdown felt by those in the gallery who had been expecting an exposé on convent life:

> [They] began to realise that the long-awaited entertainment was going to be disappointing to them. Nothing concerning the interior life of a convent was touched upon, barring references to the performances of religious duties. Soon was the convent left behind, the main portion of the plaintiff's evidence having to do with what transpired subsequent to her 'escape'.[16]

At one point during Shand's examination in chief, Campbell objected to Bridget's giving evidence about what happened on the afternoon of her leaving the convent, saying it was not relevant. Shand responded by saying he was entitled to lead evidence to show her actions were those of a rational person. Campbell replied that it was not relevant unless the bishop knew of it, seizing the opportunity to outline the defendant's case:

> We did not say that she was in fact insane. The only motive for the bishop's action was to have her sanity determined by the proper authority. As the person in charge of Miss Partridge, the bishop had the duty cast upon him of seeing that she had proper protection in the event of her mind being in a state of unreason. ... The question was, what had the bishop reason to believe with regard to her mental condition on August 3 when he took action?

Campbell had a point but the judge said, 'I think the evidence is admissible, for what it is worth.' Campbell took a similar objection when Shand asked Miss Partridge whether she had any means of support after she had left the convent. Campbell said the plaintiff had to show that the defendant knew she had means of support by legal right or natural expectation. Once again, the judge allowed the evidence.

Early in a case it is often difficult to know what is relevant. Unless the evidence is prejudicial, judges sometimes prefer to admit

---

[16] *Truth*, 3 July 1921, p. 7.

it and later instruct the jury as to whether to pay it any regard. The problem with that approach is that it can unduly lengthen a case. And much of the evidence that would be admitted during this hearing was of doubtful relevance to the case Shand had outlined to the jury. In his opening, he had said that Dwyer's allegations in the information that Bridget was deemed to be insane and was without means of support were false to the bishop's knowledge and that he had acted to get her out of the hands of the heretics and under those influences which would work in the direction of getting her back into the convent. Strictly speaking, the range of evidence relevant to those issues was narrow but, fortunately for us, trying to understand the affair a century later, the judge exercised some leniency, permitting the facts to be recounted in more detail than was strictly necessary.

Shand then questioned Bridget about her vow of obedience and what it involved. She began to explain when Campbell objected, saying she had taken her vows voluntarily and if she was dissatisfied she could leave the order. He again took the opportunity to explain the defendant's case, adding there was no connection between the burden of obedience and her leaving the convent, which was first caused by her annoyance over the dispute concerning the broom and then later by her fear she was to be murdered. The judge allowed the question and Bridget said she had 'to ask for permission to write home, to use pen and ink, or anything in the convent, no matter how small'. Mr Shand then asked,

'Were there penances you objected to?'

Bridget said, 'Yes.'

'Physical were they?'

'Yes.'

Shand moved on to another topic, leaving this orphaned titbit hanging. It would be revisited several days later.

In his cross examination, which began after lunch, Campbell KC first obtained admissions from Bridget that she had not been subject to acts of cruelty and knew she could leave convent life at any time. He then asked her about her motivation for leaving the convent on the Saturday night in the extraordinary manner she did. His purpose was to establish that she had acted irrationally, particularly in coming to believe that Mother Stanislaus, Dr Leahy, and Sister Brendan had conspired to murder her. When the day finished, Campbell's cross examination had not been completed. Bridget would have to return to the witness box the next day.

The first day had not passed entirely without sensation. An incident occurred during the lunch adjournment that threatened to disturb the peace. As Miss Partridge and Mrs Touchell were leaving the courtroom, a man suddenly sprang from the gallery and embraced Bridget. The man turned out to be Bridget's brother Joseph, whose presence in court they had not noticed. His arm around her shoulder, he then walked her into the corridor leading to King Street. Barton and two clergymen who were following behind approached the pair. Joseph said, 'I want to talk with my sister.' A scuffle then followed and Mrs Touchell was almost knocked to the ground. A couple of men in the crowd set upon Joseph but in turn they were set upon by others. According to the *Watchman*:

> A general melee seemed imminent. Men rushed at one another pugnaciously—they were rival factions without a doubt—police shouted, 'Move on!' Women backed away cautiously and in the turmoil the central figure, Miss Partridge, was buffeted from pillar to post by the swaying mob. Miss Partridge then saved the situation by stating she would see her brother in a room. Sergeant Mills and three constables assisted by court officials, eventually restored order, and hustled the combatants out into King Street. ... Mr Partridge meanwhile was adjusting his collar and tie, which had been almost torn from his neck. Having done this, he joined his sister in a room.

The *Watchman*'s report revealed that lunch was being served in the room where Bridget's group had assembled but Joseph refused to have any as it had been provided by 'that Orangeman Barton'. Instead, he engaged Bridget in conversation. If his intention was to persuade her to back away from the court case, he clearly failed. During a pause in the conversation, Barton said to him,

> 'Now are you satisfied with having an interview with your sister?'
> Joseph replied, 'Mind your own bloody business. It's nothing to do with you.'
> 'Thank you,' said Barton. 'I spoke to you as a gentleman but I now know what you are.'

After finishing their lunch, the group returned to the courtroom.[17]

At the end of the day's proceedings, a huge crowd had gathered at the main entrance to the court in King Street, hoping to get a glimpse of the 'escaped' nun. An even larger crowd was waiting at the Elizabeth Street exit, where two motor cars were parked, suggesting she might emerge there. The *Daily Express* estimated that more than 1000 people were waiting outside the court building. Bridget and her party lingered in the courtroom, hoping to avoid the mayhem of the luncheon adjournment. Bishop Dwyer had meanwhile left the court, passing through the crowd amid mingled cheers and hoots. After waiting in vain for the numbers to diminish, the trio decided to leave through the St James Road exit opposite Hyde Park, where only a small number of people had gathered. Surrounded by police they moved through the corridor and out into the street where a car was waiting. Once they were on board, the car drove towards Elizabeth Street but it was held up by traffic. The crowd immediately rushed to surround the car and the police had to hurry down to disperse the people. Finally, once the traffic thinned, the car drove off.

Day 2: Friday, 1 July

The second day began like it did the day before. According to the *Sun*, about 500 people stood in line, mostly women, the first having arrived before 7 am: 'a long queue waited in the bleak weather

---

[17] *Watchman*, 7 July 1921, p. 7.

outside the bleak court on the chance of entering the public gallery and listening to the bleak evidence all day'.[18] On taking his seat at the bench, Justice Ferguson announced that somebody had written to him a letter about the case. He said he had not read it and that he would like the public to understand that neither he nor the jury needed any assistance in the case.

Mr Campbell then resumed his cross examination of Bridget Partridge, obtaining admissions that it was her choice to join an enclosed order rather than an open one and that during her postulate and novitiate she had become acquainted with the rigid requirements of the order. He also established that, despite knowing she was free to leave by informing the bishop, she had taken no steps to let him or her mother superior know of her desire to leave the community. He then questioned her about her dissatisfaction and ascertained that the only matter about which she complained to the mother superior was her having to sleep in a passage rather than a room. He also returned to the irrationality of her belief that there was a conspiracy to murder her, a belief, she admitted, she had held for several months after leaving the convent. She also admitted that even though she believed an attempt had been made to murder her, she did not think to tell Inspector Duprez or any of the police about it, and that after leaving the Thompson house she did not want the police or anyone else to know her whereabouts.

Miss Partridge concluded her evidence at 3.20 pm after almost eight hours in the witness box. According to *Truth*:

> During the whole of the time she was there ... she answered counsels' questions calmly and promptly though at times her replies were hardly audible in the crowded court. Though she looked all through rather pale and delicate, the close cross-examination to which she was subjected by Mr Campbell showed no effect on her as she stepped from the witness box.[19]

---

[18] *Sun*, 1 July 1921, pp. 7, 8.
[19] *Truth*, 3 July 1921, p. 11.

According to the *Sun*, 'She was an excellent witness. She faced the questions of the keen-minded cross-examining counsel with equanimity and without nervousness'.[20] As is often the case with press reports of court cases, it was form rather than substance that impressed the journalists. Campbell had elicited some significant admissions that impressed the judge and jury, as would later become apparent.

Mr Shand's next witness was Arthur Blix, the clerk of petty sessions at Central Police Court. He tendered through him the order to apprehend Bridget Partridge dated 3 August 1920, the information upon which it was based, and the order of Magistrate Gale of 13 August 1920 discharging Miss Partridge. Shand next called Blayney Keys, an accountant with the Commercial Bank at Wagga Wagga to verify Bishop Dwyer's signature on the information and on Dwyer's letter of 27 July 1920 to the Thompsons.

That concluded the evidence for the day and the case was adjourned to the following Monday.

Day 3: Monday, 4 July

The crowd outside the court on Monday morning was not as large as the previous two days, probably because Bridget Partridge's evidence was finished. The *Sun*, which estimated the number at about 100, effusively described the scene:

> One striking feature was the number of fashionably dressed women included in the crowd – women with rich-coloured frocks and the latest out in overcoats and smart hats and fluffy rainbow mufflers. ... You took a first look at them and began to wonder whether they were real. They were all dressed up for the play.[21]

When the hearing resumed, Bridget's heart must have skipped a beat when Justice Ferguson immediately asked her to return to the witness box. Having completed her evidence on the Friday before

---

[20] *Sun*, 1 July 1921, p. 7.
[21] *Sun*, 4 July 1921, p. 7.

and having spent the weekend recovering from the ordeal, she must have felt somewhat relaxed when she entered the courtroom on Day 3. If she felt anxious at her recall, the anguish was short-lived as the judge simply wanted to know whether she had seen the letter addressed to her that Bishop Dwyer had attempted to deliver to her via Mrs Thompson on 27 July 1920. Bridget answered that she had left the Thompsons when it arrived and did not see it.

The next witness was Detective Sergeant James Farley. When Mr Shand asked him to tell the court what happened when he arrested Bridget Partridge, Mr Campbell objected, submitting that it was irrelevant as the arrest had nothing to do with Bishop Dwyer. Campbell again used the objection to put forward the defence's case, arguing that the making of the apprehension order under section 4 of the *Lunacy Act* was not the act of the informant, Bishop Dwyer, or a necessary consequence of that act, as there was interposed an independent judicial act of an official, Mr Camphin, who made the order. Campbell submitted that the making of a statement in a sworn information is nothing more than the ordinary duty of a citizen who believes a person to be insane and without means of support. A magistrate is not bound to issue an apprehension order under the section unless satisfied that the sworn information justifies the making of the order. He said, 'There can be no suggestion, and there is none in the evidence, that the sworn information did not express the honest belief of the defendant at the time it was sworn.' This submission would later become significant in the determination of the outcome of the case. As with Campbell's previous objections on relevance, Justice Ferguson allowed the evidence to be given. Detective Farley then narrated the events of Bridget's arrest and of his giving evidence before the Lunacy Court.

The next witness was Dr Eric Tivey who gave evidence as to his seeing Miss Partridge at the Thompson house early on Sunday morning 25 July 1920 and as to his visit to the convent and his interview with Mother Stanislaus. Mr Campbell's cross examination began with questions regarding the use of the word 'escape' to describe Sister Liguori's departure from the convent. At this point the hearing was interrupted as the judge was not feeling well. At 12.15 pm the case was adjourned but resumed at 2.10 pm. Campbell then continued his cross examination where he had left off. Dr Tivey agreed that 'escape' had been used in an inexact way and that if she had actually escaped from detention he would have regarded the matter differently. Campbell's questioning was directed at establishing that, in drawing the conclusion that Bridget was not suffering any mental abnormality, Tivey had assumed certain facts and had not been made aware of facts that were relevant, such as her belief that an attempt had been made to murder her and her complaint of nausea and being afflicted with a persistent offensive smell. But Tivey was not prepared to alter his opinion, saying that Bridget might have reasonably misinterpreted what was happening as she was expecting some form of punishment for leaving the convent in the afternoon.

The cross examination did not conclude before the day's proceedings came to an end, so that Dr Tivey was required to return the next day. Once again Bridget and her party remained behind, hoping for the crowd to clear. This time she exited via the St James Road exit, where there were fewer people than at the Elizabeth Street gates. As the car moved off a young girl thrust a rosary into her hands and said, 'Here, Sister Liguori. Take these.'

Day 4: Tuesday, 5 July

On Tuesday morning with the gallery once again packed, this time mostly with men, Mr Campbell continued his probing of Dr Tivey. His aim was to establish that when the doctor made his diagnosis he did not have all the information that ought to have been afforded to him. Campbell took him to Bridget's statutory declaration of 4 August 1920 published a month later in the newspapers. Dr Tivey agreed it was significant as to her mental condition at the time it was made and it suggested her condition was not quite normal. However, he said it indicated obsession rather than delusion. When asked whether his opinion would have been different had he known then what he now knew, he answered, 'No.' When pressed further on the point he backtracked saying, 'It is impossible to say.' He explained that if her belief was absurd and she persisted in it, that would indicate she was insane but, if her belief was not absurd, it would not. When shown the letter Sister Liguori had written the day after fleeing the convent in which she alleged she had been given poison, Dr Tivey agreed that fear of retribution did not supply a rational explanation for her leaving the convent. He agreed that the facts in those documents would have been important for him to have known when making his diagnosis.

In re-examination, Shand put to Tivey a hypothetical question that included a recitation of several of the known facts concerning the events of 24 July 1920 and asked whether he would infer from those facts that, in believing there was an attempt on her life, the hypothetical person was subject to a delusion. Tivey replied, 'No.' Shand asked whether he thought there was anything remarkable in a sane person persisting in that impression. Tivey again answered, 'No,' adding, 'The impression must have been strong to be so persistent.' Shand then asked whether Tivey had any reason now for changing the opinion he had expressed before when he saw Sister Liguori that she was quite sane, he answered, 'I have no reason.'

Before Dr Tivey stepped down from the witness box, a jury member asked whether it was possible that Sister Liguori might have been insane on the day before he made the examination and sane on other days. Tivey replied, 'In my opinion that would be impossible.' This question gave Campbell the opportunity to reopen his cross examination, which he used to elicit that Dr Tivey was a general practitioner with no particular expertise or experience in mental health.

The next witness was Inspector William Duprez, who related the facts of his involvement in the case, including his visit to the Thompsons with Bishop Dwyer and his subsequent heated conversation with the bishop, who accused him of not doing enough to locate Sister Liguori. Mr Shand then called Dr William Binns of Kogarah who, at the request of the Touchells, had examined Bridget as to her mental condition. After describing his examination, he told Mr Shand that there was nothing in the plaintiff's bearing that indicated insanity. He also said that given her experiences, it was reasonable for her to have concluded that an attempt was being made to poison her. Mr Campbell elicited from Dr Binns that he was a general practitioner and had no more experience in mental health cases than any general practitioner. Campbell then questioned him as to his claim that Bridget's conclusion she was being poisoned was reasonable. When Justice Ferguson inquired whether Binns considered it a natural deduction that the sisters were intending to murder her, he backtracked, saying it would be 'a very exaggerated deduction'. When Campbell suggested his opinion was based on a circular argument in that he had accepted as fact Bridget's assertion that Sister Brendan had prepared a 'death bed' for her, he answered, 'I was assuming that what she said was true. I was not in a position to criticise her facts.'

The next to be called was Mrs Jessie Burgess, to whose home Bridget had fled on the afternoon and night of Saturday 24 July 1920. The examination in chief was conducted by Mr Boyce. When he asked Mrs Burgess to relate the conversation she had had with Sister Liguori, Mr Campbell objected on the ground of relevance. Mr Shand submitted that the evidence went to showing her normality on the day. This time the judge took a stricter approach than before, saying, 'The question arises only indirectly as the main point is the bona fides of the defendant's belief. I think I must exclude the evidence.' Mrs Burgess then related the facts of Bridget's two visits to her house. In cross examination, Mrs Burgess agreed that in the afternoon Bridget had appeared to go back to the convent 'quite willingly'.

Dr Alexander Gibbes, one of the medical officers at Darlinghurst Reception House, was the next witness. He told the court he had examined Bridget Partridge over five days and concluded she was not insane. In cross examination, Dr Gibbes said he was a general practitioner but that he worked daily at the reception house. When pressed as to whether Bridget's belief that she was to be murdered was a fact or a delusion, he said he believed she thought it was true but that it was not a delusion so much as an inference drawn from the events that had occurred. He agreed that in the circumstances her belief was morbid and her inferences were very grave and exaggerated.

The next witness was Mrs Letitia Howell, at whose farm near Adelong Bridget had stayed after being spirited out of Wagga Wagga. Mr Boyce conducted the examination in chief. Mrs Howell gave evidence of Bridget's stay with her and her being handed over to Grand Master Barton, a person she did not know, who was to take her to Sydney. Her evidence having concluded, the court adjourned until the next morning.

Day 5: Wednesday, 6 July

When the hearing resumed on Wednesday, Mr Shand announced that the plaintiff's evidence was complete. Mr Campbell said that before Mr Shand closed his case he would like to recall Bridget Partridge. For the third time, Bridget entered the witness box. Campbell asked her about the reference she had made in her evidence in chief to physical penances—the orphaned titbit left hanging from Day 1. He must have overlooked this brief aspect of her evidence when he cross examined her but later thought it needed to be explained lest it be seized upon as evidence of cruelty. The result of his revisiting the matter was mixed. Although Bridget agreed that the physical penances were voluntary and inflicted by the nuns on themselves, she also said they involved the use of a scourge. Not sure where it might lead, Campbell said, 'I am somewhat amazed. I will leave it at that.' Campbell then took the opportunity to clarify a few other issues regarding Bridget's dissatisfaction with convent life, obtaining an admission that she had asked to be allowed to sleep on the enclosed veranda. In reply to questions about her removal from teaching duties at Ganmain, she said the diocesan inspector had been quite pleased with her teaching and that it was the mother superior who told her she was removed because she could not control the class. In re-examination Shand elicited that she had never had any trouble teaching before then.

The plaintiff's case having closed, Mr Campbell applied for a non-suit, a procedure by which the hearing of a civil action can be ended without judgment being entered for either party if the judge determines that the plaintiff's evidence is insufficient in law to prove the case. Campbell's first submission was that the plaintiff had failed to prove absence of reasonable and proper cause for the defendant's swearing of the information. The plaintiff, he said, must first establish what were the facts in the defendant's knowledge before there can be a consideration of whether those facts were sufficient. The plaintiff had put forward a lot of facts but had failed to establish what facts were in the defendant's mind that were inconsistent with his having reasonable and proper cause to swear the information. The plaintiff, he contended, had led no evidence to show that the defendant did not make proper inquiries and it would be wrong to leave the matter to conjecture. A second ground for a non-suit was put to the court by Mr Flannery KC. He submitted that there must be a non-suit unless the plaintiff establishes by evidence that the defendant misled the tribunal which issued the order under section 4 of the *Lunacy Act*. In other words, the plaintiff must prove the defendant was wilfully false and malicious in laying the information not that he laid the information on grounds that were unreasonable. The act of the magistrate, he submitted, was a judicial one and was interposed between the information and the arrest so that the defendant would only be liable if it could be proved that the information was an abuse of process.

Without hearing from Mr Shand, Justice Ferguson refused the non-suit. In relation to Flannery's submissions, he said he disagreed with his characterisation of the role of the magistrate issuing an order under section 4, saying that the magistrate may act upon the sworn information without expressing or forming any opinion as to the truth of the charge before him. As regards Mr Campbell's submissions, Justice Ferguson said:

> I think it is better I should take the opinion of the jury on questions of fact. I express no opinion myself at present. I am influenced very largely by this consideration: if I am wrong in allowing the case to go to the jury, then it will be possible for the Court [on appeal], in setting the matter right, to determine the matter finally, without putting the parties to the expense of a new trial. I refuse the non-suit.

The hearing of the application for a non-suit had occupied the rest of the day after the close of the plaintiff's case, so that on its conclusion the hearing was adjourned to the following morning when the defence case would start.

8
TRIAL – PART TWO

Day 6: Thursday, 7 July

The first witness for the defence was the defendant, Bishop Joseph Dwyer. He began by describing the extent of the diocese of Wagga Wagga, its recent establishment, and his relationship as bishop to the sisters of the Mount Erin convent. He said he had nothing to do with the administration of the convent but had a supervisory role to ensure that it was being conducted according to its rules and that its finances were satisfactory, and to inquire if any of its members had complaints about their superiors or fellow sisters. He said the role of the order was to teach the children of the poor and, if necessary, to look after the sick in hospitals. In relation to any members who wished to leave the convent he said his duty was to investigate the cause of their complaint or unhappiness and to remedy it if possible. If the sister continued in her wish to leave, he would initiate the process. The convent authorities were obliged to see that the departing nun returned in safety to her people and to supply her with reasonable expenses for the comforts and requirements of the journey. Under Canon 643 of the 1917 Code of Canon Law his duty was to ensure that was done.

Bishop Dwyer then related the events of July/August 1920, as known or as told to him, leading up to his swearing the information under section 4 of the *Lunacy Act*. He also recounted how he had called at the Darlinghurst Reception House and had asked Dr Chisholm Ross for permission to visit Sister Liguori but the doctor had denied his request. Mr Campbell then asked him a series of questions going to the nub of the case against him. In answer to those questions Bishop Dwyer said he believed the statements he made in the information to be true and that his motivation was to see and verify the state of Sister Liguori's condition, given that she had vanished. He said that if she were declared to be sane by the authorities his duty ceased so far as she was concerned. But, if she were found to be insane, the sisters and himself would have to see she was provided treatment in hospital until she was well again and then to ascertain whether she desired to remain in the convent or return to her parents. He also described the procedure for a nun to obtain a dispensation from her vows, saying that he was the channel for passing the application to the Apostolic Delegate (the papal representative in Australia), who had the power to permit the dispensation. He said that Bridget's application had been granted.

Under cross examination by Mr Shand, the bishop said he had no part in instructing Mr Ryan KC to appear at the Lunacy Court and knew nothing about it. Mr Shand then asked him about his dealings with the Inspector General of Police and with Mr Camphin. Referring to the latter, Shand asked, 'He is one of your church?', to which Dwyer answered, 'I believe he is.' This was the first time that Shand introduced this line of questioning, which had nothing to do with the merits of the case but hinted at collusion. It also gave a passing nod to the 'elephant in the room', the centuries-old ethno-religious feud that underpinned the litigation. It soon became more than a passing nod when Shand asked a series of questions aimed at undermining the bishop's credibility:

> Have you told the Court all you know of this matter?—Yes; I have answered all questions.
>
> There is no mental reservation?—No.
>
> You know that is a doctrine of some of your theologians?—I know about reservations.
>
> You know Liguori, the man this lady is named after. He is recognised as one of those whose teachings you are justified in following?—Yes.
>
> And you know he states it is justifiable to conceal in Court on oath? Don't you know that?—No, I do not know it.
>
> Are you not aware that you can mentally reserve on ...—Go on.

> Don't you know that you can properly mentally reserve in a Court of Justice?—On oath?
>
> Yes, on oath?—No, I do not know it. If mental reservation means telling a lie ...
>
> No, I do not mean telling a lie. I mean misunderstanding a question.
>
> His Honour: What is the difference, Mr Shand, between that and telling a lie?
>
> Mr Shand: One is worse than the other.
>
> Mr Campbell: I should have thought so.
>
> Bishop Dwyer: A lie on oath is perjury.
>
> Mr Shand: Were you not taught that in a crisis you could misunderstand a question?—I never learned that.
>
> Very well. I will give some of the doctrine later on and see if you subscribe to it.
>
> His Honour: I hope not.

Shand did return to it later but was met with the same denials. In re-examination by Mr Campbell, the bishop would say, 'It is a principle of moral doctrine that a lie is always a lie—always wrong—it is always a sinful act to tell a lie.'

Shand's line of questioning has an interesting pedigree. It had been used in the Coningham divorce case, mentioned in the Introduction.[1] In 1605, during one of the Gunpowder Plot trials, Sir Edward Coke had employed a similar technique, to devastating effect, in his examination of Father Henry Garnet.[2] Implicit in this line of questioning is the notion that Catholics believe themselves justified in lying on oath and that this justification is related to Catholic disloyalty to the Crown. Dwyer's rejection of Shand's claim of 'mental reservation' was beside the point. The mere suggestion was enough to raise a doubt in the jurors' minds—after all, a liar would always deny he was lying.

---

[1] Anne E. Cunningham, *The Price of a Wife?: The Priest and the Divorce Trial*, Anchor Books Australia, Spit Junction, NSW, 2013, pp. 47-50.
[2] Antonia Fraser, *The Gunpowder Plot: Terror And Faith In 1605*, Weidenfeld & Nicholson, London, 1997, pp. 239-244, 254-258.

Mr Shand then questioned Dwyer about his knowledge of the refusal by William Hazell, the clerk of petty sessions and chamber magistrate at Wagga Wagga, to issue a 'warrant':

> Didn't [Sheekey] tell you that a warrant had been refused by the local magistrate because it had not been proved that there was no lawful support?—No, because the magistrate wanted to see her himself.
>
> Didn't he tell you that the magistrate said that as she was supposed to be at the Thompsons and as they were people of substantial means, it could not be said that she was without means of support?—I don't remember that part.
>
> Will you deny it?—No. He told me the magistrate wanted to see her.
>
> Did you tell the magistrate in Sydney that a warrant had been refused at Wagga?—No.
>
> Why not?— I only told him all that I thought was necessary.
>
> You did not regard that as important?—No.

It is apparent that Shand was framing his questions on the basis that Sheekey had made an application under section 4 of the *Lunacy Act*, where a lack of means of support was relevant. Dwyer's answers, however, suggest that Sheekey had told him about an application under section 5, where it was not. So, Shand and Dwyer were at cross purposes. While it is reasonable to assume that Shand was well aware of the distinction, the same cannot be said of the bishop, nor of the jury. At no stage did Shand seek to clarify the matter with the witness. Consequently, it is likely the jury were left with the impression that the bishop was being evasive and, more critically, that he had engaged in forum shopping to find a magistrate, one of his own faith as it turned out, who would be less scrupulous than Mr Hazell, thus undermining his claim to have acted in good faith.

As would become apparent from his closing address, Shand was working on the hypothesis that Dwyer had instructed Sheekey and Leahy to apply for a section 4 order, which Mr Hazell had refused because it had not been proved that there was no means of support. Yet, Shand never put that proposition clearly and directly to Dwyer. Nor did he suggest to any of the bishop, Sheekey and Leahy that they had conspired together to give false evidence about these matters, although he would allege this in his closing address.

After the lunch adjournment, Mr Shand continued his cross examination of the bishop. He first asked him whether the Wagga Wagga solicitor William Walsh had advised him regarding the *Lunacy Act* proceedings, to which he replied in the negative. He then questioned him as to what various people had told him about Sister Liguori's mental condition. He followed that with questions regarding the penalties that might be inflicted on nuns who leave the convent irregularly, known in Canon Law as 'apostates'. When the bishop agreed that one of the penalties could be excommunication, Shand asked, 'It inflicts the heaviest curse, one which extends from the sole of her foot to the crown of her head, doesn't it?' This evoked laughter from the gallery and an interjection by Campbell, 'You are thinking of the Jackdaw of Rheims.' Campbell's quip refers to a nineteenth-century poem of that name by Richard Barham about a jackdaw that steals a cardinal's ring, which includes the lines:

> The Cardinal rose with a dignified look,
> He called for his candle, his bell, and his book!
> In holy anger, and pious grief,
> He solemnly cursed that rascally thief!
> He cursed him at board, he cursed him in bed,
> From the sole of his foot to the crown of his head.

Clearly out of his depth and embarrassed, Shand retorted, 'I am putting it somewhat higher than the Jackdaw of Rheims,' and then turning to the bishop asked, 'Aren't there physical penalties?' It was apparent that Shand was framing his questions having regard to Canon 619 of the 1917 Code of Canon Law, which provided, 'In all things in which religious are subject to the local Ordinary [i.e., the bishop of the diocese], they can be coerced by him even with penalties.' The cross examination continued:

> But you cannot coerce by dismissing them?—If a person possessed a conscience it would.
>
> Isn't it this, that where they come back they may be coerced?—Probably they may be coerced to leave again.
>
> Is that the meaning of coerced by penalties?—Yes.
>
> That is one penalty and the other possible penalty is excommunication?—Yes.
>
> Anything else?—Not that I know of.

Clearly, Shand was hoping to establish that Bridget was at risk of some harsh physical penalty of a kind that would provide a rational basis for the fear that induced her to run from the convent in bare feet and clad only in her nightgown. But instead of being captured and physically punished, the worst that could have happened to her, according to the bishop, was that she might have been expelled from the convent or excommunicated from the church, i.e., cut off from the sacraments.

Shand then questioned Dwyer on a number of subjects: his reasons for not speaking with Dr Tivey or Archdeacon Pike, which he said was their lack of knowledge and cooperation; his knowledge of pickets and search parties looking for Sister Liguori, which he said came only from the newspapers; his dealings with Inspector Duprez; and his knowledge of Nurse Bridgefoot's sister obtaining a statement from Bridget at the reception house, of which, he said, he was ignorant until it was shown to him at the presbytery.

On the conclusion of Bishop Dwyer's evidence, Mr Campbell next called as a witness Mother Stanislaus, whose baptismal name was Mary Dunne. She gave evidence of the convent's routines and the work done by the nuns in the convent. When he asked whether the duties of the plaintiff were very arduous or laborious, Justice Ferguson intervened:

> His Honour: What does it really matter? The plaintiff does

not deny that she had the right to leave for any reason whatever.

Mr Campbell: But the question has been raised here that she was driven to leave in fact by being badly treated.

His Honour: She has told us herself that she was not subjected to any ill-treatment.

This was an important intervention by the judge for it not only indicated to Campbell he need not pursue that line of questions, it also gave to the jury food for thought. For the rest of the examination in chief, Mother Stanislaus gave evidence of Sister Liguori's time in the convent and of the events of the weekend in July 1920 when she left the convent. When the day's proceedings concluded Mr Campbell had not finished his examination of Mother Stanislaus.

Day 7: Friday, 8 July

On the resumption of the hearing on the Friday, Mr Campbell asked Mother Stanislaus about the voluntary penance to which Bridget Partridge had referred, hoping to remove it from consideration in this case:

> Is it permissible for the sisters to practise self-discipline without permission?—No.
> Did the plaintiff ask your permission to practise physical discipline upon herself?—No.
> Where permission is granted, is it ever general or only temporary?—It is always temporary.

In cross examination, Mr Shand asked Mother Stanislaus about her attitude to Sister Liguori's freedom to leave the convent:

> I understand that you took the view that if she left properly, she was a free agent?—Yes.
> But if she left other than respectably, you had the right to get her back and send her to her parents?—That was my view.
> That she was not a free agent until she came back to you and left in the proper manner?—Yes.

> So that you thought you were justified in getting her back, to restore her to her parents, whatever way you could get her?—Yes.
>
> I suppose the Bishop expressed the same view to you?—Yes.

Shand left it at that, refraining from asking whether 'whatever way you could' included force. Surprisingly, Campbell did not seek to clarify the matter in re-examination, leaving it open to the jury to infer it did.

Shand next asked Mother Stanislaus about the two novices who had left the convent and were brought back and about the nun who had tried to drown herself in the dam. When questioned about what she had told Dr Tivey, she maintained she could not remember. He then questioned her about the seriousness of a nun leaving the convent without permission:

> You regarded her leaving the convent as a very serious breach?—Yes.
>
> One of the most serious breaches that one in an enclosed order could commit?—Yes, if she was responsible for her actions.
>
> Unquestionably, if she was responsible for her actions, it would bring down the wrath of the community upon her?—Yes.

Later Mother Stanislaus said that she did not reproach Bridget nor was she annoyed with her because 'I didn't think she was right in her senses at the time.'

In re-examination, Mother Stanislaus told Mr Campbell that the worst that could have happened to Bridget, if she were responsible for her actions, was that application could have been made to the bishop to have her dispensed from her vows. If that were done, she would have had to leave the convent, though she could have appealed for forgiveness. Mr Campbell also asked about the nun who attempted suicide. Mother Stanislaus said that she was treated in a mental hospital and upon recovering she returned to the convent at her own request and had continued to be a happy and contented member of the community.

The next witness was Sister Brendan, whose baptismal name was Annie Dunne, no relation of Mother Stanislaus. She was Sister Liguori's friend from their novitiate days who had helped retrieve her from the Burgess home and had looked after her just prior to Sister Liguori's leaving the convent the second time. In her evidence in chief, Sister Brendan related the events of that afternoon and evening. In cross examination, she said she considered Sister Liguori's departure from the convent in the afternoon as a serious wrong and a disgrace to herself and the community. When asked if she deserved a fright, if not punishment, Sister Brendan answered, 'Not in her frame of mind.'

Mother Clare was next to give evidence. Her baptismal name was Mary Herbert. She had been in charge of the novitiate when Sister Liguori was there and had accompanied Sister Brendan to the Burgess house. Asked about the two novices who ran away, she said they returned of their own accord to the convent and were sent back to their friends. She then described her visit to the Burgess house and the return of Sister Liguori.

Mr Campbell next called Dr William Leahy who gave evidence of Sister Liguori's medical history, his examination of her the night she returned from the Burgess house, and the later search for her. He also described the preparation of his two affidavits. In cross examination, Dr Leahy admitted that a person might appear insane one day and sane the next. He also accepted that a person with a weak mind might believe harm was intended by events such as occurred after Sister Liguori returned from the Burgess house, but otherwise he thought no one would believe it. He was closely questioned about his involvement with Sheekey and Byrnes, his discussions with Bishop Dwyer, his knowledge of Sister Liguori's whereabouts, or lack thereof, his swearing of the affidavits, and the application to the Wagga Wagga chamber magistrate, Mr Hazell. Leahy's evidence was all over the shop. At one stage he agreed with

Shand that Sheekey had asked Hazell for a warrant for the apprehension of Sister Liguori. While it is doubtful Leahy understood precisely what Sheekey had asked of the magistrate, Shand's leading question had elicited the response he was looking for. However, later Leahy said he did not remember Sheekey asking for a warrant. When pressed as to whether he denied it, he said 'I won't. He may have asked for a warrant,' thus giving the impression of evasiveness, which was reinforced by a series of 'I don't remember' answers to other questions.

Shand's cross examination of Leahy was not completed by four o'clock, so the hearing was adjourned to the following Monday.

Day 8: Monday, 11 July

According to press reports, public interest in the Liguori case remained unabated with the public gallery packed as before. When Dr Leahy returned to the witness box, Mr Shand continued to press him on his swearing of the affidavits and the timing of his knowledge of Sister Liguori's presence at the Thompson house. Shand seemed to be suggesting that, when Leahy made the second affidavit, he had lied when he swore that Sister Liguori 'is at present at a certain private dwelling-house in Wagga Wagga', because by then she had left the town. Shand was seeking to undermine Leahy's credit so that the jury would not believe him when he said he had formed the opinion that Sister Liguori was of unsound mind. Having not advanced the matter much further, Shand changed tack, asking Leahy whether he was at a concert at Wagga Wagga on Saint Patrick's day when the bishop addressed the audience. When Leahy said he was, Shand asked, 'Did you hear him referring to the soldiers as murderers and rebels?'. Shand was alluding to the conflict in Ireland where the Crown forces had been accused of atrocities against the civilian population. Campbell objected and there followed a most intriguing exchange:

> Mr. Shand: I propose to ask him, your Honour, if he heard that, and whether he remained in the room afterwards. It is to test his credit.

Mr Campbell: I submit he cannot go into this in testing credit. This is merely an attempt, after having already done his work in exciting religious animosity and creating an atmosphere of prejudice, and my friend now seeks to stimulate political feeling in the same direction in the hope that reason will become so clouded with prejudice that he will be able to appeal not to reason but to prejudice in favour of the case that he has put before the Court, there being no other hope for him but to appeal to unreasonable prejudice, political hatred, and religious animosity.

Mr. Shand: I press it as most material.

His Honour: Tending to show that Dr Leahy is not to be believed on his oath?

Mr Shand: If a man is present at a meeting, and a thing like this is said, and he remains, I submit that he is not an observer of the law, and we say that these people, were banded together to get this girl by hook or by crook.

Mr Campbell: That he is not an observer of what law?

Mr. Shand: The law of allegiance. The man who does that is the kind of man who will lend himself to what we say the doctor did here.

His Honour: A judge is very often bound to admit questions that he thinks should not be asked.

Mr. Shand: If your Honour says that I will withdraw it – if your Honour says it should not be asked.

This was more than just a passing nod to the 'elephant in the room' and although Shand did not press the point with Leahy, he returned to it later.

The next witness was James Sheekey, who was examined by Mr Flannery. He said he had not seen Bishop Dwyer in connection with the Sister Liguori affair before Saturday 31 July 1920 and that the bishop had not been his client in the matter. He described his meeting with the bishop on 31 July during which he had told him that when he saw Mr Hazell regarding section 5 of the *Lunacy Act*, the chamber magistrate had appeared unwilling to act in the matter. He said he had also spoken with the bishop about a section 4 application and had advised him to go to Sydney about it. Next he referred to the redrafting of Dr Leahy's affidavit the following day, saying he had added the two new clauses. He also related his conversation with Dr Tivey after Bridget Partridge's statutory declaration had been published in the press in September. He said that Tivey had said that based on her statement he would have considered her insane.

Shand began his cross examination by asking Sheekey, 'Have you not taken a deep interest in this case, both as a churchman and as a professional man?', to which Sheekey replied, 'Not as a churchman, but as a professional man.' Yet another nod by Shand to the 'elephant in the room'. In answer to another question, Sheekey denied he had gone to Mr Hazell's office on 29 July to obtain a warrant or an order. Rather he had gone to have Leahy's affidavit sworn so that he might take steps under section 5 of the *Lunacy Act*. He also said that he had advised Bishop Dwyer to take the matter to Sydney because a matter coming from headquarters would always receive better attention and the local police had tried and failed to find Sister Liguori. He denied that Hazell had rung him the next day and asked him to come to his office or that he had gone to Hazell's office when Leahy was there or that he had told Hazell he was awaiting instructions from the bishop or that he had said, 'All we or they want is to get her back by hook or by crook.' Knowing the difference between sections 4 and 5, Sheekey was clear and concise in his answers, unlike Leahy who was easily led by Shand into giving answers that were vague and inconsistent. In re-examination, Sheekey said that Mr Hazell had told him on 29 July that the Wagga Wagga police magistrate would issue a warrant under section 4, to which Sheekey had replied that he was not concerned with section 4 but with section 5, adding that the first affidavit had applied to section 5 only. At this point Justice Ferguson explained to the jury the difference between the two sections.

After Mr Sheekey's evidence was finished, Mr Campbell recalled

Bishop Dwyer who was examined by Mr Flannery, who questioned him first about what Mother Stanislaus had told him about Sister Liguori and her family background. He recounted that the mother superior had told him that the young nun had no relatives or friends in Australia, that her brother was living in Hong Kong, and that she had come to the convent with no money. The bishop said he told those facts to Mr Camphin, who issued the order under section 4 of the *Lunacy Act*. In cross examination, Mr Shand asked no questions about Sister Liguori or the making of the order but, instead, asked him about his speech at the Saint Patrick's day concert in Wagga Wagga. Justice Ferguson allowed these questions on the basis they could go to credit if it appeared to the jury that the opinions the bishop held, and the manner in which he expressed them, threw into light the question whether he was a person not to be believed on his oath. As *Truth* later remarked, 'any schoolboy could see that they were not aimed at questioning the Bishop's credit but at raising prejudice'.[3] Shand then read the report in the *Daily Advertiser* which quoted from the bishop's speech:

> And now because Irishmen ask that they be given what the soldiers fought for [in the First World War, i.e., the right of self-determination for small nations] and are prepared to show their resentment of any interference, an army of murderers—the mongrel scum of England in the shape of the Black and Tans are devastating and robbing the country and are telling the people that they are only rebels, and that they should be shot. The Irish people want to live in peace as well as those of foreign lands. But they are asked to bow to the ruling of England and be loyal to the British Empire. Although I try to be loyal to it because I have to, but I can't be loyal to the headquarters of it, because they have perpetrated cruelties on the Irish peasants.

After the passage was read, Dwyer agreed he had said those words, adding that he had nothing to do with England, that he was an Australian who was loyal to the laws of Australia, and that he recognised the King of England as the King of Australia.

---

[3] *Truth*, 7 August 1921, p. 9.

In re-examination by Mr Campbell, the bishop said he was simply trying to tell the people on that occasion why they held St Patrick's concerts. He said he was not born in Ireland but he had sympathies with Irish aspirations as he had with those of Belgium or any other country, adding:

> It was just a statement of the fact that the Irish were being ill-treated because, instead of having the regular forces of England to keep order there, they had sent over some auxiliaries called Black and Tans, who were recruited from the gaols of England, and that they were committing murderous reprisals upon people. I also said that they had been objected to by Mr. Asquith in the House of Commons in just as severe terms as I had used, and by a great number of the fair-minded British people, including the Archbishop of Canterbury and a great number of the Church of England prelates there.

Mr Campbell then closed the case for the defendant.

In his case in reply, Mr Shand called Mr Hazell to give evidence as to what had occurred when he was approached by Sheekey and Leahy. However, Campbell objected to Shand's questions and the only evidence allowed was Hazell's denial that he had told Sheekey that the police magistrate would issue a warrant under section 4. Shand also recalled Inspector Duprez who answered questions about his conversation with Mother Stanislaus after his visit to the Thompsons.

With the evidence complete, Mr Campbell requested the judge to direct the jury to return a verdict for the defendant on the grounds that there was no evidence of want of reasonable and proper cause, no evidence of want of bona fides, and no evidence of malice. He finished by saying that if the judge agreed with him there was no evidence, it was his duty to make that finding and direct a verdict for the defendant as there would be no benefit in leaving it with the jury. Justice Ferguson disagreed, saying if he were to do as Campbell had asked and was found on appeal to be in error, it would create great hardship on the parties as there would have to be a new trial. On the other hand, if he were found to be wrong in leaving it to the jury, the appellate court could find there was no case to answer and enter a verdict for the defendant, thus causing less inconvenience and injustice to the parties.

After the lunch adjournment, Mr Campbell began his address to the jury. He started by saying that the manner of the plaintiff's leaving the community and her allegation of attempted murder created reasonable grounds for doubting her sanity. He then turned to address the 'elephant in the room', by saying there was 'a power, a force and purpose behind this action', inviting the jury to consider how it was that Mr Barton came into the case. He then gave the jury his answer to that question:

> There could be no other reason for calling in Mr Barton except that the plaintiff's story might become an instrument which could be used to the injury of the convent at Wagga and, ultimately, against the church with which the convent was associated. ... The object of these people was to use the plaintiff as an instrument by which they might vilify the Catholic faith and Catholic institutions.

Campbell was still focussing on the sectarian issue when the case was adjourned to the next day.

Day 9: Tuesday, 12 July

On the Tuesday, Mr Campbell continued his address to the jury, briefly referring again to the sectarian issue before moving on to survey the evidence regarding the merits of the case and the questions the jury would be asked to determine:

1. Did the defendant take reasonable care to inform himself as to the true facts of the case?
2. Did he honestly believe the case which he laid before the magistrate?
3. Was he actuated by malice?

In doing so, he emphasised the duty of the bishop who was responsible for Sister Liguori and how the lies and secrecy in which the Thompsons and Barton had engaged made it impossible for the bishop to satisfy himself as to her safety and welfare, leading him to resort to the law.

Mr Shand began his address shortly before lunch. He answered Campbell's allegations of sectarianism by turning it back on him:

> He has endeavoured to obtrude the issue of sectarianism and leaves the impression that he has not been responsible for it—that I have—yet all the time it is trailing behind his coat.

In the sectarian world of early twentieth-century Australia, it was common for one side to accuse the other of engaging in sectarian conduct and for the other side to reply that such a suggestion was itself sectarian. At that time sectarianism was widespread. Yet, judging by the rhetoric, it was only ever practised by the other, never by oneself. Shand expressed his confidence that the members of the jury would do their sworn duty despite the implied threat in Campbell's words:

> He deliberately adopted these tactics and he is trying to poison your minds by suggesting that if you bring in a verdict for the plaintiff, there was no evidence upon which you could arrive at it and that, therefore, it will be charged against you that you have dealt with the issues from the point of view of sectarianism.

Shand then answered Campbell's question about Barton's involvement by saying:

> And if this girl's fears were real, there was only one way in which she could avoid being taken back to the convent, and that was by getting the protection of a body, if not as powerful as the church, at any rate, able to make its views and its influence felt.

Shand continued addressing the jury until 4 pm when the hearing was adjourned to the following day.

Day 10: Wednesday, 13 July

On Wednesday morning Mr Shand continued his address, telling the jury that the question of Leahy's affidavits was one of the most important matters throwing light on the bona fides of the bishop and going to the question of malice. With little regard to the evidence, Shand claimed that when Bishop Dwyer had rung Dr Leahy on 27 July, prior to his going to Sydney, he had instructed Leahy to take proceedings against Sister Liguori, which he did by visiting Mr Hazell's office on 29 July. He also claimed that Sheekey had acted for the bishop throughout, despite the solicitor's evidence on oath that he first spoke to the bishop about the matter on 31 July and that the bishop had never been his client. Although Shand led no evidence to contradict Sheekey's evidence, he advanced the hypothesis that Sheekey and Leahy had on 29 July applied for an order under section 4 of the *Lunacy Act* and that they had done so on the bishop's instructions.

Shand's hypothesis makes little sense. The affidavit Sheekey presented to Hazell used the wording of section 5 relating to absence of proper care and control and omitted the wording of section 4 relating to lack of means of support. To explain that discrepancy, Shand did not suggest that Sheekey was incompetent in failing to draft the correct affidavit. Instead, he said that Sheekey, being a solicitor, was not prepared to state falsely that the girl was without means of support. Lawyers, as officers of the court, have a strict obligation not to mislead the court and can be struck off for deliberately doing so. Instead, according to Shand, Sheekey sounded out Mr Hazell to see if he could get it passed him despite the deficiency. The flaw in this reasoning is that, on the one hand, Shand was arguing that Sheekey, being a solicitor, was not prepared to mislead the chamber magistrate while, on the other, he was claiming that Sheekey was prepared to conspire with the bishop to concoct a false account of their actions and to commit perjury in the Supreme Court: 'Was it not plain,' Shand told the jury, 'that Sheekey was not telling the truth?' According to Shand, Sheekey's motivation for doing so was that he was being a good churchman. Shand's allegations of criminality against Sheekey, a fellow officer of the court, in the absence of evidence and without putting the allegation to him in cross examination was improper.

Shand completed his address at 12 noon, whereupon Justice Ferguson commenced to sum up. He told the jury no religious question was involved and there was no need for religion, politics, or Irish affairs to be considered. He added that it was impossible to hide the fact that there had been sectarian feeling involved in the conduct of the case:

> We had the rather remarkable spectacle of counsel for the plaintiff (the latter being a member of the Catholic faith) asking questions in cross examination which were designed to suggest that people of her faith could not be believed on their oath.

He then spoke of the claims of mistreatment at Mount Erin convent, noting that, in her letters, her statutory declaration, and in her conversations with the doctors, the plaintiff had made no claims before the action commenced of cruelty towards her; in fact, she had stated the opposite. He said that in her evidence on the first day of the hearing Bridget had said she had not always been shown kindness at the convent but when asked for details she referred only to being overworked and to the incident of the broom. But otherwise, she spoke of the kindness of the sisters and of Dr Leahy. Justice Ferguson continued, no doubt with a touch of irony:

> That was as her evidence stood at the end of the first day. On the next day, having had the opportunity to consult with her friends and think over matters, she seemed to think she had given an incorrect impression the day before. She was then invited and encouraged to state every complaint she had to make.

He then related the matters about which she had complained. After doing so he said:

Now, gentlemen, that is the whole evidence you have about unkindness shown to the plaintiff during the years she was in the convent up to the day she left. Whatever your verdict may be, I am sure there is no fair-minded man in the community – no Protestant, however militant his Protestantism may be – who will not share with his Catholic fellow-citizens in a sense of gratification that these imputations, so far as the plaintiff is concerned, have been refuted – not by the contradiction of people interested – not by a balance of conflicting testimony—but by her own deliberate oath.

The judge then observed that although Bridget had said she was not mistreated she also said she had been for some time dissatisfied with conventual life and had made up her mind to go. He said he sympathised with her feeling that it was a difficult thing to apply to do so, being a girl who during all her adult years had submitted her will absolutely to the control of others. She was also rundown. And her nerves were probably getting unstrung when the trivial dispute over the broom occurred and she made up her mind suddenly to leave. He added, 'And I may point out here that she had no difficulty in leaving. She had no bars to break or walls to climb. The sisters do not seem to have been locked up. What kept the nuns in the convent, no doubt, was the respect they had for their vows.' Concerning Bridget's second flight, Justice Ferguson said:

> Probably if she had taken the medicine and remained in bed for a day or two— if she had taken this sedative, which the doctor said she wanted, she would have been in a much more cheerful frame of mind. She obviously misunderstood the sisters' intentions and actions. There was a sinister meaning in her mind to it all; she was in a condition of hysteria.

He related how she then left the convent in her nightdress and eventually went to the Thompsons. He added:

> We have not seen the Thompsons but I cannot help thinking that it is a very unfortunate thing for the plaintiff that at that time she did not meet somebody who would have

> shown a little common horse-sense. ... Mr Shand says, in effect, that the only way that this girl could be protected from being taken back to the convent was by leaving her in charge of some such body as the Orange lodge. I would be very sorry to think that anyone would have to go to the Orange lodge or any other community in order to be protected from the crime which this girl says was attempted. All I can say is I do not agree with that. ...
>
> There was no necessity to hurry this young woman away at midnight. The law was strong enough to deal with this girl even if she was in a convent. If the girl had been taken back to the convent against her wish anybody aware of the fact and of the girl's feelings could at once have applied for the issue of a writ of habeas corpus. ... It was very unfortunate that, at the time the whole matter was still fresh, the girl was not put into the hands of people who were capable of telling what was the right thing to do.

Justice Ferguson then referred to the fact that the Thompsons failed to inform Dr Tivey or Inspector Duprez of Bridget's claim that the sisters had tried to poison her:

> Neither was told about this complaint against the convent. On the other hand, what reason could be suggested for withholding it from the very people who were capable of dealing with it, according to law? The court had not seen Mr or Mrs Thompson and there was no means of knowing why they had omitted to tell the inspector or the doctor; all that could be done was to guess at the reason.

He continued, saying that Bridget had not been shown the bishop's letter and therefore did not know she could come back to the convent if she wished or, if not, they were prepared to find funds for her support. He asked, rhetorically, 'What possible reason could there be for withholding from her, or refusing her an opportunity of knowing, what proposals had been made and what view the convent authorities took of her conduct? She was taken away that night and disappeared into the dark.' He told the jury that the question was:

Had the plaintiff proved that the information was laid without reasonable and probable cause and that it was laid maliciously. It was not for the defendant to excuse himself or show that he had reasonable and probable cause. The plaintiff must establish those things against him.

After the lunch adjournment, Justice Ferguson continued his summing up, saying he was sure they would deal with the matter without any reference to religious beliefs and that they would regard the case as one between one citizen who believed she had been aggrieved by another. He took the jury to the evidence relating to the three questions they had to decide and summarised that evidence in a way that suggested the judge thought the bishop did take reasonable care to inform himself of the truth of the matter and did believe in its truth. Although in trials of this nature it is for the jury alone to decide the questions of fact, judges sometimes subtly make known their opinions in that regard. On the question of malice, the summing up was more neutral. The summing up finished at 2.50 pm and the jury retired.

At 8.45 pm the jury returned. According to the *Sydney Morning Herald*: 'The court was opened at 8 o'clock last night but long before that hour a crowd of people, mainly women, had assembled outside the court in order to lose no opportunity of gaining admission and of hearing the long-awaited verdict.' But the anticipation in the gallery would not be satisfied immediately. The foreman informed the judge they had not arrived at a verdict. Ferguson asked whether a majority had agreed as he could take a majority verdict. The foreman said they had, up to a certain degree. He said three of them were unanimous but they would need a few minutes to formulate their verdict. The jury went back to the jury room and returned at 9.15 pm. The foreman said they had a majority view on two questions but asked the judge whether the jury had to answer 'Yes' or 'No' regarding malice. The judge said that if their minds were in such a state of balance they could not say the bishop was actuated by malice, they must answer 'No'. The jury retired again. Mr Shand leapt to his feet and said, 'I ask your honour to direct the jury that if the defendant did not honestly believe the charge he made—that is if they are satisfied of this—that amounts to malice in law and that their answer then to the third question should be in the affirmative.' The judge said, 'I think it would be better to wait until we see what their answers are.'

At 9.42 pm the jury returned and everyone in the court room craned eagerly forward to hear its findings. When asked if they had reached a verdict, the foreman said they had reached a majority verdict on the first two questions and were unanimous on the third. The paper on which the verdict was written was handed to the judge, who said, 'The gentlemen of the jury answer each question "No".' The following exchange then took place:

> Mr Flannery: And upon those answers, if your honour pleases, I ask your honour to enter a verdict for the defendant.
>
> Mr Shand: I submit your Honour cannot enter a verdict but should direct the jury now that, having answered the second question 'No,' malice follows as a matter of fact in law and you should direct them to return a verdict for the plaintiff and assess damages.
>
> Mr Flannery: Of course, I cannot be taken to assent to that proposition in law.
>
> His Honour (after a long pause): Have you taken into consideration, gentlemen, the question of whether, if the defendant did not honestly believe the case he laid before the magistrate, he could have acted with good faith and without malice?
>
> The foreman: I think so, your honour. We have discussed it.
>
> His Honour: I understand that by a majority you find he did not honestly believe the case he laid before the magistrate.
>
> The foreman: That is so.
>
> His Honour: Have you considered whether, in that case, he

could have acted in good faith – that he could have acted from a proper motive in laying the information?

The foreman: Yes.

His honour: And you adhere to your finding that he was not guilty of malice?

The foreman: Yes.

His Honour: Then upon those answers I direct you to find a verdict for the defendant.

The foreman: By direction verdict for the defendant.

The court adjourned at 9.50 pm.

Outside the crowd spread right across King Street from the court steps. At 8 o'clock it was estimated to have been about 5000 but by the time the court adjourned some had left. According to the *Sydney Morning Herald*:

> When the verdict was known, it travelled like wildfire among the eager spectators, who charged towards the court en masse. Volley after volley of cheers were given for the Bishop, whose sympathisers could be estimated at about ten to one in the sea of faces out in front of the court. The demonstration lasted about a quarter of an hour, subsiding only when everyone had left the court.[4]

Neither Bridget Partridge nor Bishop Dwyer was in court to hear the verdict, though Bridget's brother Joseph was. He was soon surrounded by a group of enthusiasts, who warmly congratulated him on the result.

---

[4] *Sydney Morning Herald*, 14 July 1921, p. 9.

The main participants in *Partridge v. Dwyer* (Author's collection);

EX-SISTER LIGUORI.

CLAIM FOR £5000.

OPENING OF THE CASE.

Plaintiff in Witness Box.

UNPRECEDENTED SCENES OUTSIDE.

The profound and widespread interest in the case in which the young woman Bridget Mary Partridge, formerly known as Sister Liguori, is claiming £5,000 damages from Joseph Wilfred Dwyer, Bishop of Wagga, was reflected yesterday. No. 3 Jury Court, in which the case was opened, was crowded, and the scenes outside were perhaps unprecedented in the history of the law courts of this State.

Top: Report of the start of *Partridge v. Dwyer* (*SMH*, 1 July 1921, p. 9); centre: The crowd outside the Supreme Court at the start of *Partridge v. Dwyer* (*SMH*, 1 July 1921), p. 10); bottom: Joseph Partridge with Dan O'Callaghan, Fr Jerger's nephews at Coogee (Author's collection)

Top left: Reverend William Touchell (*SMH*, 19 July 1980, p. 14); top right: Report of the verdict in *Partridge v. Dwyer* (*SMH*, 14 July 1921, p. 9); bottom: Artist's drawing of Bridget Partridge giving evidence (*Sun*, 3 July 1921, p. 1)

Top: Bridget Partridge with Grand Master Barton and Mrs Touchell outside the Supreme Court (*Sun*, 3 July 1921, p. 7); lower left: Sheet music of song written by Joseph Partridge (Author's collection); lower right: Bridget Partridge in 1954 (*People*, 11 August 1954, p. 5)

Top: Bridget Partridge (second from right) with Rev. Touchell and Mrs Touchell (standing) at Hartley c. 1922 (*People*, 11 August 1954, p. 6); bottom: Mrs Touchell and Bridget Partridge in 1954 (*People*, 11 August 1954, pp. 8-9)

9
Aftermath

Those who had hoped the conclusion of the court case would mark the end of the Sister Liguori affair were destined to be disappointed. For months after the Supreme Court entered judgment for Bishop Dwyer, the affair continued to dominate the news with commentary on the jury's verdict, reports of sectarian violence in the Riverina, stories of Joseph Partridge's continued pursuit of his sister, and a censure motion in parliament.

The Jury's Verdict

Many people were shocked and perplexed by the verdict in *Partridge v Dwyer*, especially members of the Loyal Orange Institution and editors of Protestant newspapers.[1] They found it difficult to understand how the jury could have answered No to the third question after having answered No to the first two questions. Before judgment was entered, counsel for the plaintiff, Mr Shand, had tried to persuade Justice Ferguson that in light of the first two answers he should, as a matter of law, direct the jury to answer Yes to the third question. Although not prepared to do that, the judge was nevertheless puzzled as to how the jurors could logically come to the result they did. He had said in his summing up, 'If [the bishop] did not honestly believe the information he had sworn then it may be hard to escape the conclusion that he was actuated by some motive not a proper one.' And when the jury were seeking guidance from him as to the form of their verdict, he twice asked the foreman whether they were agreed on their answer to the third question.

We cannot know for certain the jury's reasoning but their verdict is not as illogical as it first appears. On the first question, the

---
[1] *Daily Telegraph*, 15 July 1921, p. 4; *Methodist*, 23 July 1921, p. 1; *Australian Christian Commonwealth*, 29 July 1921, p. 9.

majority might have considered that, by failing to speak to Dr Tivey and Archdeacon Pike, Bishop Dwyer had not taken all reasonable steps to inform himself as to the true facts of the case. On the second question, the majority might have found that, because Bishop Dwyer had been kept in the dark as to Bridget Partridge's situation, he could not have believed affirmatively that she was without sufficient means of support. Consequently, they might have concluded that he could not honestly have sworn that such was the case. When it came to the third question, it is clear they had rejected Shand's conspiracy theory and thus may have accepted that the bishop was truly concerned for Bridget's welfare and only laid the information so as to have her medically examined to establish the state of her mind.

In some ways it was a clever verdict for it enabled both sides to claim vindication, which they did. Nevertheless, it was not the result the LOI had wished for, having spent so much time, money, and effort on the case. They would have been expecting to recover their legal costs from the bishop and to recoup their expenses from the £5000 damages, as well as being provided with a propaganda brickbat with which to belt the Roman church. They were now considerably out of pocket and had little to show for it. Unlike the Grand Orange Lodge of British America after the Sister Basil case, Grand Master Barton's Grand Lodge would not be publishing a pamphlet containing 'a terrible revelation of the possibilities of wrongdoing and cruelty within convent walls'.[2] The mixed verdict did, however, provide sufficient cover for them to claim vindication and to avoid having to spend more money on an appeal. When the period for lodging the appeal expired, Mr Hill, solicitor for Miss Partridge, released the following statement to the press:

> Sister Liguori informed Bishop Dwyer, through Mr Shand in court before any evidence was given, that she did not bring the action for the purpose of recovering damages and only required that she should be vindicated in the eyes of the world. The first two questions submitted by the judge to the jury were answered by the jury as follows:

---

[2] *Watchman*, 26 September 1918, p. 6; 3 July 1919, p. 1.

1. That Bishop Dwyer did not take reasonable care to inform himself as to the true facts of the case; and

2. That Bishop Dwyer did not honestly believe the case that was laid before the magistrate.

Sister Liguori takes the view that these answers have completely vindicated her and does not see that any good purpose will be gained by appealing.[3]

However, in litigation, as in sporting contests, it is the final result on the scoreboard that matters, not the points scored along the way. The Catholics spent little time pondering the jury's first two answers, concentrating instead on the ultimate verdict, which they celebrated with tribal triumphalism.

On the Monday night following the verdict, a crowd numbering upwards of 10,000 packed the Sydney Town Hall for a monster meeting organised by the Catholic Federation and presided over by Archbishop Michael Kelly. It opened with the singing of 'Faith of Our Fathers'. When Bishop Dwyer appeared on the platform he was greeted by an outbreak of applause that lasted for several minutes, after which Patrick Cleary, president of the Catholic Federation, moved, 'That this meeting of citizens records its appreciation of his Lordship, Dr Dwyer, Bishop of Wagga, and of the manner in which he has vindicated the dignity and responsibility of his position.' After hearing from a number of speakers, including Attorney-General Edward McTiernan, the motion was enthusiastically carried. Father Maurice O'Reilly, never one to pass up an opportunity for hyperbole, hailed the result as a glorious victory for the Catholic Church of Australia.[4] O'Reilly, like Patrick Minahan, was one of those militant Catholics ever willing to take the apocalyptic fight to militant Protestants. Clearly the crowd lapped up the rhetoric, subscribing more than £1,600 to defray the bishop's legal costs.[5] On his return to Wagga Wagga, Dwyer was feted at a number of func-

---

[3] *Sydney Morning Herald*, 22 July 1921, p. 8.
[4] *Freeman's Journal*, 21 July 1921, p. 14.
[5] *Sydney Morning Herald*, 19 July 1921, p. 7; *Freeman's Journal*, 21 July 1921, pp. 14-15.

tions throughout the diocese, the state, and even interstate, where a further £7,400 was collected.[6]

Although the result of the court case meant that Bishop Dwyer was entitled to recover his legal costs, which would have amounted to thousands of pounds, he wisely decided not to pursue Bridget Partridge for them. Given her lack of means of support, she would not have been able to pay them herself and he could not be sure the LOI would stand by her to the extent of paying the costs on her behalf. It would have been a terrible look for the bishop had he chosen to force her into bankruptcy. Besides, the money he received from various sources was sufficient not only to cover his legal costs but also to enable him to complete the construction of St Michael's cathedral at Wagga Wagga.

Sectarian violence in the Riverina

The community at Wagga Wagga and the surrounding district had been deeply divided over the affair. Division turned to violence when Rev. William Touchell toured towns in the Riverina to establish branches of the Protestant Federation. On Monday 11 July, while the trial in Sydney was in full swing, a meeting was held for that purpose in Furner's Hall, Coolamon, a town 40 kilometres northwest of Wagga Wagga. According to the *Daily Advertiser*, 'From the very outset … the meeting was a stormy one and it was early apparent that a large section of the audience attended for the express purpose of putting an end to the proceedings as quickly as possible'.[7]

When Touchell rose to speak, hoots from his opponents, who had gathered at the back of the hall, were drowned out by cheers from his supporters. During his speech protesters attempted to disrupt his talk with interjections and the singing of Irish songs. But not one to take a backward step, Touchell pressed on, telling

---

[6] *Daily Advertiser*, 21 July 1921, p. 3; 25 July 1921, p. 3; *Sydney Morning Herald*, 25 July 1921, p. 8; *Catholic Press*, 26 January 1922, p. 25.
[7] *Daily Advertiser*, 13 July 1921, p. 3.

his audience the interruptions were caused by the worst elements among the Roman Catholics who had no brains and he questioned whether the church of Rome was not a menace to the country. Despite two rotten eggs being hurled at him from the back of the hall, Touchell continued undeterred. Goaded by hecklers, he strayed on to the Sister Liguori case, portraying the Catholic church as an instrument of oppression in its mistreatment of the nun. Several times he called on the two policemen who were present to eject the protesters. However, they refrained from doing so, perhaps fearful for their own safety, whereupon Touchell accused the policemen of being adherents of 'the other faith'. At the end of the meeting, Touchell was escorted out of the hall amid cheers and boos. Despite the fracas, he achieved what he had come to do, with a new branch of the Protestant Federation established at Coolamon and 200 members enrolled. As a consequence of the disturbance 19 of the protesters were convicted of riotous behaviour and fined £1 each.[8]

Worse was to happen the next night when Rev. Touchell spoke at a meeting in the Baptist church at Marrar, 15 kilometres east of Coolamon. The meeting began in an orderly manner with Touchell commencing his address without interruption. Then a large group of men entered the church. Some of them sat near the front while the rest congregated at the back. The newcomers listened to the speaker in silence except for a few interjections. But when Touchell criticised Archbishop Mannix they erupted. According to the *Daily Advertiser*:

> Suddenly, ... a man rushed to the platform and struck the speaker a heavy blow, knocking him down and rendering him unconscious. ... The platform was thereupon invaded by the crowd of disturbers who had up to this juncture remained quiet. The officer in charge of the Marrar police with the assistance of a constable from Coolamon also

---

[8] James Logan, 'Sectarianism in Ganmain: A Local Study, 1912 21', *Rural Society*, Vol. 10, No. 2, 2000, pp. 121-138; *Daily Advertiser*, 29 July 1921, p. 3; *Daily Express*, 29 July 1921, p. 1.

rushed to the platform where, standing with levelled revolvers between the unconscious man and the crowd, they warned the rioters to keep back.[9]

The assailants then left the building. When Touchell, who was bleeding from a cut near his ear, regained consciousness, an attempt was made to continue with the meeting but a huge stone was thrown through a window, scattering glass across the church and falling close to those on the platform. On the advice of the police the meeting was abandoned and Touchell left the church guarded by police. Several men were charged. Those found guilty of assaulting Touchell and the Baptist minister were fined £5 and they and several others were fined £1 for riotous behaviour.[10] It was not only in the Riverina that Touchell came under attack. At Gilgandra rotten eggs were thrown at him when he was leaving the meeting hall and at Forbes 'a company of young men attempted to count me out'.[11]

These events call to mind Jonathan Swift's aphorism, 'We have just enough religion to make us hate, but not enough to make us love one another' (*Thoughts on Various Subjects*, 1711). It is unusual today for a political meeting to result in violence. In those days, however, it was not so rare. During the conscription campaigns of 1916 and 1917 meetings often descended into brawls. And it was not only unruly Irish Catholics who were responsible. In May 1920, at a meeting in Sydney's Moore Park to protest Father Jerger's deportation, loyalist and Protestant members of the King and Empire Alliance stormed the speakers' platform. Some of the Coolamon and Marrar rioters claimed in their defence that they were provoked by Touchell's attacks on Catholics. But it is clear they had come to the meetings to cause trouble. In any event, nothing Touchell said at those meetings could justify their resort to violence. Interestingly, Touchell later claimed that the resentment against him was not so

---

[9] *Daily Advertiser,* 14 July 1921, p. 3.
[10] *Daily Express,* 14 July 1921, p. 1; 29 July 1921, p. 1
[11] Cyclostyled copy of a letter 7 November 1921 William Touchell to Mr and Mrs Thompson, Wagga Wagga Diocesan Archives.

much for what he had said but because of his having sheltered Sister Liguori.[12]

While that might in large part be true, there may also have been a political dimension to the attacks. The Protestant Federation, like the Catholic Federation, was essentially a political organisation. Both were established to lobby governments and rally voters in support of candidates sympathetic to their denominational interests. At his meetings, Rev. Touchell regularly criticised the Labor government, claiming it was dominated by the church of Rome. At Bathurst in October 1921, he told a federation meeting, 'We want to see at the next election that a government representative of the majority of this Protestant state is returned to power'. He denied the federation was anti-Labor, arguing that the federation would support the Labor party if it nominated 'the right type of strong Protestant candidate'.[13]

Not long after Touchell's visit to the Riverina, Bishop Dwyer also went on a speaking tour of the region. He too spoke in plain terms, but his meetings did not end in violence, though they sometimes provoked a Protestant backlash in the press. On 11 August the bishop addressed a meeting at St Joseph's parish hall, Temora, where the parishioners presented him with a cheque for £250 and complimented him on the successful outcome of the recent lawsuit. He told his audience the verdict was not so much the result of what a clever lawyer had done but was divine Providence's answer to the prayers of the people. He also said that, although Miss Partridge had placed him in the unpleasant position of being a defendant in court, he held no animosity towards her:

> If I could take her out of the prison she is now in, I would do so and give her back to her brother. She is more a prisoner now than ever she was before. She cannot get away from these people because they are afraid that she will speak out about what they have persuaded her to do. She has been guarded by Mrs Touchell and Mr Barton, who

---

[12] *Cootamundra Herald*, 14 July 1921, p. 2.
[13] *Sydney Morning Herald*, 12 October 1921, p. 12.

will not let her away from their power. She is now held as a prisoner because for twelve months those people behind her have done their best to make her tell lies, but she would not do so. So now they are afraid to give her freedom. I have the greatest sympathy for her and hope that someday she will get out of where she is now as easily as she got out of the Convent.[14]

If the speech had been reported only in the local newspapers, it might have passed unnoticed but it was also reported in the Sydney dailies. The *Sydney Morning Herald* published the story under the headline, 'Liguori Case/Ex-Nun's Supporters/Attacked by Bishop Dwyer".[15] In a letter to the *Herald*, Bridget Partridge gave what the newspaper called 'a spirited reply'. In it she wrote:

> I am not a prisoner. I am remaining of my own free will and intend to continue to do so. I appreciate what has been done for me by so many kind friends. I believe that he would like to take me from my friends and give me back to my brother. He need not trouble. I am not going. His great sympathy is of no use to me I do not require it. I am old enough and capable to think and act for myself.

Grand Master Barton also wrote to the *Herald* stating:

> I deny that Miss Partridge is a prisoner she has perfect liberty to please herself and does so. I have no doubt that he would like to hand her over to her brother but she has a say in that. She is a woman 30 years of age, her brother is her junior by about eight years, and surely she can please herself where she will remain and the company she will keep.

Rev. William Touchell also wrote to the newspaper:

> If there was any case in which she was a prisoner during the time she was with [us], it was entirely due to a fear that she would be captured and brought back to a Roman Catholic institution. Miss Partridge was a product of the Roman system and the fear of being handed over to Rome

---

[14] *Daily Express*, 12 August 1921, p. 1.
[15] *Sydney Morning Herald*, 12 August 1921, p. 9.

was in her heart. It was too late in the day for Bishop Dwyer to talk about his sympathy for her.[16]

The parishioners at Temora might have regarded Bishop Dwyer's statement, 'If I could take her out of the prison she is now in, I would do so and give her back to her brother' as mere rhetoric. But, in truth, it was more literal than they might have imagined, portending yet another dramatic twist in the Sister Liguori story.

Joseph Partridge's continued pursuit of his sister

During the lunch break on the first day of the court case, Bridget Partridge had told her brother that she wished to remain with her new friends. Yet, Joseph was unconvinced, believing they were holding her against her will. With the assistance of the Catholic Federation and the knowledge of Bishop Dwyer, he would make repeated attempts over the following months to persuade her to leave her Protestant friends and go with him. At this time, Joseph was staying at the home of Roger O'Callaghan in the Sydney suburb of Haberfield. Born in 1861 in County Limerick, O'Callaghan was a leading Catholic and a former publican. He had two children, Catherine (Kitty), born in 1886 and Daniel (Dan), born in 1887. Dan and Kitty were Joseph's constant companions in his endeavours to 'rescue' Bridget.

The first attempt occurred soon after the end of the trial when Bridget had gone to the Blue Mountains for a holiday. In a letter to Bishop Dwyer, Charles Lawlor, general secretary of the Catholic Federation, described what happened:

> Miss Partridge's brother approached us seeking that we track his sister. We tracked her to Katoomba. He went there to try to see her but she was spirited away. We had good men helping him at Katoomba. However, he got a letter asking him to meet her at a solicitor's office. He did so and arranged to see her as soon as he heard from her. Miss Partridge was taken to Touchell's place at Kogarah after the

---

[16] *Sydney Morning Herald*, 13 August 1921, p. 13.

interview with her brother at her solicitor's office. He saw her there the following day and had a private chat with her. He alleges that she told him that she fought them for two days to make her sign the writ; that they asked her to put her name to a statement regarding Convent Life prepared by them. Finally, that they opened some of their letters. She has expressed her willingness to go to where he is staying to see him provided that she had police protection. Her whole fear seems to be that some attack will be made on her now. She at first refused to consider going away with him but later said that they would talk the matter over when she saw him again. Our objective is, of course, to get a statement if we can keep our hand on the matter. No publicity will be given unless we have your full approval after perusal of a copy. However, that is how matters stand at present for we will do all we can do for him in the hope of getting the truth from her.[17]

Joseph also reported to the bishop on his conversations with Bridget:

I have followed her everywhere and try and see her, and of course the old story is always told her - that I have a gang with me. ... Poor Brigid saw me twice last week, and I got her to promise me that if I could by any means prove to her and give her an official assurance that the Catholic people would not injure or molest her, that then she would be willing to leave the mob she is with and come home with me. She even promised to come to Mass if two police came. Even when Dan and myself were talking to her, there were guards outside. In this way, by means of these threatened effects they are succeeding in persuading her of all these nonsensical stories about the people or yourself or me, wanting to harm her. ... She revealed to me the most dastardly doings by those who have had her. I can very well understand now, why they dread letting her under my care. The villains know quite well that all their talk about the Catholic people harming Brigid is all rot, but they realise also, only too well, that some exposure and consequent retribution is due to them when poor Brigid tells me all.

---

[17] Letter 8 August 1921 Charles Lawlor to Bishop Dwyer, Wagga Wagga Diocesan Archives.

> My first interview with Brigid took place in Hill's office. He wanted to be present during our talk but I told Brigid I refused to speak to her with him in the room. I went up to where he sat at his desk and let a roar at him to get out—to a hot spot!! He got—after asking me to be civil as he had offered me his office to speak to Brigid in. I told him he or his ilk would get no civility from me and I didn't ask for his office. He was like a lamb, Dan tells me. Actually put out of his office. These Romanists!!!
>
> I won't say more as please God I hope to see you as I have a plan to put before you. I have talked it over with the solicitor and he agreed absolutely.[18]

Clearly, it was the information in these letters that led Bishop Dwyer to claim in his Temora speech that Bridget was a prisoner of the Orange lodge. It is also clear that the Catholic Federation's continuing interest in the matter was to have Bridget Partridge provide a statement they could use in their ongoing war with the LOI.

From the outset, Lawlor had thrown himself into the task of 'rescuing' Sister Liguori. He had allowed Joseph to stay at his home at Ashfield up to the end of November 1920, when he suggested that Joseph would be better off living near Kogarah on the off chance of his meeting with Bridget. So, he arranged accommodation for the young man in a nearby suburb.[19] Later, Lawlor would tell Bishop Dwyer, 'Looking back, I have enjoyed every bit, every incident, of the case'.[20] Nevertheless, not everyone in the Catholic Federation was happy with Lawlor's handling of the affair. Lawlor's priority was to restore Bridget to her brother. He therefore opposed those who wanted to use Joseph for broader propaganda purposes. In December 1920 Lawlor wrote to Bishop Dwyer:

> I have made a number of enemies, but because I have held

---

[18] Letter 8 August 1921 Joseph Partridge to Bishop Dwyer, Wagga Wagga Diocesan Archives.

[19] Letter 2 December 1920 Charles Lawlor to Bishop Dwyer, Wagga Wagga Diocesan Archives.

[20] Letter 14 February 1921 Charles Lawlor to Bishop Dwyer, Wagga Wagga Diocesan Archives.

> – and held until I could not prevent—that he had come to get his sister not to be made a show puppy of. I felt and still feel, that his appearance at the meetings which he was asked to attend by Minahan and others, did no good. I could not prevent finally his appearance at the Hippodrome concert but have done my best to stay him at other publicity stunts. That can come when his sister is right.[21]

The concert to which Lawlor referred was held on 9 November 1920 at the 4,000-seat Hippodrome Theatre in Sydney (now the Capitol Theatre) where Father Maurice O'Reilly delivered to a full house what the *Catholic Press* described as 'a stirring address on Ireland'. In his lecture, entitled 'John Bull and his Island', O'Reilly sang the praises of Archbishop Mannix. The *Freeman's Journal* reported that Joseph, 'the possessor of a well-trained light tenor voice', was given a most enthusiastic welcome and had to respond to no fewer than four encores.[22]

During his stay in Australia, Joseph performed at a number of concerts in support of Irish nationalist causes. He soon became an audience favourite with the *Freeman's Journal* describing him as having 'established himself as the most popular tenor in Sydney'.[23] He also wrote and composed some of his songs, including 'My Little Thatched Home in Kildare'. The *Catholic Press* enthused, 'Partridge's beautiful tenor voice rouses the blood of all Irish people in his truly national rendering of Gaelic melodies'.[24] In April 1921 he appeared at a concert organised by the Irish National Association for the relief of distress in Ireland.[25] The following month he sang at concerts that accompanied screenings of *Ireland will be Free*, an Irish nationalist propaganda film.[26] The film comprised a collage

---

[21] Letter 2 December 1920 Charles Lawlor to Bishop Dwyer, Wagga Wagga Diocesan Archives.

[22] *Freeman's Journal*, 11 November 1920, p. 24; *Catholic Press* 11 November 1920, p. 20.

[23] *Freeman's Journal*, 5 May 1921, p. 27.

[24] *Catholic Press*, 5 May 1921, p. 32.

[25] *Catholic Press*, 21 April 1921, p. 17.

[26] Jeff Kildea, 'Ireland Will Be Free: "Fanning the Flames of Sectarianism" in

of images of 'the martyrs' of Easter Week 1916 and other heroes in the Irish nationalist pantheon as well as film footage of the 1920 Melbourne St Patrick's Day parade. The parade had been a carefully stage-managed event during which Archbishop Mannix was escorted by 14 Victoria Cross recipients on horseback followed by 10,000 ex-servicemen marching in uniform. The purpose was to turn the parade into a political statement: a graphic rebuttal of persistent allegations that Australian Catholics of Irish descent had been shirkers during the war and were disloyal.

Ireland will be Free angered Protestant loyalists who called for it to be banned. Tom Hoskins MLA wrote to the Chief Secretary a letter of complaint in which he referred to Joseph Partridge's appearance at the screenings: 'Amongst [the artists] is a Mr Partridge, brother of Miss Partridge, who sings a song, "That Dirty Rotten Flag", referring to the Union Jack'.[27] The allegation was denied, but Rev. Touchell told a meeting of the Protestant Federation he 'could not conceive anything that was more calculated to stir up the greatest hatred of the Union Jack and the administration of British justice'.[28] Grand Master Barton's criticism of the film was overtly sectarian declaring that Ireland 'will never be free while they have priests there. Clear the priests out of Ireland and you will clear away the trouble, and the people there will be all right. Clear the priests out of Australia and the people here will be all right'.[29] Joseph's association with such events no doubt reinforced Barton's and Touchell's jaundiced opinions of the young man, rendering it less likely they would permit him to take Bridget with him, which had been Charles Lawlor's main aim.

Apart from his opposition to using Joseph as a show puppy, Lawlor's handling of the finances was another source of concern to his enemies within the federation. The fund the federation had set

---

Australia, 1920-21', *Australasian Journal of Irish Studies*, Vol. 18, 2018, pp. 130-154.
[27] NSWPD, 22 September 1921, p. 644.
[28] *Lithgow Mercury*, 27 May 1921, p. 6.
[29] *Sydney Morning Herald*, 17 May 1921, p. 8.

up in September 1920 to raise money to send Joseph and Bridget home to Ireland had been severely reduced. More than £240 had been collected but because Joseph had declined to get a job, he was paid £2 per week out of the fund for his living expenses. In his letter to Bishop Dwyer Lawlor explained:

> I have asked and recommended to him again and again the need for at any rate trying to secure a position. He saw Minahan. P.J. promised to think it over. That's all. Now Joe says that he hardly likes to tie himself down to a position as he might be needed by Brigid.[30]

Lawlor also told the bishop he had heard from a priest that the new bishop of Bathurst, Dr Michael O'Farrell, had expressed the opinion that the Catholic Federation had prevented Joseph from getting his sister back even though she wanted to go with him. Despite the criticisms, Lawlor remained upbeat, adding: 'I can put up with Joe and things—rumours included—if it's for the good of the Cause.'

When Joseph and Bridget met in Mr Hill's office in Sydney on 4 August 1921, they spoke for two hours. They spoke again for another two-and-a-half hours at the Touchell house. On this latter occasion, Kitty O'Callaghan joined in, trying to persuade Bridget to leave with them. As with all previous attempts, Bridget refused.[31] As things stood at the end of August, it was difficult to ascertain definitively whether Joseph was right to believe that Bridget was under some form of duress or whether he was tone deaf to her expressed wish to remain with her Protestant friends. Joseph's next and most dramatic attempt would provide the answer.

But first there were things to attend to. After his August meetings with Bridget, he travelled to Wagga Wagga, where he stayed with Mr and Mrs J.J. Byrnes. He told the press that he journeyed to the town 'to fulfil certain commissions on her behalf'.[32] Presum-

---

[30] Letter 2 December 1920 Charles Lawlor to Bishop Dwyer, Wagga Wagga Diocesan Archives.
[31] *Daily Express*, 15 August 1921, p. 1.
[32] *Southern Cross*, 2 September 1921, p. 720 (Trove page: p. 12).

ably he carried messages to the sisters at Mount Erin for whom Bridget retained affection. On 19 September Joseph told the press he would be leaving Australia in November as it was useless for him to remain any longer in consequence of his sister's expression to him of her fear of molestation from Roman Catholic people. He added that if his sister wished to leave with him she would be very welcome to do so.[33] In the following weeks the two communicated through her solicitor with Bridget rejecting his offer.

Once again the matter might have ended there, but Joseph was nothing if not persistent. Towards the end of October, he wrote to Bridget informing her he had booked a passage on the S.S. *Ceramic*, which would be leaving Sydney in a few weeks. He requested that she return with him to Ireland. At that time Bridget also received a cable from her father advising her to go with Joseph. But she had made up her mind. On Tuesday 25 October, she replied to Joseph's letter, once more informing him she did not wish to go with him and reaffirming that she wanted to remain with Mr and Mrs Touchell.[34] Bridget's latest rebuff was not good enough for Joseph. He was convinced that, if he could get Bridget away from the overbearing influence of her Protestant guards and have her for a few days in the home and company of respectable Catholics, he could prove to her that the stories she had been told were untrue. She would then see sense and return to Ireland with him. That night he put into effect a plan he had hatched with his friend Dan O'Callaghan.

The Abduction of Bridget Partridge

At about 11 pm on Wednesday 26 October, Bridget was walking along Gray Street, Kogarah towards the Touchell house at the corner of Chapel Street. With her were Rev. Touchell, his wife, his sister, and his father aged 87, and a neighbour, Mr Ellard. They were returning home after attending a Home Mission Festival in the city. As they neared the front gate, the party was set upon by a gang of

---

[33] *Sun*, 19 September 1921, p. 7.
[34] *Daily Telegraph*, 27 October 1921, p. 5; *Sydney Morning Herald*, 27 October 1921, p. 7.

men. According to Rev. Touchell there were twenty of them; Joseph would later say there were nine. In any event, they were an overwhelming force. Mrs Touchell was knocked to the ground and Bridget snatched off her arm. Then, suddenly, a car pulled up and one of the men bundled Bridget inside and others climbed in after her. The car then raced away, with some of the assailants mounted on the running boards.

The car was driven by Edward Morris, a licensed hire-car driver employed by Australian Motor Services, who had been sent by his despatcher to the Catholic Club in Castlereagh Street, in the city, where he picked up Joseph Partridge and four other men. Morris was told, 'We are going out to Kogarah to get one of the men's sisters.' As they were driving along, one of the men mentioned Touchell's name. Morris then realised they were going to get Bridget Partridge. One of the men said, 'If [Touchell] will not let her come we will just take her.' When they arrived outside Touchell's house at about 8 pm Morris was told to park in Chapel Street where they waited. Joseph introduced himself and told Morris he had come to Kogarah to get his sister and take her away from the Touchell's control. After a long wait, one of the men instructed Morris to bring the car around the corner into Gray Street, whereupon two men on the footpath carried Bridget to the car and placed her in the back seat where Joseph was sitting. When the others climbed aboard, one of the men told Morris to drive to Ashfield.[35]

Rev. Touchell, having noted the car's registration number, ran to the nearby Kogarah police station to report the incident. The police immediately sent out an alert and began a search for Bridget Partridge and her abductors. The search was hampered by the fact that the registration number Touchell supplied was wrong. It proved to belong to a car located out of Sydney, leading Touchell to claim the number plate was a fake. However, according to Joseph there was no alteration to the number plate. This was true – Morris's registra-

---

[35] NSWPD, 17 November 1921, p. 1740.

tion was 32-402; Touchell told the police the number was 3204.³⁶ Interviewed by a reporter from *Truth*, Joseph would confirm that Morris was not in on the plan:

> The taxi was not a private one. It was hired off a public rank and the driver, in addition to being a Protestant, was a sport. I asked him if he was 'a tyke'. He said, 'No'. He knew what he was wanted for. He was paid for what he did and was dismissed.³⁷

On the drive to Ashfield, Bridget berated Joseph for having taken her the way he did. He told her there was no other way to get her alone as the Touchells would have prevented her from going with him. They drove to a house in Church Street, Ashfield known as 'Elleray', the residence of John Francis (Jack) Carlton and his wife Maria Agatha (Queenie) Carlton.³⁸ There Joseph said he would draw up a statutory declaration stating that Bridget had voluntarily forsaken the persons with whom she had recently lived and wished to go with her brother. He promised her she would not be interfered with or forced to go back to the convent. His idea was that, freed from the influence of the Touchells, she would willingly sign such a declaration which he would then provide to the press. He wrote out the declaration and she signed it in the presence of Mr Carlton, a justice of the peace, who witnessed her signature. Carlton was an engineer, a leading Catholic and a member of the Catholic Federation. Bridget would later claim, 'I did not sign willingly but thought discretion the better part of valour'.³⁹ According to Joseph, there was no duress. He told a reporter for *Truth* that he had invited her to dictate any conditions she required in the declaration and she signed it willingly after saying she was satisfied with what he had written.⁴⁰

---

36 *Daily Advertiser*, 28 October 1921, p. 2.
37 *Truth*, 30 October 1921, p. 7.
38 *Daily Telegraph*, 16 November 1921, p. 8; https://www.wikitree.com/wiki/Carlton-2151.
39 Ibid.
40 *Truth*, 30 October 1921, p. 7.

As Bridget was too agitated to sleep, the two siblings spent the rest of the night talking. In his interview with *Truth*, Joseph said that Bridget had told him that her Protestant friends had warned her that if the Jesuits ordered him to murder her, he would not dare disobey. She had also said that one of those responsible for the litigation against Bishop Dwyer had upbraided her for having let the side down during the trial. He told the reporter he had reassured her that he did not want her to return to the convent, that nobody wished to force her to go back, and that no convent would want to take her, anyway. He also claimed they had agreed to cancel his passage on the *Ceramic* and to travel home together in the spring to avoid the Irish winter: 'I told her I would do anything she liked'.[41] According to Bridget, Joseph refused to allow her to ring Mrs Touchell to let her know she was all right. She claimed he also told her that all the men in the car carried arms and that they had been watching the Touchell house for weeks and the whole business had been carefully planned.[42] Joseph would deny that his men were armed or that he told her they were.[43]

Whatever was said during their conversation, Joseph must have been satisfied that he had done all he could to bring Bridget back into the fold, for the next morning he agreed that she could go into the city. He later confided to Bishop Dwyer:

> She wanted to get out into the air, she said. We all suspected that she wanted to get away. I told her that so long as we had proved to her by talking to her, that our Church or our Catholic people had no spite against her, then, if she still wanted to get back to her so-called friends, she could go, for I wouldn't try to stop her. We could have prevented her from going out, but that would not have cured her. She can never say, nor can non-Catholics say now, that we Catholics forced her in any way.[44]

---

[41] *Truth*, 30 October 1921, p. 7.
[42] *Sun*, 15 November 1921, p. 7
[43] Ibid.
[44] Letter 2 November 1921 Joseph Partridge to Bishop Dwyer, Wagga Wagga Diocesan Archives.

According to Joseph, Bridget had said she wanted to visit the Botanic Gardens. According to Bridget, she had told him she wanted to do some shopping, but only as a pretext to enable her to pass a note to a shop assistant requesting the police be called. In the morning, Bridget and Joseph walked up and down the street in front of the house talking until Dan and Kitty O'Callaghan arrived. It was agreed that Joseph would remain behind to have a rest while Bridget and Dan would go into town and Kitty would return home. They would all meet up later in the Botanic Gardens and perhaps take an excursion up the Parramatta River.

Accompanied by Dan, Bridget caught the tram into the city and they walked up Hunter Street towards Phillip Street, on the corner of which stood police headquarters. Shortly before 11 am, Bridget was spotted in the street by Mr T.H. Roach of Burwood, a member of the LOI known to Bridget, who then followed the pair. When they stopped to buy a drink at a fruit shop, Roach, who had signalled to Bridget he recognised her, ducked into the police station and informed the detectives. A few minutes later, as Bridget and Dan were walking along Macquarie Street towards the Botanic Gardens, a voice from behind called Bridget's name. When the couple stopped and turned, Roach, accompanied by Detective Inspector Arthur Leary and Detective Sergeant Louis Pether, approached. Bridget said to Roach, 'For God's sake, don't leave me.' He replied, 'I won't. It's all right now, you are with friends.' At this point the detectives stepped in and after a few questions, Bridget said, 'I want protection. I was taken away forcibly last night.' The detectives then invited the pair to accompany them to headquarters. At the station, 59-year-old Superintendent William Bannan, head of the Criminal Investigations Division (CID), interviewed Bridget in the presence of her solicitor, Mr William Hill, who had been summoned by a phone call.

What then followed was extraordinary and unimaginable in the present day. Instead of detaining O'Callaghan and sending police to arrest Joseph, Superintendent Bannan convened a conference of interested parties. Over the next couple of hours 'the usual suspects' began arriving at police headquarters: Rev. and Mrs Touchell, Grand Master Barton, Tom Hoskins MLA and two other Orangemen, Mr Ken Cottle and Rev. Edward Crawford. They were followed by Joseph Partridge, who arrived shortly before 1.30 pm. He was accompanied by Dan O'Callaghan, who, instead of being detained, had been sent to find Joseph, and two of his friends.[45] Another solicitor was also in attendance. This was J.J. Carroll, a leading Catholic lawyer and member of the Catholic Federation. Given the federation's involvement in the affair, it is likely that Charles Lawlor had asked him to attend. Mr Peter Gallagher, private secretary to Attorney General McTiernan was also there.

When all had assembled, they were ushered into a large office in which there was a long rectangular table. Bridget's friends sat on one side of the table, while Joseph and his friends sat on the other. Members of the press were allowed in and they assembled at the far end of the room. The last to enter was Bridget Partridge, who sat in a chair near the head of the table. Superintendent Bannan stood next to her. Irish-born William Patrick Bannan had served in the Royal Irish Constabulary before emigrating to New Zealand and then Australia, where he joined the New South Wales police force in 1886. He was well regarded and rose through the ranks to head the CID. He was flanked by several other police officials, including Detective Sergeant Farley, who had arrested Bridget at the Touchell house in August 1920. The fact that Bannan was Irish and a Protestant might have calmed the atmosphere sufficiently to enable him to assume the role of mediator. In a rather lyrical description of the scene the reporter for the *Daily Telegraph* observed: 'Mr Partridge fought for his sister. He carried a sworn declaration to help his cause. But others also claimed her. And the Solomon who had to find a way out was Mr Bannan'.[46]

Judging by Bannan's opening words, the idea of a conference

---

[45] *Sun*, 27 October 1921, p. 7.
[46] *Daily Telegraph*, 28 October 1921, p. 5.

had been approved at the highest level of the police force. Turning to Bridget, he said slowly and deliberately,

> I represent the Inspector General of Police. It is our duty to give you all the protection the law entitles you to. There is your brother on one side with a solicitor who claims to represent you, on the other side is Mr Hill, your solicitor. I want you to understand clearly that you can elect to go with whoever you like and you can choose wherever you wish to go.

After a short pause, Bridget, who had been sitting with her hands folded in her lap and her gaze fixed on the wall in front of her, gulped, wrung her hands nervously, and said in a soft voice,

> I wish to go with Mr. Hill and Mr and Mrs Touchell. I am not going back to the Catholic Church. I am not going back to my brother. It shows plainly they are not our friends. I don't want any more worry. I've had quite enough. And I ask God to forgive them for their treatment of me.

According to Barton's account of the conference, 'There was a dramatic pause. Mr Joseph Partridge seemed stunned'.[47] Joseph then produced the statutory declaration and said,

> 'But this is your statement you signed last night.'
> Bridget replied, 'It is not my statement. You wrote it.'
> Mr Hill said, 'Do you wish to go back to your brother?'
> Bridget turned to face her brother and said, 'No.'

The meeting over, Joseph and O'Callaghan were allowed to leave the station. Bridget and the Touchells went into an adjoining room, where they remained a while before being smuggled out of the building to a waiting car, disappointing the large crowd of spectators who had gathered outside the headquarters building to get a glimpse of Miss Partridge.[48]

In Sydney and across the country the newspapers that morning

---

[47] *Watchman*, 3 November 1921, p. 5.
[48] *Daily Advertiser*, 28 October 1921, p. 2.

had been full of the news of the abduction. Even before Bridget had been located it was mentioned in parliament. At 2.36 that morning, during the adjournment debate, Mr Hoskins had called on the government to see that every effort was made to find the people who had taken part in the kidnapping of ex-Sister Liguori and to secure her freedom.[49] Later in the day, Sir Thomas Henley also raised the matter in parliament, asking the premier what action he proposed to take in bringing to justice those 'ruffians and criminals' who assaulted Rev. Touchell and kidnapped Sister Liguori. The premier replied that he considered it a very serious matter and had asked the police for a report.[50] Most of the press coverage told the story from the Touchell's point of view, with the *Daily Telegraph* strongly supportive of their interest. Only *Truth* carried an interview with Joseph. In that interview he said:

> I want everybody to understand that I have done my duty as a brother to Bridget. She has received word from home to go home with me. I am going back to Ireland on November 15 by the *Ceramic* with or without her. I have done all I intend doing as far as trying to speak or have any more intercourse with my sister. If she wishes to become a Congregationalist she can please herself and they are welcome to her.[51]

The abduction provided militant Protestants with retrospective validation of their claims that ever since Sister Liguori left her convent she had been hunted by Catholics who wanted to return her to her convent prison. It provided an ideal opportunity to intensify their propaganda campaign against the Catholic church. The chief secretary of the Protestant Federation, Mr W. Wallace, issued a statement:

> The spirit of Rome is clearly illustrated by the forcible seizure of Miss Partridge (ex-Sister Liguori) at Kogarah by the Pope's Irish. It is a question if any ex-Roman Catho-

---

[49] NSWPD, 26 October 1921, p. 1152; *Daily Telegraph*, 27 October 1921, p. 5.
[50] NSWPD, 27 October 1921, p. 1179; *Sun*, 27 October 1921, p. 7.
[51] *Truth*, 30 October 1921, p. 7.

lic ever escaped without being persecuted and boycotted to some extent. Many have suffered bodily injury. Others have been burned out of house and home simply because they turned Protestant. Practically every ex-priest—and there are a good number of them—has been slandered, threatened, mobbed, and beaten in some way or other.[52]

Sir Thomas Henley wrote to the press:

> The kidnapping by violence of ex-Sister Liguori by a gang said to be Roman Catholic ruffians, who are clearly in a secret service, and are doing the dirty work of a foreign disloyal priesthood, means for Australia a good deal more than the assault upon the Rev. Mr Touchell's party and the capturing of that innocent girl. ... The kidnapping of Miss Partridge is the extremists' challenge in the Roman Catholic Church to the right to introduce into Australia all the frightful crimes she is known to be guilty of in Ireland and other parts of the world. ... In taking by force ex-Sister Liguori, the actors for the Romish Church in Australia removed the mask.[53]

Rev. Touchell claimed that before the events of Wednesday night, he had received a warning from 'a Romanist friend' that an attempt would shortly be made to secure Miss Partridge. He was told that a large sum of money was to be paid to those who were about to undertake the task.[54]

Initially Mr Hill had requested the police to delay any investigation of the matter so he could consult his clients. The following Monday, accompanied by Rev. Touchell and Mr Barton, he called on Inspector General Mitchell and requested a thorough investigation be made and that appropriate action be taken. When Mitchell asked them if they desired any particular officer to lead the investigation, Hill nominated Detective Sergeant Farley. That day Farley commenced his inquiry. After taking statements from

---

[52] *Watchman*, 3 November 1921, p. 2.
[53] Ibid.
[54] Ibid., p. 5.

those involved, Farley submitted them to the crown solicitor, who advised that the offence disclosed by the statements was one of riot, a charge, which, if proved, carried a maximum penalty of £5. Neither kidnapping (the term most frequently used by the press) nor abduction were mentioned in the advice. The Inspector General decided not to prosecute. On 14 November he wrote to Mr Hill advising him of the nature of the offence mentioned by the crown solicitor and added:

> As, however, the occurrence took place several weeks ago and that the evidence of identification, except against Joseph Partridge, is not at present of a conclusive character, it is not intended to institute police proceedings. This decision is also guided by the manifest reluctance on the part of Miss Partridge to give evidence against her brother.[55]

A censure motion in Parliament

Bridget and her supporters were angered by the news. In a letter to the *Daily Telegraph*, Rev. Touchell complained, 'Clearly, here is a concrete case of condoning lawlessness in the interests of sectarianism, which may yet lead to an outbreak of very serious trouble in this state'.[56] Bridget told a reporter for the *Telegraph*, 'There is sufficient evidence in my opinion for the police to take action and I am annoyed that they have not done so. I feel insecure from my enemies and I never go out alone'.[57] At a Protestant rally at Kogarah Congregational Hall on 17 November, William Bagnall MLA referred to the 'impudence or arrogance of the government' and called the assailants of Miss Partridge 'a gang of hoodlums'. He predicted some sinister influence at work and urged Protestants to keep their powder dry, 'for the great offensive has only

---

[55] Report of the Inspector General of Police to the Chief Secretary dated 17 November 1921, quoted in NSWPD 17 November 1921, pp. 1732-1733.
[56] *Daily Telegraph*, 16 November 1921, p. 8.
[57] Ibid.

commenced'.⁵⁸ Sir Thomas Henley told a meeting at Leichhardt, 'The Dooley government had shown by its inaction in the recent kidnapping that the influence of the Roman church was controlling it'.⁵⁹

In the eyes of Henley and other militant Protestants, the insidious influence of Rome had recently increased following the death on 5 October 1921 of Premier John Storey, a Presbyterian. His replacement as Labor leader and premier was James Dooley, a Catholic. Not content to confine the protests to public meetings and the press, the leader of the opposition in the New South Wales parliament, Sir George Fuller, moved against the government a censure motion:

> That the failure of the government to bring to justice the persons involved in the assault upon miss Partridge and others, and the subsequent abduction of Miss Partridge, constitutes a flagrant violation of its trust and is deserving of the censure of this house.

A censure motion is a parliamentary procedure used only in the most serious cases of alleged government malfeasance. All other parliamentary business in the chamber is suspended until the motion is dealt with. That the Sister Liguori affair had been elevated to being the subject of such a motion indicates how deeply sectarianism had infected the state's politics.

The decision not to prosecute had been taken by the inspector general in the exercise of his discretion. It was not a government decision to make. Unless the opposition could show that the government had put pressure on the inspector general and had thereby influenced his decision, the censure motion was without foundation. Fuller, despite denying any sectarian intent in bringing the motion, produced no such evidence. Rather he insinuated that 'there is some sinister and unseen force behind all this' and waxed lyrical about the citizen's right to liberty. This led Premier James

---

⁵⁸ *Daily Telegraph*, 18 November 1921, p. 5.
⁵⁹ *Watchman*, 24 November 1921, p. 5.

Dooley to congratulate the opposition leader on his lecture but suggesting it was more appropriate for a School of Arts debating society than a busy parliament. He then said:

> With all due respect to the leader of the Opposition I am inclined to think that this case has been selected to a great extent because of the history of this unfortunate woman who—and I say it emphatically and deliberately—has been used and made a tool of by certain people, in order to inculcate the prejudices and bitternesses of hundreds of years ago.[60]

The debate was cut short when a Labor member successfully moved that the motion be put. That having been agreed to, the censure motion was put and it was lost 34 votes to 44, with three opposition members siding with the government. *Truth* commented that it was fortunate that the debate was terminated as Sir Thomas Henley was to speak next and had he taken the floor 'there would have been a Donnybrook fair'.[61]

The debate on the censure motion took place on 17 November, two days after Joseph Partridge had left Sydney. He had departed at 4 pm on the S.S. *Ceramic* farewelled by a large gathering of friends who serenaded him with Irish songs.[62] No doubt many on both sides of the Sister Liguori divide breathed a sigh of relief when it was confirmed he had gone.

The End of the Affair

After almost 16 months of drama that had begun with a squabble over a broom, the Sister Liguori affair had finally come to an end. Over the next few months, Catholics continued to hold testimonials celebrating Bishop Dwyer's gallant defence of Catholicism while Protestants continued to hold rallies attacking the evils of the convent system as exemplified by the mistreatment of Sister Liguori. But apart from the occasional rumour that Bridget Partridge had escaped from the Touchells or had been abducted again, the citi-

---

[60] NSWPD, 17 November 1921, pp. 1724-1742.
[61] *Truth*, 20 November 1921, p. 1.
[62] *Evening News*, 16 November 1921, p. 3.

zens of New South Wales were relieved to be able to put the affair behind them.[63]

The end of the Sister Liguori affair did not mark the end of sectarianism in New South Wales or its influence on the state's politics. Although the censure motion was doomed to fail because of Labor's majority, albeit a thin one, it was not without its purpose. In modern political parlance we would call it 'throwing red meat to the base'. Sir George Fuller was well aware that an election was imminent, even though it was not due until 1923. Labor's hold on government was precarious, as it depended on Daniel Levy, a member of the Nationalist party, continuing to hold the position of Speaker. Consequently, James Dooley was widely expected to call an early election in the hope of improving the party's position.

The election was eventually called for 25 March 1922. But instead of Labor increasing its majority, it was heavily defeated. In contrast to 1920, the campaign was bitterly sectarian and the coalition's base responded accordingly. The *Methodist*, after recounting how the Roman Catholic church had effectively captured the Labor Party and dominated the public service, urged, 'It is high time the Protestant electors woke up'.[64] The irony is that the Labor Party comprised a mix of Catholics, Protestants, and secularists with most of its Catholic members being non-religious. The Nationalist and Progressive parties, on the other hand, contained no Catholics with the only non-Protestant being a Jew, Daniel Levy, who had enabled Labor to govern by holding the speakership. And, as we have seen, many of the coalition's Protestant members were strongly militant. The Protestant Federation and the Orange lodges exhorted the people to elect Protestant candidates and they even trotted out Bridget Partridge to urge electors to vote for the champions of liberty.[65] The Catholic Federation once more ran candidates under the banner

---

[63] *Catholic Press*, 26 January 1922, p. 25; *Watchman*, 4 May 1922, p. 5; *Newcastle Sun*, 11 May 1922, p. 5.

[64] *Methodist*, 25 March 1922, p. 1.

[65] *Sydney Morning Herald*, 23 March 1922, p. 11; *Truth*, 2 April 1922, p. 1.

of the Democratic Party. This time it achieved some success. Its candidate in the electorate of the Eastern Suburbs, Dr Cyril Fallon, won a seat.

The Nationalist-Progressive coalition government under Sir George Fuller was not long in office before it confirmed in the minds of many Catholics that the rhetoric of the election campaign would be reflected in government policy. It appointed to the Legislative Council former Grand Master James Robinson, who started his parliamentary career with a bitter sectarian speech denouncing Catholics, their churches, and their schools. He also made a strong attack on Bishop Dwyer and resurrected the sorry saga of the Liguori affair.[66] Under a headline sub-titled "Persecution Begins", the *Catholic Press* commented on a report in the *Daily Telegraph* that the Government would introduce legislation in relation to Catholic marriage laws:

> It looks as if Premier Fuller and his Orange Ministry are about to begin a persecution of Catholics. We have been threatened with war upon Catholic orphans, and with the inspection, if not the suppression of convents, and now the Government are contemplating the regulation of Catholic marriages.[67]

In November 1923 the government introduced the *Marriage Amendment Bill (No. 2)*, commonly referred to as the Ne Temere Bill. *Ne Temere* was the name of a decree issued by Pope Pius X that came into force in 1908, which made it a condition of the validity of a marriage to which a Catholic was a party that the marriage be contracted before a priest and two witnesses. In other words, a mixed marriage contracted before a Protestant minister or a registrar would be regarded as null and void by the Catholic church. Although *Ne Temere* had no effect on the civil recognition of such marriages, militant Protestants regarded it as an unwarranted

---

[66] *Daily Standard*, 5 July 1922, p. 5.
[67] *Catholic Press*, 18 May 1922, p. 21.

priestly interference with domestic harmony evidencing Rome's desire to dominate Australian society. It became a priority issue for militant Protestants that legislation be enacted to outlaw compliance with the *Ne Temere* decree. The bill was introduced by Thomas Ley, the Minister for Justice, who was one of its most fervent supporters. This 'virulently sectarian' dispenser of harsh justice would gain even greater notoriety in 1947 when he was convicted of murder.[68] The proposed legislation made it an offence punishable by fine and imprisonment to allege 'expressly or by implication, that any persons lawfully married are not truly and sufficiently married'. The bill passed through the lower house but was defeated in the Legislative Council when Catholic and moderate Protestant members combined to defeat it.[69]

The *Ne Temere* affair marked the low point of the era of rabid sectarianism that had divided the people of New South Wales for a decade or more. But it also signalled its demise. One by one the issues that had caused the level of sectarianism to rise from chronic to acute a decade and a half before began to fall away. The establishment in 1922 of the Irish Free State as a dominion within the British Empire resolved the Irish question so far as the Australian Irish were concerned, thus eliminating Protestant claims of Irish Catholic disloyalty. In 1924 the Catholic church, having learned from the election of the Fuller government the downside of engaging in sectarian politics, dismantled the Catholic Federation and shelved its demand for state aid for Catholic schools, not to be reactivated in any significant way for four decades. With the passing of Irish self-government, state aid, and empire loyalty as issues dividing the

---

[68] The description 'virulently sectarian' is taken from Ley's entry in the *Australian Dictionary of Biography*. A more detailed account of his political and criminal career and the bizarre story of his part in the 'Chalkpit Murder' is contained in Dan Morgan, *The Minister for Murder*, Hutchinson of Australia, Richmond, Vic., 1979.

[69] Brigid Moore, 'Sectarianism in NSW: The Ne Temere Legislation 1924-1925', *Journal of the Australian Catholic Historical Society*, Vol. 9, No. 1, 1987, pp. 3-15.

Australian people along ethno-religious lines, the rancour between Catholics and Protestants, demonstrated most graphically during the Sister Liguori affair, began to subside. Although sectarianism did not disappear—some say it still exists today—it no longer dominated social and political discourse in the way it did in the first quarter of the twentieth century.

10
Conclusion

This book, which is the first full-length study of the Sister Liguori affair, does not claim to be the last word on the subject. Others will see it through a different lens, such as Amanda Bromfield, who told the Australian Broadcasting Corporation that Bridget's story is profoundly engaging as a feminist parable. One of the reasons the story continues to be told a century after Sister Liguori fled her convent is because it is multi-faceted and open to many interpretations.

To me, as an historian of sectarianism in early twentieth-century Australia, the Sister Liguori affair is essentially a story of a desperately unhappy Catholic nun who felt trapped in her surroundings and who in a moment of panic took flight and sought refuge among Protestant strangers who exploited her situation for their own ends. The involvement of the Loyal Orange Institution and the Protestant Federation provoked militant Catholics in the Catholic Federation to intervene, purportedly on her behalf but in reality to defend the church and its convent system from attack by militant Protestants. The escalation of the personal crisis of one individual into a political and ethno-religious conflict that excited the press and parliament in the nation's largest state for more than fifteen months was testimony to the pernicious influence of sectarianism in early twentieth-century Australia.

An historian of the Presentation sisters at Wagga Wagga provides another insight into why the affair got out of hand:

> Hidden by their Enclosure, the Sisters remained a mystery to most, and to some, they were a group involved in superstitious practices. The unknown, coupled with what some considered the unnatural lifestyle of the enclosed religious,

in this case, bred fear and suspicion in the minds of the ordinary citizens. Bizarre customs were attributed to the Sisters, and in the Ligouri Case [sic], as in other incidents, melodramatic newspaper accounts played upon the credibility and ignorance of the populace.[1]

At many points along the way, the controversy, which began with an argument over a broom, could have been avoided or minimised. Things might have been different had Sister Liguori not panicked when she formed the mistaken impression she was about to be murdered; had the Thompsons not lied to the police and the search parties; had Sister Liguori not been made to vanish when those responsible for her welfare held grave concerns for her health and safety; had Grand Master Barton not intervened; had Bishop Dwyer spoken to Dr Eric Tivey and informed him of Sister Liguori's delusion of which he was unaware or to Archdeacon Joseph Pike on a clergyman-to-clergyman basis; had Barton not pressured Bridget Partridge into suing her bishop; had Joseph been less impetuous and more accepting of Bridget's wish to remain with the Touchells; had sectarian warriors refrained from using Bridget's plight as a brickbat with which to beat their opponents; had MPs refrained from using Bridget's plight to score political points; etc., etc., etc. Justice Ferguson summed it up well when he said, 'It is a very unfortunate thing for the plaintiff that at that time she did not meet somebody who would have shown a little common horse-sense.'

For the people of Wagga Wagga and indeed the country as a whole the Sister Liguori affair was a cathartic experience stretching far beyond its genesis in the argument over the broom. At its peak it called into question the way in which the Catholic church operated its vast network of convents. Ironically, recent media reports and official inquiries have exposed malfeasance in several institutions run by orders of nuns both in Australia and overseas. These reports have mostly concerned Magdalen laundries, orphanages,

---

[1] Noela M. Fox, *In this Land: A History of the Presentation Sisters, Wagga Wagga*, The Trustees of the Presentation Sisters Wagga, New South Wales, Wagga Wagga (NSW), 2003, p. 179.

and industrial schools rather than convents such as Mount Erin. So, it is tangential to the present discussion. Nevertheless, because there are points of crossover, particularly the role of sectarianism in drowning out the individual's cry for help, I have addressed the subject in the Appendix.

During the Sister Liguori affair, and in particular during the hearing in the Supreme Court, the Mount Erin convent and Bishop Dwyer came under close scrutiny. Both emerged with their reputations intact, as Justice Ferguson's summing up to the jury makes clear. That is not to say they were without fault. It does seem harsh that Sister Liguori was demoted from a teaching role to that of a domestic servant because she was unable to control a class of boys, particularly when the evidence suggests the children were fond of her. However, we do not have sufficient information regarding the whole of her teaching record to make a definitive judgment on that score. Having regard to what emerged at the trial, her domestic duties were not particularly onerous and, in her evidence, Bridget spoke of the kindness of the sisters, with a few minor exceptions. Moreover, Mother Stanislaus seems to have adopted a pastoral approach to the young nun. Nevertheless, it appears she might not have detected soon enough how miserable she had become. So miserable that the trivial incident of the broom led her to walk out of the convent in contravention of the rules. But in a convent with almost 80 nuns and 90 resident boarders to look after, it would be remarkable if some problems did not escape the mother superior's full attention.

The LOI and elements of the press were quick to portray Bishop Dwyer as the villain in the piece. Even after he won the court case, they used the jury's mixed verdict to claim vindication of their condemnation of him. Yet, as explained in chapter 9, the verdict is perfectly explicable and provides exoneration of the bishop's motivation in laying the information that led to Bridget Partridge's arrest. While it is arguable he should have spoken to Dr Tivey and to Archdeacon Pike in an endeavour to do all that was reasonably possible before putting in train the legal processes of the *Lunacy Act*, in the end it might not have made any difference. Yes, Dr Tivey might have changed his mind if he had been given all the relevant facts, including Sister Liguori's belief that an attempt had been made to murder her. But at the trial, when confronted with those facts, he stuck to his opinion as to her sanity. Perhaps at an earlier stage, when not under public gaze, he might have been more flexible. But that is speculation. Similarly, as regards Bishop Dwyer's refusal to speak with Archdeacon Pike. As senior clergymen, both men had the common experience of being responsible for those in their care, particularly those who were vulnerable. Perhaps if Bishop Dwyer had gone to him and said, 'Help me out. Tell me what's happening. I'm responsible for this young woman,' Pike might have been willing to set his mind at rest. But, again, that is mere speculation. At that stage, Grand Master Barton was calling the shots and he had bigger fish to fry. Even if Dwyer had spoken to Tivey and Pike but was still in the dark concerning Sister Liguori's whereabouts and welfare, his options would have been the same as they were before: to turn to the law or do nothing. Had he done nothing he would rightly have been criticised for dereliction of his duty of care to Sister Liguori.

One might be tempted to say that Sister Liguori was the author of her own misfortune in not telling Mother Stanislaus that she believed she had lost her vocation, in not seeking dispensation from her vows in the regular way, in overreacting to the incident with the broom, in panicking over the treatment she received on returning to the convent after her first flight, in agreeing to vanish without trace when those responsible for her care needed to know she was safe and well, and in allowing herself to be used for propaganda purposes by the militant Protestants into whose hands she had found herself. But, even taking those facts into account, it would be unfair to conclude that the debacle that followed was her fault. It was the officious intervention of third parties, the LOI and the Catholic Federation, that transformed Sister Liguori's personal crisis into a public one. It would have taken a much more streetwise person than Bridget Partridge to resist the gaslighting that was inflicted on her in the months she was under the control of Barton and the Touchells. Although her public utterances indicate she absorbed many of the LOI's talking points on the evils of Roman Catholicism, she resisted sufficiently to eschew criticism of the sisters at Mount Erin convent.

And what do we say about Joseph? Initially, Joseph was seen by all as the white knight come to solve the problem. Bridget had delayed making decisions about her future until his arrival. The Catholic Federation saw him as the person who would rescue her from the 'heretics'. The LOI hoped he would join them in condemning the bishop and the convent for mistreating his sister. Hence the manoeuvring to get to him first. In that regard, the Catholics were better prepared in the timing of their interception but the LOI still held the high cards in terms of controlling his access to Bridget. Once it became clear Joseph did not buy into the LOI's narrative he was cut off from contact with his sister. One can admire him for his persistence thereafter, but he was no match for the wily pair of Barton and Touchell, and his impetuosity played into their hands. But it needs to be remembered he was only 23 with limited life experience, whereas the 54-year-old Barton and the 51-year-old Touchell possessed well-honed skills in dealing with people and the press. Yet, more intriguing is Joseph's personal relationship with Bridget.

How was it possible that they could each give such conflicting accounts of their conversations, which sometimes lasted many hours, often in private? Did Bridget say one thing to her brother and another to Barton, the Touchells, and the public? Did Joseph misunderstand what Bridget was telling him? Did Joseph falsify his accounts of their conversations? Did Barton pressure her to say and write the things she did? Perhaps there is a bit of each involved. A common defence mechanism for vulnerable people is to tell their listeners what they think the listeners want to hear. Also, it is common for people emotionally invested in a situation to hear what they want to hear.

Another consideration is that Joseph seems to have enjoyed himself while he was in Australia and appeared less than anxious to return home to his wife in Ireland. After all, the Catholic Federation was providing him with free board plus living expenses and he was free to show off his musical talents to adoring Irish-Australian audiences. While it was the LOI's involvement in the affair that prompted the Catholic Federation to intervene, it was Joseph's continued pursuit of his sister that kept the federation engaged and the sectarian conflict simmering. The federation continued to back him in the hope he would bring Bridget back into the fold, even to the extent of condoning her botched abduction. Bishop Dwyer, too, seems to have backed Joseph when it might have been wiser to counsel him to abandon his pursuit, which Joseph eventually did but only after he had caused considerable mayhem.

Looking back more than 100 years, it is difficult for us living in a largely secular world to understand what the fuss was all about and why the Sister Liguori story has continued over decades to fascinate the public imagination. To this author, who has researched the affair for more than a quarter century, the answer lies in the fact that it is more than just an episode in Australia's political and religious history. It is a universal story, dating back at least to the Mycenaean age with the saga of Helen of Troy popularised by Homer. We have seen it played out in our own times, most spectacularly in 2005 with the severely brain-damaged Terri Schiavo over her 'right to die' and in 2000 with Elián González, a five-year-old Cuban refugee, over his repatriation to Cuba.[2] It is a tale in which powerful adversaries pull at a hapless victim like children fighting over a rag doll, in a struggle they frame in Manichean terms, while at the same time proclaiming their motivation is the individual's best interests.

---

[2] 'Thousands of Cuban Mothers Demonstrate for Boy's Return', *New York Times*, 15 January 2000; 'Schiavo's Case May Reshape American Law', *New York Times*, 1 April 2005.

Epilogue

After more than 15 months at the centre of one of the most bitter episodes in Australia's long sectarian history, Bridget Partridge had at last found the settled life for which she had been searching ever since her dramatic departure from the convent at Mount Erin that dreary Saturday afternoon in July 1920. By the end of 1921 the Sister Liguori affair had ceased to excite public attention and Bridget was able to live the remaining 45 years of her life relatively quietly as a member of the Touchell household. Whenever Rev. Touchell's work required him to change districts, Bridget travelled with them: to Cessnock, Cronulla, and finally Hurstville.

That is not to say that her life after the affair was trouble free. Sadly, in January 1939 Bridget returned to the Darlinghurst Reception House, where, in an echo of her visit there in August 1920, the Lunacy Court remanded her for a week for medical examination. Dr John McGeorge, a well-known psychiatrist, believed her condition to be serious. He informed the court, 'I saw the patient at the Royal Prince Alfred Hospital and I consider her to be insane. She needs medical treatment.' Rev. William Touchell told the court:

> There has been a gradual development towards mental embarrassment. This has culminated in the past three weeks, when she became so sick that we lost control of her. She became obsessed with delusions and she made complaints of persecution by her neighbours. For some years her case might be described as psychopathic. She has been causing the neighbours trouble.[1]

Bridget was eventually allowed to return to the Touchell home. On 21 January 1954 Rev. Touchell died aged 84. Thereafter, Bridget continued living with Laura Touchell. She received a brief return to fame when in August 1954 *People* magazine ran a six-page fea-

---
[1] *Daily Telegraph*, 14 January 1939, p. 2; *Truth*, 22 January 1939, p. 26.

ture article on the two women. The article described 63-year-old Bridget as 'a grey-haired, plump, rubicund, shy, silent woman who each day plods around the Sydney suburb of Hurstville, carrying her shopping in a brown cardboard suitcase'. Mrs Touchell was then 82. They were firm friends, with Bridget calling Mrs Touchell 'Mike' and Mrs Touchell calling Bridget 'Paddy' or 'Pat'. Bridget spent her days drawing, painting in watercolours, writing simple short stories, and playing the piano – mostly sacred pieces. She was nervous about going out, ever fearful of being kidnapped, and only did so to do the shopping.

Two years after the article was published, a former student at Mount Erin primary school, Mrs Sheila Tearle, who was living in Hurstville, saw a copy of it in the library.[2] Born in Victoria in 1911, Sheila Byrne and her family had moved to Wagga Wagga in 1917. When Sister Liguori was on playground duty, young Sheila used to bring her flowers. After reading the *People* article, which contained contemporary photographs of Bridget, Mrs Tearle would sometimes see her at the local shops. One day they ran into each other in the bank and Bridget asked, 'Where did I know you?' Mrs Tearle replied, 'Wagga'. Bridget asked, 'In the playground?' and Mrs Tearle said it was. They then began to meet up in the street and chat about the old days, with Bridget inquiring about several of the nuns she had known. Soon after, Father Peter Morrissey, the curate from 1955 to 1957 at St Michael's Catholic church, Hurstville, visited Bridget at Mrs Tearle's suggestion. He recalled:

> Plump little Bridget sat meekly with her knitting, as nun-like as ever, tired old eyes behind small steel-framed spectacles, rosary beads in her lap, and we spoke of generalities. The two or three rooms in view reminded me of Dickens' Miss Faversham and her preservation of the remnants of her life's tragedy. The tables and other surfaces were littered

---

[2] Sheila Tearle wrote a lengthy memorandum dated 18 November 1991 relating her relationship with Bridget Partridge (Maureen McKeown Papers). A shorter account is in Sheila Tearle, 'I Remember Sister Liguori', *Footprints*, April 1977, pp. 9-10.

with the newspapers of thirty-five years ago, the family still reliving, apparently, the bitter drama of 1921's court case in Wagga. Mrs. Touchell said she'd leave us alone for a while. At my ever-tactful invitation, Bridget said yes, she would like to have Confession and Holy Communion, but at that moment Mrs. Touchell sang out from the kitchen telling 'Pat' not to take any notice of me, and I was over-ruled.[3]

That was his one and only visit to their home. However, Father Thomas Dunlea, parish priest at Hurstville from 1952 to 1968, also visited the two women. Bridget told Mrs Tearle they liked him because he made them laugh.

In late 1962, when Mrs Touchell was in her 90s, the two women were admitted to North Ryde hospital as they were finding it difficult to look after themselves. They were then transferred to Rydalmere Psychiatric Hospital, more than 20 kilometres from their Hurstville home. Father Dunlea arranged for news of the move to be sent to Joseph Partridge, who wrote a lengthy letter to the priest thanking him for his goodness in the matter and providing a potted history of the Sister Liguori affair. He admitted to having kidnapped Bridget, adding that he had said goodbye to her after she had refused to go with him. But after more than 40 years, it seems Joseph had not given up on his hope she would return to the church:

> Since [the kidnapping], the Touchell's have kept her filled with this nonsense of fearing to speak to anyone or to go into a Catholic Church. ... To sum up as far as I can judge my own sister, she is innocent in the sight of God, I believe, of any wrong. But she was not at the time of the incident in Wagga capable of forming a sensible judgment. I think that is quite clear. Her fears at the time and for the past 40 years have been kept alive and I doubt if she is more capable today of a sound judgment. BUT she is not insane and never was. Now I am delighted to hear she has been in touch with you, Father. ... Please God she is coming around. And, of course, I need not say that you have my full support in

---

[3] *Newsletter of the Australian Catholic Historical Society*, Vol. 25, No. 3, August 2012, p. 3.

anything you will have the goodness to do to get her away from the evil influences that surround her.[4]

On 9 September 1963 Mrs Touchell died aged 92, leaving Bridget all alone. Seeing the death notice in the newspaper, Mrs Tearle decided to visit Bridget at Rydalmere. From then on she did so regularly. On one occasion she took Father Dunlea and another priest, Father Edward Wilkinson. Wilkinson had just returned from Ireland and had brought back for Bridget a letter from her brother and her girlhood prayer book. The visitors sat with Bridget in the garden while Mrs Tearle read the letter to her. Among other things Joseph wrote, 'I made a visit to the Holy Land and to Calvary, where I prayed for you, Bride.' At that point Bridget, fingering through her prayer book, began to cry.

On the morning of 5 December 1966, the hospital rang Mrs Tearle to say that Bridget had died during the night of bronchopneumonia, and asked whether she would take possession of the body, as there were no relatives and no other known friends in Australia. Mrs Tearle said that was not possible. She contacted Father Dunlea who rang Joseph, who asked that she be given a Catholic burial. The hospital said that was not possible because Bridget had already expressed her wish to be buried with Mrs Touchell. Although it turned out that Mrs Touchell had been cremated, the hospital still declined to allow a Catholic burial as Mrs Touchell had left money to pay for Bridget's funeral. Mrs Tearle rang Father Morrissey and asked him to conduct the funeral at Rookwood. But he declined, saying he did not wish to start another sectarian war.[5]

At St Michael's, Hurstville on the two Sundays after her death, the name 'Bridget Partridge' was read out in the list of masses for the dead. According to Mrs Tearle, 'The announcement caused not the slightest ripple, not a gesture of surprise, not a questioning

---

[4] Letter 29 November 1962 Joseph Partridge to Father Thomas Dunlea (Maureen McKeown Papers).
[5] *Newsletter of the Australian Catholic Historical Society*, Vol. 25, No. 3, August 2012, p. 4.

glance, nor a remark of any kind. How different the reaction would have been had the name "Sister Liguori" been read out instead of "Bridget Partridge".

On the morning of 16 December, Mrs Tearle arrived at the funeral parlour of William H. Timmins of Parramatta, where she met a Congregationalist minister Rev. G. Riley. Mrs Tearle later recalled:

> Mr. Riley asked me who was Miss Partridge. Did she come from a particular district family? He soon realised who she was and said something not complimentary re Mr Touchell. I told him I was a Catholic. He pointed to an Ecumenical badge on the lapel of his coat. He was a very nice man. ... At Rookwood, when the coffin was being removed from the hearse, one of the undertaker's men said to another, 'They said she used to be a nun.' Mr. Riley and I were the only ones present at the graveside. He said some prayers and I answered. Her only flowers were a handful of gardenias from our place.

Bridget, whose death at age 76, finally ended the Sister Liguori story, had outlived all the other major players apart from her brother and her sole mourner.

Bishop Joseph Dwyer had continued to administer the diocese of Wagga Wagga until his death on 11 October 1939, one day short of his 70th birthday. In 1933 on a trip to Ireland he had visited Bridget Partridge's mother in Kildare. Dwyer's nemesis, Grand Master Robert Elvin Barton had died a few months before the bishop on 28 July 1939 aged 73. Mother Mary Stanislaus had remained at Mount Erin convent until her death on 26 September 1934, a few years after retiring from active administration. She is buried in the grounds of the convent.

Mrs Mary Elizabeth Thompson died on 7 May 1962 at Sydney Hospital. She outlived by 33 years her husband Robert, who had died at Wagga Wagga on 2 December 1928. Members of the Orange lodge had been requested to attend his funeral.

Justice David Gilbert Ferguson retired from the Supreme Court bench in 1931 and was knighted in 1934. He continued in public service in various forms until his death on 2 November 1941, aged 80. Superintendent William Patrick Bannan retired from the police force less than six months after chairing the mediation conference at police headquarters. He died on 8 December 1939, aged 77 years.

After departing Australia in November 1921, Joseph Partridge arrived at Southampton on 4 January 1922 and made his way to his home at Newbridge, County Kildare. There he was reunited with his patient and long-suffering wife Evelyn, whom he had farewelled almost two years before, just days after their wedding. On his return to Ireland, he took up a teaching position. He and Evelyn had a daughter Eithne, born in 1925. After a few years, Joseph was appointed principal of a school in the diocese of Kildare-Leighlin. On 6 May 1948 Evelyn died three years after being diagnosed with a brain tumour. Joseph lived for another 21 years when he suffered a cerebral thrombosis and died on 16 September 1969, aged 72.

Sheila Tearle, the sole mourner at the funeral of the former nun who had once divided the nation, outlasted them all. She lived for another 36 years after Bridget's funeral, dying on 3 January 2003, aged 91 years.

REQUIESCANT IN PACE

Appendix

Magdalen laundries, orphanages, and industrial schools

The Sister Liguori affair was not the propaganda coup the Loyal Orange Institution had hoped for. The absence of convent horror stories and a verdict for the bishop were bad enough, but anyone reading Justice Ferguson's summing up would have detected displeasure behind his Honour's restrained language. Clearly, he was less than impressed with the LOI's intervention in the affair. Furthermore, he had told the jury that, after a thorough investigation, imputations that the plaintiff had been ill-treated at Mount Erin had been refuted by Bridget herself and that, apart from a few trivial tiffs, the sisters had been kind and friendly to her.

While Mount Erin emerged from the trial with its reputation intact, not all religious institutions may have fared so well after such scrutiny. Given what we now know of Magdalen laundries and industrial schools run by orders of nuns in Australia and overseas, all was not well in such institutions. The LOI might have been on to something in its criticisms of such establishments. Yet, because of its zeal to expose the evils of Roman Catholicism, those criticisms were too easily dismissed as sectarian rants. As in the case of Mount Erin, militant Protestants too often cried wolf.

Today, with the benefit of reports of inquiries in Australia and Ireland, we know that abuses occurred in many orphanages and industrial schools run not only by Catholic nuns but also by Protestant charities and the state. In its 2004 report into children in institutional care, *Forgotten Australians*, the Senate Community Affairs References Committee found:

> Upwards of, and possibly more than 500,000 Australians experienced care in an orphanage, Home or other form

of out-of-home care during the last century. ... Children were placed in a range of institutions including orphanages, Homes, industrial or training schools that were administered variously by the state, religious bodies and other charitable or welfare groups. ... The Committee received hundreds of graphic and disturbing accounts about the treatment and care experienced by children in out-of-home care. ... Their stories outlined a litany of emotional, physical and sexual abuse, and often criminal physical and sexual assault. Their stories also told of neglect, humiliation and deprivation of food, education and healthcare. Such abuse and assault was widespread across institutions, across States and across the government, religious and other care providers.

Similar findings were made in respect of child migrants in the 2001 report *Lost Innocents: Righting the Record* and Aboriginal children in the 1997 report *Bringing them Home*.[1] In Ireland, the 2013 McAleese Report contained even more damning findings.[2] How widespread it was in early twentieth-century Australia we do not know as the reports generally do not go back that far. Nevertheless, we do have a report from 1904 dealing with one institution that was investigated following an 'exposé' by the *Watchman* which alleged mistreatment of inmates at the Manly Industrial School and Orphanage run by the Sisters of the Good Samaritan.

This institution, which operated from 1881 to 1910, catered to orphaned and abandoned infants and school-aged children as well as destitute females placed there by courts and welfare authorities. In the industrial school, the aim was to teach a set of skills which would eventually lead to employment and independence.

---

[1] Senate Community Affairs References Committee, *Lost Innocents: Righting the Record*, Report on Child Migration, August 2001; Human Rights and Equal Opportunity Commission, *Bringing them home*, Report of the National Inquiry into the Separation of Aboriginal and Torres Strait Islander Children from Their Families, April 1997.

[2] Report of the Inter-Departmental Committee to establish the facts of State involvement with the Magdalen Laundries (McAleese Report, 2013), http://www.justice.ie/en/JELR/Pages/MagdalenRpt2013.

The training was in the practical trades of laundry work, sewing, and domestic service. Basic literacy instruction was given at night to those who needed it. The laundry work was unpaid and mostly manual and backbreaking, a consequence of the lack of equipment due to chronic underfunding. In the absence of government funding, the money earned from the laundry was applied towards living expenses and ongoing maintenance. Many of the girls who found jobs upon leaving the school and eventually married and raised families were grateful to the nuns. But others were critical of their treatment. Many resented the hard manual work, frugal living, and strict discipline of the industrial school.[3]

In June-July 1903 the *Watchman* ran a series of four articles critical of the Manly industrial school based on the testimony of a former inmate, whose identity was not disclosed. The articles, later published in a pamphlet entitled, 'Convent Horrors', were accompanied by an editorial declaring, 'The horrors which are so graphically described demand an immediate enquiry by Parliament'.[4] When the matter was raised in parliament the government immediately set up an inquiry. It was conducted by Mr Alfred W. Green, Chief Officer under the *Children's Protection Act 1902*, and Sub-Inspector William J. Tindall of the New South Wales Police, neither of whom was a Catholic. Their report dated 11 February 1904 found:

> The closest investigation has failed to elicit any evidence in corroboration of the statements of ill-treatment or neglect of the children in any particular, either at the date (six years ago) when the cruelties were alleged to have been inflicted, or at the present time. Dr Watkins was visiting medical officer six years ago, and his evidence is typical of the unanimous testimony in support of the good care and

---

[3] Margaret Walsh, *The Good Sams: Sisters of the Good Samaritan 1857-1969*, John Garratt, Mulgrave, Vic., 2001, pp. 105-120; Manly Industrial School and Orphanage (1881 - 1910): https://www.findandconnect.gov.au/ref/nsw/biogs/NE00155b.htm

[4] *Watchman*, 20 June 1903, pp. 4, 5; 27 June 1903, p. 4; 4 July 1903, p. 5; 11 July 1903, p. 5; 19 March 1904, p. 8.

kindly treatment bestowed on the children by the officers of the institution.[5]

While the Catholic newspapers welcomed the report and condemned the 'Sectarian Jackals' who are 'constantly barking their anti-Catholic calumnies', the *Watchman* was silent until it launched its next foray a few months later concerning an escape from a Magdalen refuge in Redfern of an inmate who used a rope to climb over the wall. The *Freeman's Journal* scoffed at the allegations with an article in which it retorted, 'Sydney was treated last week to its annual horror about an escape from a convent' and suggested the reason the woman escaped was to get a drink.[6] As if to vindicate the *Freeman's Journal*'s cynicism, the *Watchman* ran stories in the two following years of cruel treatment suffered by inmates who had escaped from Magdalen refuges at Redfern and Tempe, respectively. Both accounts were exposed as fraudulent. In the latter case, the *Watchman* admitted that the 'escaped' inmate had lied to them about her circumstances in a statutory declaration, leading the newspaper to refer the matter to the police.[7]

The exoneration of the Manly Industrial School and Orphanage and the *Watchman*'s cries of wolf should not lead us to conclude that problems did not exist in such institutions in the early part of the twentieth century. James Franklin, editor of the *Journal of the Australian Catholic Historical Society*, wrote a lengthy article surveying the phenomenon of Magdalen laundries in Australia.[8] In it he wrote:

---

[5] 'Roman Catholic Orphanage, Manly: report respecting management', NSW Legislative Assembly, V&P, 1904, Vol. 2, pp. 901-910.

[6] *Watchman*, 15 October 1904, p. 5; *Freeman's Journal*, 22 October 1904, p. 27.

[7] *Watchman*, 4 February 1905, p. 4; 14 July 1906, p. 8; 4 August 1906, p. 4; *Freeman's Journal*, 8 July 1905, p. 13; 14 July 1906, p. 16; 21 July 1906, p. 19; 28 July 1906, p. 15. See Jeff Kildea, '"The Missing Magdalens": the ABC resurrects a "hidden story" discredited more than a century ago', *Journal of the Australian Catholic Historical Society*, Vol. 44, 2023, pp. 42-49.

[8] James Franklin, 'Convent Slave Laundries? Magdalen Asylums in Australia', *Journal of the Australian Catholic Historical Society*, Vol. 34, 2013, pp. 70-90.

> Each Australian state capital had, from about the 1890s to the 1960s, a large convent which contained a commercial laundry where the work was done by mostly teenage 'fallen women' who were placed in the convent, voluntarily or involuntarily, for reasons such as being destitute, uncontrollable, picked up by the police and similar.

In attempting to explain what happened with many of those institutions, Franklin observed:

> They began as refuges but turned into prisons. ... As the laundries came to be used as dumping grounds for girls picked up by the police, got rid of by their parents and stepparents, or sent on by jails and other institutions, they turned into penal institutions with locks, barred windows and walls. The attitudes of inmates followed suit.

In his conclusion, Franklin made the following points:

> First, the sisters faced an immensely difficult task, and one that only they were prepared to take on. It was a task they performed without material benefit to themselves. ... Second, there is an issue about the perceptions of people from backgrounds as disturbed and deprived as many of the girls in the laundries. Put simply, those who do not receive love early have difficulty perceiving positive human interactions. ... Yet when all that is fully taken into account, the consistent story of former inmates includes a high level of gratuitous positive cruelty and emotional deprivation.

Sister Liguori's story is different from those of girls who ended up in laundries, orphanages, and industrial schools in that she was an adult when she took her final vows and she had knowingly volunteered to subject herself to a life of sacrifice detached from the world. In those days when individualism and speaking up for oneself was discouraged and strict discipline was the norm, it is easy to see how Bridget, once dissatisfied with conventual life, might have felt trapped in the system until the dispute over the broom caused her to snap, leading to her 'escape'. Even so, Sister Liguori was hardly the best example of victimhood upon which to base the

LOI's campaign against the Catholic church and its convent system. A bit more objective inquiry and less anti-Catholic venom might have uncovered genuine cases of mistreatment that lay unexposed until late in the century when sectarian rancour no longer aided in obscuring them.

Note on Sources

Bibliographical details of the sources used are contained in the footnotes. Below are some general comments on sources.

On the subject of sectarianism in early twentieth-century Australia there are not many secondary sources. The standard work is Michael Hogan's *The Sectarian Strand: Religion in Australian History* (Penguin, 1987), which looks at sectarianism in Australia from the convict era to the 1980s with chapters covering the period under review. My own *Tearing the Fabric: Sectarianism in Australia 1910-1925* (Citadel Books, 2002) is a study of the Catholic Federation of New South Wales and covers the Sister Liguori affair in the context of the sectarian episodes of 1920.

On the Sister Liguori affair itself, there are several published sources, which I list here with comments regarding some of them:

> Anonymous, *People* 11 August 1954, pp. 5-10. This is the article referred to in the Epilogue in which Bridget Partridge and Laura Touchell were interviewed in their home.
>
> Barlass, Tim, 'The "escaped nun" on the run who fled in the night', *Sydney Morning Herald* 9 April 2019, p. 9. This is an article about Maureen McKeown's *The Extraordinary Case of Sister Liguori*.
>
> Barlass, Tim, 'Pregnant to a priest, nun on run defied church over child, *Sydney Morning Herald* 3 April 2023, pp. 14-15. This article asserts, without any credible evidence, that Sister Liguori left the convent because she was pregnant to a priest. Of the many allegations the Loyal Orange Institution levelled at the Catholic church over the Liguori affair, this was not one of them. The article also contains several factual errors. I wrote a let-

ter refuting the article, which the *Herald* published on 7 April 2023.

Blacklow, Nancy and West, Elizabeth, 'Sectarianism and Sisterhood: Research in Progress', *Rural Society*, Vol. 10, No. 2, 2000, pp. 243-248.

Darlow, Justin, *Consider the Crows: The History of the Diocese of Wagga Wagga*, Triple D Books, Wagga Wagga (N.S.W.), 2020, pp. 21-23.

Dowd, B. T. and Tearle, Sheila E., *Centenary, Sisters of the Presentation of the Blessed Virgin Mary, Wagga Wagga, New South Wales, 1874-1974*, The Sisters of the Presentation of the Blessed Virgin Mary, Wagga Wagga, N.S.W., 1973, pp. 64-67.

Fox, Noela M., *In this Land: A History of the Presentation Sisters, Wagga Wagga*, The Trustees of the Presentation Sisters Wagga, New South Wales, Wagga Wagga (NSW), 2003, pp. 176-181.

Gill, Alan, 'The Fate of Sister Liguori', *Sydney Morning Herald* 19 July 1980, Good Weekend section, p. 14. Fascinated by the Sister Liguori affair, Alan Gill intended to write a book on the subject but died in 2018 before doing so. His article contains some factual errors.

Kildea, Jeff, 'Where Crows Gather: The Sister Liguori Affair 1920-21', *Journal of the Australian Catholic Historical Society*, Vol. 27, 2006, pp. 31-40.

Lee, Andrew, 'The Nun in the Nightgown: The Public Airing of Private Prejudice and the Sister Ligouri [sic] Scandal, 1920-21', *Journal of Australian Studies*, Vol. 21, No. 52, 1997, pp. 34-42.

Logan, James, 'Sectarianism in Ganmain: A Local Study, 1912-21', *Rural Society*, Vol. 10, No. 2, 2000, pp. 121-138. This article contains details about the violence at Coolamon and Marrar.

McKeown, Maureen, *The Extraordinary Case of Sister Liguori*, Leo Press, Downpatrick, Nth Ire., 2017. This is a 'narrative non-fiction' account of the affair written purely from Bridget Partridge's point of view without taking into consideration the sectarian aspects of the case, thus presenting a distorted view of the case. See my review of this book: Jeff Kildea, 'Review of Maureen McKeown, The Extraordinary Case of Sister Liguori', *Journal of the Australian Catholic Historical Society*, Vol. 40, 2019, pp. 173-175.

Swan, Keith, *A History of Wagga Wagga*, City of Wagga Wagga, Wagga Wagga, N.S.W., 1970, pp.166-169.

Tearle, Sheila, 'I Remember Sister Liguori', *Footprints*, April 1977, pp. 9-10.

Walsh, Sylvia, *'Neath the Mantle of Saint Michael: Saint Michael's Catholic Church and Parish Wagga Wagga, 1858-1987: A History*, Sylvia Walsh, Wagga Wagga, 1987, pp. 41-42.

In terms of unpublished sources, Bishop William Brennan granted me access to the papers concerning the Sister Liguori affair in the Wagga Wagga Diocesan Archives. I was also given access to the archives of the Loyal of Institution of New South Wales. However, little remains in the LOI archive of the period under review. Maureen McKeown (Bridget Partridge's great niece) and Eithne Flanagan (Joseph Partridge's daughter) provided me with various documents, letters, and photographs from their family collections. Some records are held in the NSW State Archives (MHNSW-StAc) as indicated in the footnotes.

Much of the narrative, especially in the early chapters, was derived from the extensive newspaper reports of the hearings in the Lunacy Court and the Supreme Court and of the mediation conference at police headquarters. Using the National Library of Australia's online newspaper archive, Trove, I have accessed each of the

Sydney dailies, both morning and evening, and the two Wagga Wagga dailies, as well as weekly newspapers, both secular and religious. Although at first sight the newspaper reports of the evidence given in the court cases and of the discussion at the mediation conference appear to be verbatim accounts, a comparative study revealed that some reports omitted details that appeared in other reports, while several of the accounts were inconsistent. I have therefore had to exercise a subjective assessment as to which of the reports were the most accurate, often constructing an account from several sources. Furthermore, in narrating conversations, I have sometimes turned indirect speech into direct speech and vice versa.

Index

Adams, Frederick Sigismund (Juryman) 132–33
Adelong 36, 46–47, 58, 146
Arthur MLA, Dr Richard 71
Australian Protestant Defence Association 15

Bagnall MLA, William 101–02, 200
Bannan, Superintendent William Patrick
  abduction of Bridget Partridge 195–97
  death of 218
Barclay, Sister Margaret vii
Barham, Richard 153
Barlass, Tim
  SMH article on Sr Liguori vi, 225–26
Barry, Fr Thomas 20–21, 26–27, 33, 38–40, 43, 51, 115
Barton, Grand Master Robert Elvin 12, 16, 58, 68, 71, 91, 115, 131, 164, 178, 208, 210
  abduction of Bridget Partridge 196–97, 199
  allegations re gunmen of Berry 95–99
  biographical details 8
  Bridget Partridge stays with 85
  Bridget Partridge brought to Sydney 48, 146
  campaign against convents 69, 83–84, 94, 105, 163
  campaign to rally Protestants 65–66, 76, 78, 93–94, 116
  criticises *Ireland will be Free* (movie) 189
  death of 217
  describes Bridget Partridge's escape 35, 37–38
  Ferguson J criticises 167–68
  gaslighting of Bridget Partridge 83–84, 118–19, 120–21, 210–11
  rejects claim Bridget Partridge is imprisoned 183–84
  relations with Joseph Partridge 110–13, 116–17, 122, 138–39, 211
  visit to Adelong 46–47
  visit to Wagga Wagga 44, 46
Barton, Mrs 117
Barton, Prime Minister Edmund 130
Basil, Sister Mary 14–15, 178
Bavin, Thomas 72
Berry, allegations re gunmen 95–99
Binns, Dr William
  evidence in *Partridge v. Dwyer* 145
  opinion as to sanity of Bridget Partridge 60, 145
Blacklow, Nancy 13
Blix, Arthur 141
Blowick, Fr John (China Mission) 114
Bourke, Mons Thomas (Townsville PP) 114
Boyce, Francis Stewart (Barrister)
  biographical details 72–73, 130
  examination of witnesses in *Partridge v. Dwyer* 145, 146

legal teams in *Partridge v. Dwyer* 129

Lunacy Court hearing 1920 72–75, 76, 77, 81–82

Boyce, Reverend Francis Bertie 72

Brendan, Sister
evidence in *Partridge v. Dwyer* 157
flight from Mount Erin convent - first 21–23
flight from Mount Erin convent - second 24–25, 59, 138, 145

Brennan, Bishop William vii, 227

Bridgefoot, Anne 77

Bridgefoot, John 77

Bridgefoot, Nurse Harriet
biographical details 77
interview with Bp Dwyer 79, 154

Bringing them Home 1997 Human Rights report 220

Bromfield, Amanda
exhibition at Wagga Wagga Art Gallery vi
interview with ABC vii, 207

Broom, incident of the 17–19, 23, 134, 137, 166, 167, 202, 208, 209, 210, 223

Brownlee, Constable James 26–27

Burgess, Gelette (*Find the Woman*) 16

Burgess, Jessie Ada
evidence in *Partridge v. Dwyer* 145
flight from Mount Erin convent – first 20–22, 32, 157
flight from Mount Erin convent – second 25–27, 34

Byrnes, John Joseph
interview with Dr Leahy 43–44, 157

interview with James Sheekey 43, 45, 51
Joseph Partridge stays with 190
visit to Thompson house 42–43

Campbell KC, James Lang
address to the jury 163–64
applies for a non-suit 147–48
biographical details 130
defendant's case 149–62
plaintiff's case 135–47
requests verdict by direction 162–63

Camphin, William Joseph (Clerk of Petty Sessions) 55, 62, 142, 150, 161
issues order under *Lunacy Act*, s 4 56

Canon Law 52, 91, 149–50, 153–54

Carlton, John Francis 193

Carlton, Maria Agatha (Queenie) 193

Carroll, JJ (Solicitor) 196–97

Castro, Thomas 2

Catholic Church
convents 208–09
opposition to freemasonry and Orangeism 10–12
state aid for Catholic schools 5

Catholic Club 67, 192

Catholic Federation of NSW 44, 79
assists Joseph Partridge's pursuit of Bridget 115, 119–20, 121, 185–87, 193, 196, 211–12
criticism of Charles Lawlor 187, 190

defence of Catholic church and convents 207
demise of 205
Democratic Party 10, 102, 203–04
foundation and role 10, 27, 67, 183, 225
NSW parliament elections 1920 102
NSW parliament elections 1922 203–04
organised Town Hall celebration of Bp Dwyer 179
response to LOI 99
Town Hall meeting after verdict 179
Catholic response to Protestant campaign 66, 84, 94–95, 98–99, 119–21, 127–28, 207
censure motion in parliament 200–02
Clare, Mother
evidence in *Partridge v. Dwyer* 157
flight from Mount Erin convent – first 21–23
flight from Mount Erin convent – second 32–33
Cleary, Patrick (Catholic Federation president) 179
Collins, Neil (Solicitor) 77, 81
Coningham affair 1–2, 151
Connell, Sister Rosaria vii
convents, Protestant campaign against 13–16, 35, 38, 66, 67, 76, 82–83, 84, 91–94, 99, 105–07, 119, 202, 207, 223
Coolamon riot 180–82

Cooney, Kathleen
arranges for Bridget to meet Bp Dwyer 79–81
biographical details 79
Bridget breaks arrangement to meet Bp Dwyer 83
Cooney, Lawrence 79
Cooper, Constable 30, 32
Cootamundra
Adelong to Sydney with GM Barton 47–48
NSW parliament elections 1920 67
Cottle, Ken (Orangeman) 196
Craig, Mr (Adelong) 47
Crawford, Reverend Edward (Orangeman) 196
Cullen, Fr Paul 95

Darlinghurst Reception House
Bridget Partridge admitted 1920 65
Bridget Partridge admitted 1939 213
Bridget Partridge Lunacy Court hearing 71–75
Bridget Partridge's stay 75–83
Bridget Patrridge released 1920 83
Democratic Party 10, 102, 203–04
Dooley, James 45
abduction of Bridget Partridge 198
allegations re Berry gunmen and Mount Erin attack 95–99
censure motion in parliament re abduction 202

NSW parliament elections 1922
203

premier from 5 October 1921 201

refuses inquiry into convents 93

Duhig, Archbishop James

communications with Bp Dwyer
114–15

meets with Irish China Mission
114

speaks on Sr Liguori affair 95

Dunlea, Fr Thomas

communications with Joseph
Partridge 215–16

meetings with Bridget Partridge
215, 216

Dunne, Annie – see Brendan, Sister

Dunne, Mary – see Stanislaus,
Mother

Duprez, Inspector William
Alexander 37, 140, 154, 168

biographical details 29–30

communications with Bp Dwyer
40, 49–51

communications with Dr Tivey
51

communications with Inspr Gen
Mitchell 45, 48, 55, 57, 96

denies he forbade visits to Sr
Liguori 33

evidence in *Partridge v. Dwyer*
144–45, 162

interview with Mother Stanislaus
32–33

knowledge of Sr Liguori's
whereabouts 52, 58, 62

visits Thompson house 30–32,
40–42

Durschmied, Erik (*The Hinge
Factor*) 17–18

Duval, Helen 105

Dwyer, Bishop Joseph Wilfrid 15,
17n, 37, 63, 64, 99, 102, 104, 112,
116, 128, 130, 135, 141, 171, 177,
178, 204, 208

action for damages by Bridget
Partridge 12, 15, 17n, 102,
125–71, 126

alleges Sr Liguori of unsound
mind 12, 56, 62

assists Joseph Partridge 185, 212

attitude to Archdeacon Pike
49–50, 154

attitude to Dr Tivey 50–51, 154

biographical details 12

Canon Law, duty under 52, 66,
91, 149–50, 153–54

claims Bridget Partridge is a
prisoner of LOI 183–85, 187

communications with Abp Duhig
114–15

communications with Bridget
Partridge 20, 40, 42, 78, 142

communications with Charles
Lawlor 121, 185–86, 187–88, 190

communications with Inspector
Duprez 40, 49–51

communications with Inspr Gen
Mitchell 48

communications with Joseph
Partridge 186–87, 194

communications with
Thompsons 39–40, 42

consults Dr Leahy 44

courtroom demeanour 131–32

death of 217
denies involvement with Patrick Minahan 76
denies requested Byrnes consult Sheekey 43
Dr Leahy's second affidavit 54–55
evidence in *Partridge v. Dwyer* 149–54, 161–62
feted after verdict 179–80, 183–85, 202
informed re Joseph Partridge's movements 115
interview with A.G. McTiernan 44
interview with Inspr Gen Mitchell 45, 55–56
interview with James Sheekey 51–52, 53–54
interview with Joseph Partridge 111
interview with Mother Stanislaus 42, 161
interview with Mr Camphin 56
interview with Nurse Bridgefoot 79, 154
interview with Sol Gen Sproule 56
proposed meeting with Bridget Partridge 79, 83, 85
questioned re mental reservation 150–51
refused permission to visit Bridget Partridge 77, 149
reputation intact 209–10
return from Albury 38
return from Sydney 48
St Patrick's Day speech 158–59, 161–62

visits Partridge family in Ireland 1933 217
visits Sydney 44–45, 55–57, 76–77
visits Thompson house 40–42

Edney, Worshipful Master George 36, 47, 57–58
Enright, Reverend John 68–69, 71, 78, 82–83
escaped nun trope 12–15, 35, 84
Evans, Ada 133
Fallon MLA, Dr Cyril 203–04

Farley, Detective Sergeant James 83, 85
abduction of Bridget Partridge 196–97, 199–200
arrests Bridget Partridge 64–65
evidence in *Partridge v. Dwyer* 142
Lunacy Court hearing 1920 73–74

Ferguson, Justice David Gilbert
biographical details 129
career after *Partridge v. Dwyer* 217–18
criticises GM Barton and LOI 167–68
criticises Mr and Mrs Thompson 167–68
death of 217–18
exonerates Mount Erin convent 166–67, 219
Partridge v. Dwyer, presiding judge 132, 133–71
questions jury 169–71
refuses non-suit 147–48

refuses verdict by direction 162–63

summing up to jury 166–69, 177, 208, 209, 219

Ferry, Bryan 27

Ferry, Michael 27, 29–32, 35

Finn, Alexander Donald 79

Flanagan (née Partridge), Eithne vii, 218, 227

Flannery KC, George Ernest
  biographical details 130
  examination of witnesses in *Partridge v. Dwyer* 159–60, 161–62
  submissions on non-suit 147–48
  submissions on verdict 170

Forgotten Australians 2004 Senate report 219–20

Fox, Sister Noela 207–08

Franklin, Professor James viii, 222–23

Freemasonry 11–12

Fuller, Sir George 201, 203, 204

Gale SM, Charles Henry 71–75, 81–82, 83, 141

Gallagher, Peter 196

Gallaher, Sergeant Sam 26–27, 37, 42–43, 57–58

Ganmain 4, 18, 79, 147

Garnet, Fr Henry 151

Gibbes, Dr Alexander 75, 79
  evidence in *Partridge v. Dwyer* 145–46
  opinion as to sanity of Bridget Partridge 146

Gill, Alan 13, 226

González, Elián 212

Grand Orange Lodge of British America 15, 178

Green, Alfred W. 221–22

Gunpowder plot 1605 151

Hall, Dianne 14

Harkness, Edward Burns 45

Harrowsmith, Detective 64

Hartigan, Fr Patrick 4

Hazell, William George (Clerk of Petty Sessions)
  evidence in *Partridge v. Dwyer* 162
  interview with Sheekey and Leahy 45–46, 51, 152–53, 157–58, 159–60, 162, 165

Heathwood, Ethel 29–30, 36

Helen of Troy 15, 212

Henley MLA, Sir Thomas 68, 69, 81, 201–02
  abduction of Bridget Partridge 198–99
  biographical details 67
  campaign against convents 105–07
  first raised Sr Liguori affair in parliament 104

Herbert, Mary – see Clare, Mother

Heydon, Justice Charles 99, 100–01, 120

Higgins, Percy Reginald (Barrister) 129
  biographical details 130

Hill, Walter (Solicitor) 129, 178, 187
  abduction of Bridget Partridge 195–97, 199–200

Holman, William 67

Hoskins MLA, Mr Tom 71, 104
   abduction of Bridget Partridge 196–97, 198
   criticises *Ireland will be Free* (movie) 189
Howell, Frank 36
Howell, Letitia
   evidence in *Partridge v. Dwyer* 146
   shelters Bridget Partridge 36, 46–47, 57–58
Hughes, Prime Minister Billy 8–9

Industrial Workers of the World 103
Ireland will be Free (movie) 188–89
Irish Free State 205
Irish Mission to China 114
Irish National Association 188
Irish War of Independence 7, 158–59, 161–62

Jackdaw of Rheims 153
Jerger, Fr Charles 7–8, 104, 122, 182
Joan, Sister 17–18

Kells, Grand Secretary Ian vii
Kelly, Archbishop Michael 122, 179
Kennedy, Alphonsus 115
Keys, Blayney 141
Kildea, Michael viii
Kildea, Robyn viii
King and Empire Alliance 182
Knights of the Southern Cross 67

Labor Party 6, 9, 67, 73, 78, 102–03, 106, 183, 202, 203

Lane, Fr Maurice (Brisbane) 115
Lawlor, Charles (Secretary of Catholic Federation)
   assists Joseph Partridge 115, 187–88, 196
   communications with Bp Dwyer 121, 185–86, 187–88, 190
   criticism of by Catholic Federation members 187–88, 189–90
   response to LOI 99–100, 119–20
Lazzarini MLA, Carlo Camillo 106–07
Leahy, Dr William
   affidavit, first 43, 46, 51, 157–58, 160
   affidavit, second 53–54, 54–55, 56, 157–58, 160
   belief as to Bridget Partridge's location 43, 46, 157–58
   biographical details 19
   Bridget Partridge spoke of his kindness 166
   evidence in *Partridge v. Dwyer* 157–59
   flight from Mount Erin convent - first 32, 58–59
   flight from Mount Erin convent – second 25, 26–27, 138
   interview with Bp Dwyer 157
   interview with CPS Hazell 45–46, 152–53, 157–58, 162, 165
   interview with JJ Byrnes 43, 157
   interview with James Sheekey 43, 157–58
   opinion as to sanity of Bridget Partridge 23–24, 33, 34, 44, 157–58

questioned re Bp Dwyer's St Patrick's Day speech 158–59

Leary, Detective Inspector Arthur 195

Levy MLA, Daniel 102, 203

Ley MLA, Thomas 205

Liguori, Sister – see Partridge, Bridget

Liguori, St Alphonsus 3–4

Lost Innocents 2001 Senate report 220

Loyal Orange Institution 1, 8, vii, 26, 36, 56, 58, 67, 68n, 82, 227
  allegations Bridget is a prisoner of LOI 183–85, 187
  allegations re Berry gunmen and Mount Erin attack 95–99
  Catholic opposition to 94–95
  Ferguson J criticises 167–68
  history 10–11
  Joseph Partridge's arrival in Australia 110–11, 114
  jury's verdict disappoints 177–78
  NSW parliament elections 1920 103
  NSW parliament elections 1922 203–04
  opposition to Catholicism 10–12, 14–15
  promotes legal action against Bp Dwyer 125
  Sr Liguori affair 16, 38, 65–66, 76, 84, 92–93, 102, 104, 118–21, 180, 207, 209, 210, 211–12, 219, 223–24, 225

Lunacy Act 1898 12, 43, 45–46, 51, 52, 53–54, 56, 63, 74, 91, 134–35, 142, 147–48, 149, 152–53, 159–60, 161

Lunacy Court hearing 1920 71–75

Magdalen laundries 208–09, 219–24

Maguire, Mons. Edward 114, 115

Mahon, Hugh 9, 122

Manly Industrial School and Orphanage 220–22

Mannix, Archbishop Daniel 8, 100, 104, 122, 181, 188, 189

Marie, Byles 133

Marrar riot 181–82

Matthews JP, Frederick (Juryman) 132–33

Matthews, Jane 133

Maund, John (Solicitor) 77, 83, 85, 111

Maxwell, Alan Victor (Barrister)
  biographical details 130

McAleese Report 2013 (Ireland) 220

McGeorge, Dr John 213

McIntyre, Dr Perry viii

McKeown, Maureen viii
  The Extraordinary Case of Sister Liguori (2017) vii, 227

McTiernan, Attorney General Edward 9, 55, 67, 196
  interview with Bp Dwyer 44
  speech at Marist Brothers' Darlinghurst 122
  Town Hall meeting after verdict 179

Minahan MLA, Patrick Joseph
  assists Joseph Partridge 188, 190

biographical details 67
defence of Catholic church and convents 66, 106, 119, 179
Lunacy Court hearing 1920 71–75, 76–77, 82–83
NSW parliament elections 1920 103
visits Darlinghurst Reception House 67–69, 68–69, 77, 104

Minahan, Elizabeth
Lunacy Court hearing 1920 71–75
visits Darlinghurst Reception House 67, 68–69

Mitchell, Inspector General James
abduction of Bridget Partridge 197, 200, 201
allegations re Berry gunmen and Mount Erin attack 98
biographical details 45
communications with Bp Dwyer 48, 51, 52, 150
communications with Inspector Duprez 50, 56–57, 58
interview with Bp Dwyer 45, 55–56
interview with GM Barton and Rev. Touchell 199
Lunacy Court hearing 1920 83, 85

Moran, Cardinal Patrick 1

Morris, Edward
abduction of Bridget Partridge 192–93

Morrison, Sibyl 133

Morrissey, Fr Peter
declines to officiate at Bridget Partridge's funeral 216
meeting with Bridget Partridge 214–15

Mount Erin Convent
allegations re attack on 96–97
Ferguson J exonerates 166–67, 219
founded 1876 2
reputation intact 209, 219

Mount Pleasant 36, 46

Murphy, Fr Peter
telegram to Archbishop Duhig 114–15
visits Darlinghurst Reception House 81

Nationalist Party 6, 72, 102, 203, 204

Ne Temere Bill 204–05

Ness, Alderman John
biographical details 8
campaign against convents 76, 84, 91–92
visit to Wagga Wagga 127

Newing, Thomas 95

NSW State Elections 1917 67

NSW State Elections 1920 9, 10, 67, 102–03

NSW State Elections 1922 203–04

O'Callaghan, Daniel 187
abduction of Bridget Partridge 191–97
biographical details 185
meeting with Joseph Partridge 195

O'Callaghan, Kitty
   biographical details 185
   meeting with Bridget Partridge 190
   meeting with Joseph Partridge 195
O'Callaghan, Roger 185
O'Connor, Justice Richard 130
O'Farrell, Bishop Michael (Bathurst) 190
O'Gorman, Edith 14, 15
O'Haran, Monsignor Denis 1–2
O'Keeffe, J.F.D.
   Joseph Partridge's arrival in Australia 114, 115
O'Regan, John 27
O'Reilly JP, J.K. 54–55
O'Reilly, Fr Maurice 179, 188
O'Rourke, Sergeant Patrick 26–27, 29
Orton, Arthur 2
Outcault, Richard Felton 71

Partridge (née Johnson), Evelyn 110, 218
Partridge v. Dwyer (Supreme Court of NSW)
   action for damages by Bridget Partridge 12
   build up to the trial 126–27, 128–29
   Campbell KC presents defendant's case 149–62
   cause of action and defence 126
   Ferguson J refuses non-suit 147–48
   Ferguson J refuses verdict by direction 162–63
   Ferguson J's summing up to the jury 166–69, 177
   jury deliberation 169–71
   jury selection 132–33
   jury's verdict 171, 177–80, 209
   legal teams 129–30
   public interest in 127, 131, 139–40, 141, 143, 158, 169, 171
   settlement discussions 135
   Shand KC opening address 133–35
   Shand KC presents plaintiff's case 135–47
   Shand KC presents plaintiff's case in reply 162
   trial begins 132
   Witnesses
      Arthur Blix 141
      Blayney Keys 141
      Bp Joseph Dwyer 149–54, 161–62
      Bridget Partridge 135–41, 141–42, 146–47
      Det. Sgt. James Farley 142
      Dr Alexander Gibbes 145–46
      Dr Eric Tivey 142–44
      Dr William Binns 145
      Dr William Leahy 157–59
      Inspr William Duprez 144–45, 162
      James Sheekey 159–60
      Jessie Burgess 145
      Letitia Howell 146
      Mother Clare 157

Mother Stanislaus 154–57
Sr Brendan 157
William Hazell 162
Partridge, Anne (née Cardiff) 3
Partridge, Bridget
  abduction of 191–200
  action for damages against Bp Dwyer 12, 17n, 125–71, 171
  Adelong stay with Mrs Howell 46–47
  Adelong to Sydney with GM Barton 47–48
  Adelong, flight to 35–36
  admission to North Ryde Hospital 215
  admission to Rydalmere Psychiatric Hospital 215
  arrest of 64–65
  assessment of 210–11
  Berry, visit to 95–97
  biographical details 3–4
  censure motion in parliament re abduction 200–02
  communications with Bp Dwyer 34, 42, 78, 80, 81, 142
  communications with Joseph Partridge 121, 191
  communications with Mrs Thompson 57, 85
  communications with Mrs Touchell 80
  courtroom demeanour 131–32
  Darlinghurst Reception House 1920 65, 75–83, 213
  death and burial of 216–17
  declines to appeal *Partridge v. Dwyer* verdict 178–79
  evidence in *Partridge v. Dwyer* 135–41, 141–42, 146–47
  examination by Dr Binns 60
  flight from Mount Erin convent – first 15–16, 17–18, 19–24, 58–59
  flight from Mount Erin convent - second 24–27, 58–59, 61–64
  gaslighting by GM Barton 118–19, 120–21
  interview with Mr and Mrs Minahan 68–69
  life after the affair 213–17
  Lunacy Court hearing 1920 12, 71–75, 91
  meetings with Joseph Partridge 111–12, 138–39, 185–87, 190, 193–94
  messages to sisters at Mount Erin 190–91
  NSW parliament elections 1922 203
  People magazine article 213–14
  proposed meeting with Bp Dwyer 79, 83–84
  refuge in Thompson house 29–35
  rejects claim she is imprisoned 184
  reluctant to sue Bp Dwyer 125
  rumours about escape or abduction 202
  Sr Liguori affair 1, 2, vi–iii, 207–08, 223
  statement of 11 August 1920 77–78, 154
  statement re alleged poison 93

statements re Joseph Partridge 115–16, 117–18

statutory declaration of 4 August 1920 58–59

stays with Rev. and Mrs Touchell 12, 48–49, 54, 57

Partridge, Catherine (aka Kathleen) 3

Partridge, Edward 3, 109, 191

Partridge, Elizabeth (aka Lizzie) 3, 109

Partridge, Joseph

abduction of Bridget Partridge 191–200

action for damages against Bp Dwyer 171

arrival in Australia 80, 109–11, 113–15

assessment of 210–11

biographical details 3, 109–10, 218

Catholic Federation financial support 189–90

censure motion in parliament re abduction 200–02

claims Bridget reluctant to sue Bp Dwyer 125

communications with Bp Dwyer 194

communications with Bridget Partridge 47, 121, 121–22, 191, 216

communications with Fr Dunlea 215–16

death of 218

informed of Bridget's admission to hospital 215

informed of Bridget's death 216

interview with Bp Dwyer 111

leaves Australia on *SS Ceramic* 202

letter to Bp Dwyer 186–87

meetings with Bridget Partridge 111–12, 138–39, 185–87, 190, 193–94

meetings with GM Barton 111, 116–17

meets Mr and Mrs Touchell 111

meets Mrs Barton 117

musical performances 188–89

pursuit of Bridget Partridge 185–200, 208

responds to criticism 116

settlement discussions in *Partridge v. Dwyer* 135

visit to Wagga Wagga 121, 190–91

Partridge, Susan 3, 109

Pether, Detective Sergeant Louis 195

Pike, Archdeacon Joseph 49–50, 57, 63, 85, 154, 178, 208, 209–10

confronts J.J. Byrnes 42–43

Pius X, Pope 204

Presentation order – see Sisters of the Presentation of the Blessed Virgin Mary

press coverage of the Sr Liguori affair 61–64, 84, 94–95, 98–99, 118

Progressive Party 102, 203, 204

Protestant Federation 8, 10, 49, 71, 75–76, 92, 104, 120, 127, 180–83, 189, 198, 203, 207

Protestant protests re Sister Liguori 65, 66, 76, 78, 91–93, 116, 200
Prowse, Mr (Adelong) 47

Reilly, James Joseph (Juryman) 132–33
Returned Soldiers' League, Wagga Wagga 96–97
Riley, Reverend G. 217
Riverina, violence in 180–83
Roach, T.H. (Orangeman) 195
Robinson, Past Grand Master James 71, 92, 204
Ross, Dr Chisholm 74–75, 79, 79
  opinion as to sanity of Bridget Partridge 81
  refuses Bp Dwyer permission to visit Bridget Partridge 77, 149
Ryan KC, MP, Thomas Joseph
  Lunacy Court hearing 1920 73–76, 81–82, 92, 119, 150
Rydalmere Psychiatric Hospital 215–16

Saurin, Susann (Sister Scholastica) 13
Schiavo, Terri 212
sectarianism
  'elephant in the room' 150, 159, 160, 163–64, 166
  history of 4–16, 35
  Irish War of Independence 188–89
  Nationalist government 1922-1925 203–06
  Sr Liguori affair 1, 17, 27, 69, 72, 84, 91–95, 96–97, 99, vi–vii, 102,

119–20, 122–23, 200–01, 207–09, 212, 213, 216, 219–24
  violence in the Riverina 177, 180–83
Shand C, Alexander Barclay
  address to the jury 164–66
  biographical details 129–30
  defendant's case 149–62
  opening address 133–35
  plaintiff's case 135–47
  plaintiff's case in reply 162
  questions Bp Dwyer re mental reservation 150–51
Sheekey, James Patrick (Solicitor)
  affidavit of Dr Leahy, first 43, 157
  affidavit of Dr Leahy, second 53–54, 55, 160
  communications with Bp Dwyer 51
  denies Bp Dwyer was his client 43, 159–60, 165
  evidence in *Partridge v. Dwyer* 159–60
  interview with Bp Dwyer 51–52, 53–54, 159–60
  interview with CPS Hazell 45–46, 152–53, 158, 159–60, 162, 165
  interview with Dr Tivey 160
  interview with JJ Byrnes 43
  Shand KC improperly alleges criminality 165–66
Sisters of the Good Samaritan 105–06, 220–22
Sisters of the Presentation of the Blessed Virgin Mary 2–3, vii, 53, 134, 207–08

Smith, John William (Juryman) 132–33
Smith, Lydia 105, 105
Smith, Mr (Adelong) 47
Sproule, Robert (Solicitor General)
   interview with Bp Dwyer 56, 104
   Partridge v. Dwyer, arrangements for trial 127
St Magdalene's Retreat, Tempe 105–06, 222
Stanislaus, Mother
   assessment of 209
   biographical details 20
   Bridget Partridge was on good terms with 135
   communications with Bridget Partridge 118
   communications with Dr Tivey 48
   communications with Joseph Partridge 110
   communications with Thompsons 34
   death and burial of 217
   evidence in *Partridge v. Dwyer* 154–57
   flight from Mount Erin convent – first 20–24, 58–59
   flight from Mount Erin convent – second 25, 26, 32–34, 37, 138, 142
   interview with Bp Dwyer 42, 161
   interview with Inspector Duprez 162
Stocker, Charles Harold (Grand Secretary)
   allegations re Berry gunmen and Mount Erin attack 95–97, 99
   biographical details 58
   campaign to rally Protestants 76
   Joseph Partridge's arrival in Australia 110–11
Storey, Premier John 102, 201
Swift, Jonathan 182

Tearle, Sheila
   biographical details 214
   death and burial of Bridget Partridge 216–17
   death of 218
   meetings with Bridget Partridge 214–15, 216
Thomas, Sylvia (habeas corpus case) 105–06
Thompson, Mary
   communications with Bp Dwyer 141
   communications with Bridget Partridge 84
   communications with GM Barton 37–38
   death of 217
   Ferguson J criticises 167–68
   flight from Mount Erin convent – second 15, 25–27, 29–36, 61n, 63, 134
   interview with Bp Dwyer 40–42
   interview with Inspector Duprez 30–31, 40–42, 144
   Lunacy Court hearing 1920 82
   meeting with Bridget Partridge 85
   refuses to accept letters 33–34, 40, 42–43, 142
   refuses to disclose Bridget

Partridge's location 36–37, 164, 208
visit by JJ Byrnes and Sgt Gallaher 42–43
Thompson, Robert 15, 26, 27, 46, 48, 57
death and burial of 217
Ferguson J criticises 167–68
Tichborne affair 2
Tindall, William J. 221–22
Tivey, Dr Eric 85, 154, 156, 178, 208
biographical details 29
evidence in *Partridge v. Dwyer* 142–44
interview with James Sheekey 160
interviewed by reporter 61, 63
opinion as to sanity of Bridget Partridge 33, 34, 48, 50–51, 50, 56, 143–44, 160, 168, 209–10
visit to Thompson house 30–33
Toohey, James Francis 43
Touchell, Mrs Laura
abduction of Bridget Partridge 191–92, 196–97
accompanied Bridget Partridge in Supreme Court 131, 138
admission to North Ryde Hospital 215
admission to Rydalmere Psychiatric Hospital 215
arrest of Bridget Partridge 64–65
biographical details 48–49
Bridget Partridge lives with Touchells 54, 57, 213
campaign against convents 93
communications with Bridget Partridge 80

death of 216
Lunacy Court hearing 1920 12, 71–72, 75, 91
meeting of Bridget and Joseph Partridge 113
meeting of Bridget Partridge and Fr Dunlea 215
meeting of Bridget Partridge and Fr Morrissey 214–15
meets Joseph Partridge 111, 112
People magazine article 213–14
Touchell, Reverend William
abduction of Bridget Partridge 191–93, 196–97, 198, 199, 200
arrest of Bridget Partridge 64–65
associated with Rev. John Enright 68
biographical details 48–49
Bridget Partridge lives with Touchells 54, 57, 213
campaign against convents 93
criticises *Ireland will be Free* (movie) 189
death of 213
foreshadows legal action against Bp Dwyer 101–02
gaslighting of Bridget Partridge 211
Joseph Partridge's arrival in Australia 113–14
Lunacy Court hearing 1920 12, 71, 91
meeting of Bridget and Joseph Partridge 113
meets Joseph Partridge 111, 112
mental illness of Bridget Patridge 1939 213

rejects claim Bridget Partridge is imprisoned 113, 184–85

responds to Justice Heydon 101

settlement discussions in *Partridge v. Dwyer* 135

violence in the Riverina 180–83

visit to Wagga Wagga 127

Twain, Mark 2

Universal Service League 72

Unlawful Detention Bill 1920 105

Wade, Justice Sir Charles 106

Wagga Wagga 2, 4, 6, 127–28, 208

Wallace, W. (Secretary of Protestant Federation)

abduction of Bridget Partridge 198–99

Walsh, Dorothea

visits Darlinghurst Reception House 77–78

Walsh, Mr (Farmer) 43

Walsh, William (Solicitor) 38–39, 128

Watchman attack on Catholic institutions 220–22

West, Elizabeth 13

Wilkinson, Fr Edward

meeting with Bridget Partridge 216

Zillwood, Leila (The Broken Rosary) 15